THE PORTFOLIO ARCHITECT

HOW TO BUILD INTELLIGENT, RESILIENT, AND PURPOSE-DRIVEN WEALTH IN THE AGE OF ALTERNATIVES

ARUN JAIN

Published by Kubera Capital Investments LLC.

ISBN: 9781971316000

DEDICATION

To those who work hard but wonder if it's ever enough.

To those who have been excluded from the wealth-building strategies of the ultra-wealthy—not because they lack intelligence or discipline, but because no one bothered to translate them clearly.

To my family, whose encouragement to pursue excellence across technology, business, and investing shaped my belief that financial autonomy is not a luxury for the few—it's a right accessible to all.

And to every reader who refuses to accept that financial freedom is years away. Your freedom is closer than you think. This book is the roadmap.

ACKNOWLEDGMENTS

This book exists because of the thousands of investors who shared their stories, failures, and successes. To the architects who built systems that work and generously taught others: thank you.

To the pioneers of alternative investing who democratized access to private markets, real estate syndications, and venture capital—you expanded opportunity for millions.

To my family, who supported the research, writing, and revision process: your patience made this possible.

To every reader who takes these principles and builds their own path to freedom: this is for you.

Financial autonomy isn't a privilege reserved for the wealthy. It's a system available to anyone willing to learn, adapt, and persist.

May you design freedom. May you achieve autonomy. May you teach others.

The future belongs to architects.

ABOUT THE AUTHOR

Arun Jain is the founder of Kubera Capital, a wealth management and alternative investment company serving family offices, institutions, and individual investors. With two decades of investment banking and technology leadership, he brings deep expertise in financial systems innovation and capital markets strategy. Since its inception, Kubera has invested in assets and companies valued at $1B+, driven by Arun's thematic approach to investing that consistently delivers measurable performance across diversified asset classes.

He holds a BTech in Engineering from IIT and an MBA from UNC. ***The Portfolio Architect*** captures the wealth-building frameworks and alternative investment strategies he has pioneered and witnessed firsthand — translating institutional methodologies into actionable blueprints for investors seeking true financial autonomy.

CONTENTS

INTRODUCTION

The year is 2026, and the rules of wealth-building have fundamentally changed.

Maria, a 34-year-old nurse in Phoenix, checks her phone during a break. Three notifications appear: $847 deposited from her rental property syndication, $112 from her micro-royalty investment in a music catalog, and a quarterly distribution notice from her private credit fund. Combined with her salary, these streams now cover 60% of her living expenses. She's not wealthy by traditional metrics—her net worth is $180,000—but she's architecting something more valuable: freedom.

Across town, James, a 58-year-old former tech executive, has successfully built a $4.3 million portfolio through decades of disciplined investing in index funds. By most measures, he's achieved remarkable success. Yet despite his substantial wealth, he remains uncertain about retirement. His portfolio only grows when markets rise, provides no consistent income, and offers no protection against inflation. He's wealthy on paper but constrained by the very strategy that built his fortune.

This book is about why Maria is winning the game James doesn't even know he's playing.

THE SHIFT HAPPENING RIGHT NOW

Three seismic forces are reshaping personal wealth:

1. The democratization of elite assets. Private equity, venture capital, real estate syndications, and alternative investments—once reserved for institutions and the ultra-wealthy—are now accessible to individuals. Technology has shattered the minimum investment barriers that protected these assets for centuries.

2. The failure of traditional diversification. The 60/40 portfolio (60% stocks, 40% bonds) delivered 8-10% annual returns for decades. Between 2022-2024, it lost money in real terms. Bonds no longer hedge equities. Cash loses 3-5% annually to inflation. The old playbook is obsolete.

3. The rise of income engineering. Wealth is no longer about accumulation alone—it's about designing cash flow systems that fund your life while your capital continues to compound. The new metric isn't net worth; it's "freedom number": the moment your passive income exceeds your expenses.

WHO THIS BOOK IS FOR

This book speaks to five distinct groups, each at different stages of their wealth journey:

The Starter ($0-$50K investable): You're building your foundation, learning to convert earned income into assets that work for you. You need clarity on where to begin, what to avoid, and how to build momentum.

The Accumulator ($50K-$500K): You've saved but feel stuck in traditional investments. You're ready to explore alternatives but don't know how to access them or evaluate opportunities.

The Diversifier ($500K-$2M): You have wealth but limited sophistication. Your portfolio is concentrated in 401(k)s, your home, or company stock. You seek resilience and income, not just growth.

The Freedom Seeker ($2M+): You have capital but lack autonomy. You want to replace active income with systematic cash flow and design a portfolio that serves your life vision.

The Legacy Builder (any level): You're thinking beyond yourself—about family, impact, and continuity. You want to build systems that outlast you and teach others to thrive.

This book works whether you're 23 or 63, earning $50,000 or $500,000, starting from zero or stewarding millions. The principles of portfolio architecture scale across all demographics.

HOW THIS BOOK WORKS

This isn't a theory. Every concept is paired with implementation steps, real-world case studies, and decision frameworks you can use immediately.

Section I destroys the myths holding you back and introduces a new way of thinking about wealth—not as a number, but as a system.

Section II teaches you the foundational principles of portfolio design: how to engineer risk, structure capital, and build for resilience rather than speculation.

Section III opens the door to modern investments: real estate, private equity, startups, and alternatives that generate income and appreciation simultaneously.

Section IV shows you how to construct your own Freedom Portfolio: a cash-flowing, tax-efficient, antifragile wealth system aligned with your life.

Section V elevates beyond money into legacy, teaching you to measure true freedom, transmit values, and adapt to the future of finance.

Throughout, you'll encounter the **Portfolio Architecture Pyramid™, Freedom Flow Matrix™, Kubera Framework**, and other proprietary tools designed to simplify complex decisions.

THE PROMISE

By the end of this book, you will:

- Understand how wealth compounds in the modern economy
- Know how to evaluate any investment opportunity with confidence
- Build a diversified portfolio beyond stocks and bonds
- Design income streams that fund your life indefinitely
- Create a system that thrives in volatility rather than fears it
- Align your capital with your purpose and values

You won't become rich overnight. But you will become an architect—someone who designs intentionally rather than speculates blindly.

The markets are unpredictable. Your system doesn't have to be. Let's begin.

DISCLAIMER

All characters and examples in this book are fictional. Any resemblance to actual persons, living or dead, or actual events is entirely coincidental. The narratives, case studies, and investor profiles presented are composite illustrations designed to illuminate concepts and frameworks, not to represent actual individuals or their specific outcomes.

This book is for educational and informational purposes only and does not constitute investment advice, financial advice, legal advice, or tax advice. The strategies, frameworks, and insights presented are general in nature and should not be construed as personalized recommendations for your specific financial situation, goals, risk tolerance, or circumstances.

Past performance is not indicative of future results. The returns, outcomes, and metrics cited throughout this book are illustrative and based on historical data, market conditions, and specific transaction structures. Your results may differ materially based on market conditions, timing, selection, execution, and numerous other factors beyond your control.

All investments carry risk, including the potential loss of principal. Alternative investments are generally illiquid, carry higher fees, require longer holding periods, and may not be suitable for all investors.

Before making any investment decision, consult with qualified professionals, including a financial advisor, tax accountant, and attorney who understand your complete financial picture, risk tolerance, time horizon, and goals.

The author and publisher disclaim all liability for any direct, indirect, incidental, special, or consequential damages arising from the use of or reliance on the information contained in this book, including but not limited to investment losses, missed opportunities, or tax consequences.

The information in this book is current as of publication date and subject to change. Markets, regulations, tax laws, and investment opportunities evolve continuously, and some frameworks or strategies may not remain applicable.

This book does not guarantee any specific outcomes. Building sustainable wealth requires discipline, time, market conditions, proper execution, and often professional guidance.

By reading this book, you acknowledge that you understand these disclaimers and assume full responsibility for your financial decisions.

SECTION I

THE SHIFT

From Earning to Architecting Wealth

CHAPTER 1:

THE DEATH OF THE 60/40 PORTFOLIO

On December 31, 2021, Sarah reviewed her retirement accounts with satisfaction. Twenty years of disciplined investing—60% in stock index funds, 40% in bonds—had grown to $1.2 million. Every financial advisor, every book, every calculator told her she was on track.

By December 31, 2022, that portfolio was worth $960,000. Stocks fell 18%. Bonds, supposed to be her hedge, fell 13%—the worst year for bonds since 1788. Her "diversified" portfolio did exactly what it wasn't supposed to do: both components declined together.

She had followed every rule and lost a decade of progress in twelve months.

The Great Unraveling

The 60/40 portfolio was the genius solution to a specific era. From 1980 to 2020, it worked because of a unique convergence:

Declining interest rates: When rates fall, bond prices rise. The 40-year bull market in bonds propped up portfolios during stock crashes. In 1980, 10-year Treasury yields were 15%. By 2020, they were 0.5%. That one-way trip is over. Rates can't fall below zero (for long), and rising rates devastate bond portfolios.

Negative correlation: Historically, when stocks fell, bonds rose, and vice versa. This relationship broke after the 2008 financial crisis. Central bank intervention tied both asset classes to the same puppet strings. Now they often move together—especially downward.

Low inflation: From 1990-2020, inflation averaged 2.3%. Cash lost purchasing power slowly enough that modest bond yields could keep pace. Post-pandemic inflation spiked to 9%, evaporating the real returns of both stocks and bonds. A 7% nominal return minus 4% inflation equals 3% real growth—barely enough to outpace lifestyle expansion.

Limited alternatives: Forty years ago, ordinary investors had few choices. Today, technology has democratized access to private markets, real assets, and alternative income streams that were once reserved for institutions.

The 60/40 portfolio wasn't designed for a world of:

- Zero-to-negative real interest rates
- Synchronized global markets
- Persistent structural inflation
- Algorithmic trading destroying traditional correlations
- Democratized access to private market returns

The New Math of Diversification

True diversification isn't owning different stocks. It's owning different types of returns.

Consider three $100,000 portfolios:

Portfolio A (Traditional):

- 60% S&P 500
- 40% Aggregate Bond Index
- Expected return: 6-7%
- Income generated: $2,400/year (2.4%)
- Correlation to market crashes: 95%

Portfolio B (Modern):

1. 25% Index funds (Core stability)
2. 25% Real estate syndications (Cash flow + appreciation)
3. 20% Private credit funds (High current income)
4. 15% Venture/PE (Asymmetric upside)
5. 10% Cash/liquid alternatives (Dry powder)
6. 5% Commodities/Real assets (Inflation hedge)
7. Expected return: 8-12%
8. Income generated: $6,500-8,000/year (6.5-8%)
9. Correlation to market crashes: 40%

Portfolio C (Architect's Portfolio):

- 20% Core equities (Foundation)
- 30% Income-producing real estate (Stability)

- 20% Private market opportunities (Growth)
- 15% Cash-flowing alternatives (Royalties, revenue shares)
- 10% Venture/startup exposure (Asymmetry)
- 5% Inflation hedges (Commodities, TIPS, hard assets)
- Expected return: 10-15%
- Income generated: $8,000-10,000/year (8-10%)
- Correlation to market crashes: 25%

Portfolio C not only targets higher returns—it produces 3-4x the income while being dramatically less correlated to stock market crashes.

The Rise of Personal Family Offices

Traditionally, family offices managed wealth for dynasties worth $100 million+. They invested in private deals, formed syndications, negotiated direct access to funds, and built diversified portfolios across dozens of asset classes.

Today, technology is democratizing that model:

- Syndication platforms allow $25,000-$50,000 minimums for institutional-quality real estate
- AngelList and Republic provide venture access starting at $1,000
- Private credit platforms offer 9-12% yields to accredited investors
- Masterworks and Rally enable fractional ownership of art and collectibles
- Yield-farming protocols in DeFi offer alternative income streams

You don't need $100 million to build a family office approach. You need $100,000 and the knowledge to deploy it intelligently.

The Intelligent Diversification Framework

Moving beyond 60/40 requires understanding what you're actually diversifying:

1. Return drivers: Don't just diversify by asset class. Diversify by what generates the return—equity appreciation, contractual income, inflation pass-through, asymmetric bets.

2. Time horizons: Some capital should be liquid (emergencies, opportunities). Some should be locked for 5-10 years (compounding, tax efficiency). Traditional portfolios are entirely liquid, which seems safe but limits access to higher-returning illiquid investments.

3. Risk types: Stocks carry market risk. Real estate carries tenant and refinancing risk. Startups carry execution risk. Private credit carries default risk. When properly uncorrelated, these risks offset each other.

4. Income vs. growth: The old model assumed you'd accumulate for 40 years, then sell down assets in retirement. The new model generates income throughout, never forcing you to sell during downturns.

Case Study: The Nurse Who Designed Freedom

Maria (from our introduction) didn't start wealthy. At 29, she had $35,000 saved—purely in a Vanguard Target Date Fund.

Year 1-2: She educated herself (books, podcasts, communities) while continuing to max her Roth IRA in index funds. Core foundation: stability first.

Year 3: She joined a real estate syndication with $25,000—a 200-unit multifamily property in Texas. Projected returns: 7% annual cash distributions, 15-18% IRR over 5 years.

Year 4: Her first distribution: $1,750. She reinvested it into a second syndication (different market, different operator—diversification).

Year 5: She allocated $10,000 to a private credit fund yielding 11% annually. Another $5,000 to a music royalty investment platform.

Year 6 (current): Five income streams now generate $15,000/year—25% of her expenses. Her net worth is $180,000, but her "freedom progress" is 25% (passive income as % of expenses).

Maria's freedom number is $60,000/year passive income. At her current trajectory, she'll reach it in 8-10 years—at age 42. Not through spectacular bets, but through systematic architecture.

The Architect's Shift

The death of 60/40 isn't a crisis. It's an invitation.

An invitation to stop being a passive portfolio collector and become an active portfolio architect. To stop accepting average returns and start designing superior outcomes. To stop fearing volatility and start building systems that thrive in chaos.

The next chapter explores the three types of investors and why only one achieves true freedom.

Key Takeaways:

- The 60/40 portfolio worked for a specific era that has ended
- True diversification means different return drivers, not different stocks
- Modern investors can access institutional-quality alternatives
- Income generation is as important as capital appreciation
- The new goal: design cash flow, not just accumulate net worth

CHAPTER 2:

THE INVESTOR'S EVOLUTION

Not all investors are created equal. After observing thousands of portfolios and wealth journeys, I've identified three distinct archetypes. Most investors cycle through all three before reaching mastery—if they ever do.

The Three Investor Archetypes

Type 1: The Collector

Mindset: "I need to own everything the experts recommend."

The Collector reads every article, watches every YouTube video, and follows every guru. Their portfolio is a junk drawer of investments: 12 different ETFs with overlapping holdings, a few individual stocks from Reddit, cryptocurrency from a 2021 FOMO moment, a robo-advisor account, a 401(k) they haven't reviewed in years, and maybe a rental property they wish they never bought.

They confuse activity with progress. Complexity with sophistication.

Example: David, 41, has accounts at Vanguard, Fidelity, Robinhood, Coinbase, and Betterment. He owns 47 different positions. When asked about his investment thesis, he says, "I'm diversified." When asked about his expected return, he shrugs. When asked about his passive income, he says "$0—but my net worth is up when markets are up."

The Collector's Portfolio:

- Average return: Market return minus fees and mistiming (5-6%)
- Income generation: Minimal
- Stress level: High (constantly monitoring, reacting)
- Time to freedom: Never (no systematic plan)

Collectors operate from scarcity. They fear missing out, so they chase everything. They fear loss, so they over-diversify into meaninglessness. They accumulate assets but never architect a system.

Type 2: The Speculator

Mindset: "I can beat the market with the right trade."

The Speculator graduated from collecting to conviction—but in the wrong direction. They believe they can predict markets, time trades, and identify the next Amazon or Bitcoin. They read The Intelligent Investor but internalized only the stories of Buffett's wins, not his discipline.

Speculators allocate heavily based on narratives. They loved tech in 2021, energy in 2022, and AI in 2023. They make bold bets, experience spectacular wins, and give it all back (plus more) on subsequent losses. Their portfolio returns look like an electrocardiogram.

Example: Jennifer, 38, turned $50,000 into $190,000 in 2020-2021 trading tech stocks and crypto. She felt like a genius. By 2023, she was back to $35,000. She's now "rebuilding" with options trading. When asked about her strategy, she says, "High risk, high reward—you have to play big to win big."

The Speculator's Portfolio:

- Average return: Highly volatile—big wins and bigger losses (2-4% long-term)
- Income generation: None (capital gains only)
- Stress level: Extreme (obsessive monitoring)
- Time to freedom: Never (always one bad bet away from reset)

Speculators operate from ego. They need to be right, to be exceptional. They confuse luck with skill and randomness with pattern. Ironically, they work harder than Collectors and achieve worse outcomes.

Type 3: The Architect

Mindset: "I design systems that generate freedom regardless of market conditions."

The Architect doesn't predict. They prepare. They don't chase returns. They design outcomes. They understand that wealth is built through compounding, diversification, cash flow, and discipline—not brilliance.

Architects ask different questions:

- "What income does this generate annually?"
- "How is this uncorrelated to my other holdings?"
- "What's the risk-adjusted return over 5-10 years?"

- "Does this move me closer to financial autonomy?"

They build portfolios like engineers design bridges: with load calculations, stress testing, redundancy, and safety margins. They prioritize resilience over brilliance.

Example: Marcus, 45, has $850,000 allocated across:

- 30% index funds (foundation)
- 35% real estate syndications (cash flow)
- 15% private credit (income)
- 10% venture/PE (asymmetric upside)
- 10% cash/opportunities (dry powder)

His portfolio generates $52,000/year in passive income—covering 75% of his family's expenses. His target: 100% coverage by age 50. He doesn't check his portfolio daily. He doesn't react to market crashes. He rebalances annually and deploys capital into opportunities during downturns.

The Architect's Portfolio:

- Average return: 10-14% (less volatile than Speculator, higher than Collector)
- Income generation: 6-8% annually
- Stress level: Low (system-driven, not emotion-driven)
- Time to freedom: Defined and trackable

Architects operate from purpose. They know their "why" and build accordingly. They measure progress by freedom gained, not wealth accumulated.

The Evolution Path

Most successful investors progress through these stages:

Stage 1: Unconscious Collector (Ages 20-30) You're saving in a 401(k) because HR told you to. You have no strategy beyond "buy index funds." This is fine—you're building the foundation.

Stage 2: Conscious Collector (Ages 28-35) You've educated yourself. You're maxing tax-advantaged accounts. You're comparing expense ratios. You're diversifying across asset classes. This is good—you're optimizing the basics.

Stage 3: Tempted Speculator (Ages 30-40) You've had some wins. You think you've figured it out. You make a concentrated bet. Maybe you win big. Maybe you lose hard. Either way, you learn.

Stage 4: Humbled Architect (Ages 35-50) You've experienced full market cycles. You've learned that no one can consistently predict markets. You shift from speculation to architecture—building systems, not chasing returns.

Stage 5: Evolved Architect (Ages 45+) Your system is mature, diversified, and cash-flowing. You focus on preservation, legacy, and teaching others. You've achieved financial autonomy and use it to pursue meaning, not more money.

The goal isn't to skip stages—it's to shorten them. To learn from others' mistakes rather than repeating them. To recognize which archetype you currently embody and deliberately evolve.

The Architect's Advantage

Why do Architects win when Collectors and Speculators don't?

1. **Systems Over Predictions**: Architects don't need to predict interest rates, earnings reports, or market crashes. Their diversified, cash-flowing systems perform across scenarios.

2. **Income Over Appreciation**: While Collectors and Speculators rely entirely on asset price increases, Architects generate income regardless of valuations. In a sideways or down market, they still eat.

3. **Compounding Through Reinvestment**: Regular cash flow creates reinvestment opportunities. Architects deploy into weakness while others panic-sell.

4. **Emotional Resilience**: When you've architected resilience, you don't fear crashes—you welcome them as buying opportunities. Your system has shock absorbers.

5. **Freedom as the Metric**: Collectors measure net worth. Speculators measure returns. Architects measure autonomy. When passive income exceeds expenses, the game changes entirely.

Case Study: The System Income Revolution

Tom spent 15 years as a corporate attorney earning $280,000/year. He hated it but felt trapped—his lifestyle expanded with his income. At 42, he had $1.4 million saved, entirely in index funds.

Then he discovered architecture.

Over three years, he methodically repositioned his portfolio:

- Kept $350,000 in index funds (foundation)
- Deployed $600,000 into real estate syndications (projected 7% annual distributions)
- Allocated $300,000 to private credit and income-producing alternatives (9-11% yields)
- Kept $150,000 liquid (opportunities + emergency)

His new system generated $85,000/year in passive income—more than covering his family's $72,000 annual expenses.

At 45, Tom quit his job. Not to retire, but to pursue what he always wanted: teaching financial literacy to underserved communities. His system income gave him the freedom to do meaningful work without financial stress.

He's not richer than when he was a lawyer. He's freer. And freedom, it turns out, is the ultimate return.

The Architect's Mindset Principles

To evolve into an Architect, adopt these mental models:

1. Wealth is a system, not a destination. There's no finish line. Even billionaires face financial insecurity if they depend entirely on asset appreciation. Build systems that feed you indefinitely.

2. You can't predict, but you can prepare. No one knows what markets will do tomorrow. Everyone can build portfolios that thrive across scenarios.

3. Income is freedom; net worth is score. A $5 million portfolio generating no income is a prison. A $500,000 portfolio generating $50,000/year is liberation.

4. Risk is not volatility—it's ruin. Stock prices fluctuating 20% isn't a risk if you don't need to sell. Losing your job with no passive income is a risk.

5. Time is the ultimate asset. Money is renewable. Time is not. The goal is to buy time—through passive income, through autonomy, through optionality.

Your Evolution Begins Now

Where are you today? Collector? Speculator? Architect?

The answer doesn't matter as much as the direction you choose tomorrow.

In the next chapter, we redefine what wealth actually means—and why freedom, not fortune, is the goal worth pursuing.

Key Takeaways:

- Three investor types: Collectors accumulate, Speculators gamble, Architects design
- Evolution requires self-awareness and deliberate mindset shifts
- The Architect advantage: systems, income, compounding, resilience, freedom
- Success is measured by autonomy gained, not wealth accumulated
- You can't skip stages, but you can accelerate through them with learning

CHAPTER 3:

FREEDOM AS THE TRUE RETURN

Let me tell you about two people.

Person A: Net worth \$3.5 million, age 52. Works 60 hours/week in a job she tolerates. Terrified of market crashes because her portfolio is entirely in stocks—if it drops 40%, her retirement plan collapses. Takes one week of vacation per year. Passive income: \$0.

Person B: Net worth \$600,000, age 48. Works 15 hours/week on projects she loves. Portfolio generates \$48,000/year in cash flow, covering 90% of expenses. Took three months off last year to travel. Completely unbothered by market volatility because her income streams are contractual and diversified.

Who's wealthier?

By traditional metrics, Person A is winning. By every metric that matters—time sovereignty, stress levels, optionality, life satisfaction—Person B is in a different universe.

This chapter rewrites the equation. Wealth isn't money. Wealth is freedom. And freedom has a precise, calculable formula.

The Failure of Net Worth

Net worth is a terrible proxy for financial health.

It's backward-looking (what you've accumulated), not forward-looking (what you can access). It's static (a snapshot), not dynamic (a flow). It measures score, not capability.

Consider:

- A \$2 million home you live in adds to net worth but generates no income
- A \$1 million retirement account you can't touch for 15 years is "wealth" you can't use
- A \$500,000 brokerage account in stocks might crash 50% tomorrow

Meanwhile:

- A $100,000 investment in a rental property syndication generating 7% annual distributions produces $7,000/year—forever
- A $50,000 stake in a private credit fund yielding 10% generates $5,000/year in passive income
- A $25,000 venture investment that 5x's to $125,000 creates capital you can redeploy

Net worth tells you where you've been. Cash flow tells you where you're going.

The Freedom Equation

Here's the formula that changes everything:

Passive Income ≥ Living Expenses = Infinite Optionality

Let me break it down:

Passive Income: Money that arrives regardless of your active effort. Rental income, dividends, royalties, business cash flow, fund distributions, interest from lending.

Living Expenses: Your annual cost to maintain your chosen lifestyle. Not what you could spend. What you need to spend to feel content.

Infinite Optionality: The moment passive income exceeds expenses, work becomes optional. You can still work—many do—but it's from desire, not necessity. You've bought back your time.

The Three Financial Horizons

Most people think in two dimensions: working and retired. Architects think in three:

Horizon 1: Dependent (Passive Income < 25% of Expenses)

You're entirely reliant on active income. If you stop working, your lifestyle collapses within months. This isn't shameful—it's the starting point for 90% of people.

Goal: Build foundation. Max tax-advantaged accounts. Eliminate high-interest debt. Start accumulating capital.

Psychology: Scarcity. Fear of job loss. No optionality.

Example: Derrick, 28, earns $72,000. Spends $55,000/year. Saves $15,000 annually. Has $40,000 invested, generating $800/year in dividends. Status: 1.5% financially free.

Horizon 2: Augmented (Passive Income = 25-75% of Expenses)

You've built meaningful income streams. You're not free yet, but you have a cushion. Job loss is stressful, not catastrophic. You can take lower-paying work you enjoy because passive income fills the gap.

Goal: Accelerate income-producing investments. Diversify. Optimize tax efficiency.

Psychology: Confidence. Reduced fear. Growing optionality.

Example: Shanice, 39, needs $65,000/year. Earns $90,000 in salary. Passive income: $32,000/year (49% of expenses). Status: She could take a $58,000 job doing something she loves—the passive income covers the gap.

Horizon 3: Autonomous (Passive Income ≥ 100% of Expenses)

You've crossed the threshold. Work is optional. You might still work because you enjoy it, but you're not dependent on it. You've achieved financial freedom—not retirement, autonomy.

Goal: Preserve and grow. Legacy planning. Optimize lifestyle and impact.

Psychology: Abundance. Time sovereignty. Infinite optionality.

Example: Raymond, 51, needs $80,000/year. Passive income: $95,000/year (119% of expenses). Status: He quit his corporate job and now advises startups for equity. He travels six months per year. He works because he wants to, not because he has to.

Redefining ROI

Traditional investing measures ROI as Return on Investment—a simple percentage.

Architects measure three types of returns:

1. Return on Investment (Traditional ROI)

The financial gain. A 12% annual return on capital.

Important but incomplete. A speculative stock might return 30% one year and -40% the next. A real estate syndication might return a steady 15% IRR over five years. Which is better? Depends on your system.

2. Return on Intent (Purposeful ROI)

Does this investment align with your values and goals?

- If you value impact, does it support businesses solving real problems?
- If you value autonomy, does it generate income or just appreciation?
- If you value learning, does it expose you to new markets or models?

Example: Investing in a local affordable housing project might return 10% financially but also create community impact, teach you real estate, and align with your values. Purposeful ROI: high.

3. Return on Impact (Systemic ROI)

Does this investment move you closer to freedom or lock you in?

- A 401(k) generates compounding but no access for decades—low impact on near-term freedom
- A cash-flowing syndication generates immediate income—high impact on freedom progress
- A speculative crypto bet might 10x but contributes nothing to systematic wealth—low impact

Example: You have $50,000 to deploy. Option A: Growth stock projected 15% annual return, $0 income. Option B: Private credit fund projected 11% annual return, $5,500/year income. Traditional ROI favors A. Impact ROI favors B—it generates immediate progress toward autonomy.

The Freedom Number

Your Freedom Number is the single most important metric you'll calculate. It's not your net worth goal. It's your annual passive income target.

The Formula:

Freedom Number = Annual Expenses ÷ Conservative Income Yield

Let's say your annual expenses are $75,000 (housing, food, insurance, discretionary). You determine you can build a diversified portfolio yielding 7% annually in cash flow (realistic with modern alternatives).

Freedom Number = $75,000 ÷ 0.07 = $1,071,428

When you've allocated roughly $1.07 million into income-producing assets averaging 7% yield, you've achieved financial autonomy.

Notice: This is far less than the typical "$2-3 million retirement target" financial advisors suggest. Why? Because you're engineering income, not relying purely on asset appreciation.

The Time-Money Tradeoff Reimagined

Traditional wisdom says: Work hard for 40 years, save aggressively, retire at 65 with $2-3 million.

Architect wisdom says: Build income systematically, reach financial autonomy in 10-20 years, use your 40s-60s to pursue meaning rather than money.

Traditional Path:

- Age 25-65: Work full-time (80,000 hours)
- Age 65-85: "Freedom" (but declining health, limited time)
- Passive income during career: $0
- Autonomy gained: 20 years (after physical peak)

Architect Path:

- Age 25-45: Work full-time + build income systems (40,000 hours)
- Age 45-85: Passive income covers expenses (60,000 hours of freedom)
- Passive income during career: Growing annually
- Autonomy gained: 40 years (during physical and mental peak)

Same career length. Double the freedom years. And you experience autonomy when you can most enjoy it.

The Lifestyle Design Question

Most people increase spending as income rises. They're on a hedonic treadmill—always needing more to feel satisfied.

Architects ask: "What's my enough number?"

- How much do you need annually to feel content, not deprived?
- What lifestyle actually makes you happy versus impresses others?
- Where's the point of diminishing returns on spending?

Research shows life satisfaction increases with income up to roughly $75,000-90,000/year (adjusted for location). Beyond that, marginal happiness gains are minimal.

If you can design a fulfilling life on $70,000/year, your Freedom Number might be $1 million. If you need $150,000/year, it might be $2.1 million. If you're disciplined enough to live well on $50,000/year, it might be $715,000.

The less you need, the faster you're free. This isn't about deprivation—it's about intentionality.

Case Study: The Portfolio That Bought Time

At 33, Elena was a marketing director earning $135,000. She was miserable. She wanted to write novels but couldn't afford to quit.

She ran the numbers:

- Annual expenses (lean lifestyle): $48,000
- Freedom Number (at 7% yield): $685,714

She had $180,000 saved (in index funds) and committed to aggressive allocation:

- Save $60,000/year for 5 years = $300,000
- Reallocate existing $180,000 into income-producing assets
- Target portfolio: $480,000 by age 38

Projected income at 7% yield: $33,600/year (70% of expenses).

She wouldn't be fully free, but 70% coverage meant she could take a part-time job earning $20,000/year and write the rest of the time.

Her actual outcome: By 38, her portfolio was at $520,000 (market performance + compounding). Annual passive income: $36,400.

She now works 15 hours/week as a freelance strategist (earning $30,000/year), writes 25 hours/week, and has published two novels.

Her net worth is modest by societal standards. Her freedom is extraordinary by any measure.

The Freedom Index

Forget tracking net worth obsessively. Track your Freedom Index:

Freedom Index = (Passive Income ÷ Annual Expenses) × 100

Examples:

- Passive income $15,000, Expenses $60,000 = Freedom Index of 25%
- Passive income $45,000, Expenses $60,000 = Freedom Index of 75%
- Passive income $72,000, Expenses $60,000 = Freedom Index of 120%

At 100%+, you've achieved financial autonomy. But meaningful milestones happen earlier:

- 25% Freedom: You can weather job loss for 3+ months without panic
- 50% Freedom: You can take lower-paying work you enjoy
- 75% Freedom: You can work part-time or take extended sabbaticals
- 100% Freedom: Work becomes entirely optional
- 150% Freedom: You're building legacy wealth and can increase lifestyle

Track this quarterly. Celebrate every 5% gain. This number tells you what your net worth doesn't: how close you are to sovereignty.

The Misconception of Sacrifice

People hear "live on less" and think of deprivation. Architects think optimization.

You're not sacrificing—you're choosing. You're not restricting—you're prioritizing.

Poor trade: $800/month luxury car lease for 40 years = $384,000 spent, $0 remaining
Smart trade: $300/month reliable car for 40 years + invest the $500/month difference at 8% = $1,397,000 accumulated

Same 40 years. One choice bought status. One choice bought freedom.

The question isn't "What can I afford?" It's "What serves my freedom?"

Freedom Beyond Finance

Here's what changes when passive income exceeds expenses:

Time sovereignty: Your calendar becomes yours. No more trading time for money.

Relationship quality: Financial stress destroys relationships. Financial security allows presence, generosity, and patience.

Health improvements: Chronic stress from financial insecurity causes measurable health damage. Autonomy reduces cortisol, improves sleep, and extends longevity.

Risk tolerance: When you're not dependent on a paycheck, you can take intelligent risks—start businesses, change careers, relocate.

Authenticity: You stop doing what you "should" and start doing what resonates. You can afford to be yourself.

Generosity: Financial margin creates capacity to help others—family, community, causes.

Legacy: You shift from surviving to contributing. Your focus expands beyond yourself.

This is why freedom is the true return. Money is a means. Autonomy is the end.

The Two Freedoms

Understanding this distinction is critical:

Financial Independence (FI): Passive income ≥ expenses. You don't need a job.

Financial Freedom (FF): Passive income significantly exceeds expenses. You have the margin to be generous, take risks, and absorb setbacks without stress.

Many pursue FI and stop. They've reached the threshold but live tight. Every market dip causes anxiety. They achieved independence but not freedom.

Architects target 125-150% coverage—enough to feel abundant, not just adequate. Enough to say yes to opportunities, not just no to necessity.

Your Freedom Equation

Pull out a calculator. Let's run your numbers:

1. What are your true annual expenses? (Housing + food + insurance + transportation + utilities + discretionary) = $_______

2. What's your target passive income yield? (Conservative: 6-7% | Moderate: 8-9% | Aggressive: 10%+) = _______%

3. Your Freedom Number: (Annual Expenses ÷ Income Yield) = $_______

4. Your current passive income: (Dividends + rental income + distributions + royalties + interest) = $_______/year

5. Your Freedom Index: (Current Passive Income ÷ Annual Expenses × 100) = _______%

6. Years to freedom: (Assuming you deploy $X/year at Y% return) = _______ years

This is your starting point. This is your North Star.

Every investment decision should be evaluated against one question: Does this accelerate my path to 100%?

The Mental Shift

From this moment forward:

- Stop comparing net worth to peers
- Start tracking Freedom Index
- Stop chasing maximum returns
- Start engineering systematic income
- Stop accumulating for accumulation's sake
- Start building for autonomy

The game changes when you realize: The goal was never to be rich. The goal was always to be free.

And freedom, unlike wealth, has a finish line. You'll know the moment you cross it.

Key Takeaways:

- Wealth is freedom, not net worth
- The Freedom Equation: Passive Income ≥ Expenses = Infinite Optionality
- Three horizons: Dependent, Augmented, Autonomous
- Calculate your Freedom Number and Freedom Index
- Track progress toward autonomy, not arbitrary wealth targets
- Financial freedom enables time sovereignty, health, relationships, impact, and authenticity

CHAPTER 4:

THE PORFTFOLIO AS A LIVING SYSTEM

On a spring morning in 1988, a seemingly small event would reshape our understanding of complex systems forever.

Yellowstone National Park, after decades of wolf extinction, had become overpopulated with elk. The elk overgrazed riverside vegetation. Riverbanks eroded. Beaver populations collapsed. Songbirds disappeared. The entire ecosystem was dying.

Then, in 1995, biologists reintroduced 14 wolves.

What happened next stunned ecologists. The wolves didn't just control elk populations—they changed elk behavior. Elk avoided valleys and gorges where they could be trapped. Vegetation regenerated. Riverbanks stabilized. Beavers returned and built dams. The dams created habitats for otters, ducks, and fish. Songbirds returned. Bears found more berries. The rivers literally changed course.

Fourteen wolves transformed an entire ecosystem through cascading effects no one predicted.

Your portfolio is the same type of system.

Beyond the Mechanics: Systems Thinking

Most investors view portfolios mechanically: inputs (contributions) + operations (investments) = outputs (returns).

Architects view portfolios organically: living systems with feedback loops, emergent properties, and evolutionary adaptation.

Consider these parallels:

Ecosystem: Wolves → Elk behavior → Vegetation → Rivers → Biodiversity Portfolio: Income assets → Cash flow → Reinvestment → Compounding → Freedom

Ecosystem: Species diversity creates resilience against disease, climate change, invasive species Portfolio: Asset diversity creates resilience against crashes, inflation, policy changes

Ecosystem: Energy flows through trophic levels, each supporting the next Portfolio: Capital flows through asset classes, each feeding the system differently

Ecosystem: Adaptation occurs through natural selection over generations Portfolio: Adaptation occurs through learning, rebalancing, and strategic evolution

The lesson: You can't control a complex system through micromanagement. You design initial conditions, monitor feedback, and intervene strategically.

The Four Properties of Living Portfolios

Property 1: Diversity = Resilience

In nature, monocultures collapse. A field of only corn is vulnerable to corn-specific diseases, pests, and weather. A forest with 40 species of trees survives.

In finance, concentration is fragility. A portfolio of only tech stocks collapses when tech crashes. A portfolio across asset classes, geographies, and return drivers survives.

But diversity isn't just owning different stocks. It's owning different types of returns:

- Contractual returns: Bonds, private credit (you're owed a specific payment)
- Equity returns: Stocks, real estate appreciation (you own a piece of value)
- Arbitrage returns: Market inefficiencies, mispricing (you exploit temporary dislocations)
- Inflation-linked returns: Commodities, TIPS (you benefit from rising prices)
- Asymmetric returns: Venture capital, options (unlimited upside, limited downside)

When one return driver fails, others continue feeding the system.

Property 2: Feedback Loops Create Acceleration

In ecosystems, positive feedback loops amplify growth. Plants grow → more shade → better moisture retention → more plants.

In portfolios, income reinvestment creates exponential compounding:

Year 1: $100,000 portfolio generating 7% income = $7,000 Year 2: You reinvest the $7,000 + add $10,000 = $117,000 portfolio → $8,190 income Year 3: Reinvest $8,190 + add $10,000 = $135,190 portfolio → $9,463 income Year 10: Portfolio = $247,000 → $17,290 income

The feedback loop (income → reinvestment → larger income) accelerates without additional effort.

Negative feedback loops stabilize the system. When stocks become overvalued, you rebalance into undervalued assets. When cash flow exceeds needs, you deploy into growth. The system self-corrects.

Property 3: Emergence (The Whole > Sum of Parts)

Ant colonies exhibit intelligence no individual ant possesses. Birds flock in complex patterns without a leader. Markets discover prices through millions of independent decisions.

Portfolios exhibit emergent properties:

- Risk reduction through diversification: Ten 20%-volatile assets create a portfolio with 8% volatility
- Income stability through variety: Five income streams, each varying 30%, create combined variance of 10%
- Antifragility through optionality: A portfolio with 10% in high-risk asymmetric bets becomes stronger during chaos

You design components, but the system behavior emerges from their interactions.

Property 4: Adaptation Through Evolution

Species evolve. Successful traits proliferate. Failed experiments die. The system learns.

Portfolios should evolve:

- Learning from cycles: After experiencing a crash, you add uncorrelated assets
- Responding to life stages: In your 30s you prioritize growth; in your 50s you prioritize income
- Incorporating new opportunities: When private credit democratizes, you add it to your mix
- Pruning failures: When an investment thesis breaks, you exit rather than hope

Static portfolios are dead portfolios. Living portfolios adapt.

The Portfolio Architecture Pyramid™

Every ecosystem has layers—forest floor, understory, canopy. Each serves a different function.

Your portfolio needs the same structure:

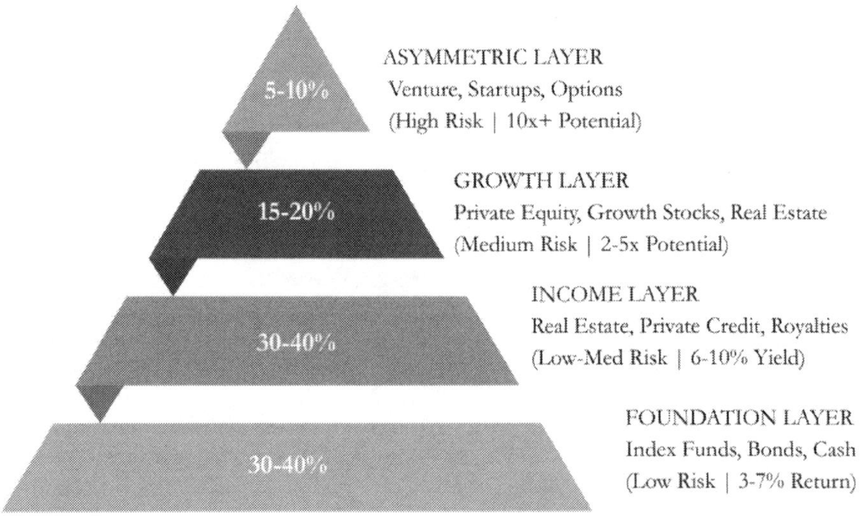

Foundation Layer: Stability

Purpose: Survive. Provide liquidity. Weather storms. Assets: Index funds, bonds, cash, short-term treasuries Characteristics: Liquid, low-volatility, reliable Role: This is your bedrock. It doesn't excite you. It protects you.

Allocation: 25-35% (higher when young or risk-tolerant, lower when nearing autonomy)

Income Layer: Cash Flow

Purpose: Generate systematic passive income. Fund freedom. Assets: Real estate syndications, private credit, dividend stocks, royalties, revenue shares Characteristics: Semi-liquid to illiquid, contractual or predictable income, moderate risk Role: This is your oxygen. It feeds you monthly/quarterly regardless of market conditions.

Allocation: 30-40% (the core of the freedom portfolio)

Growth Layer: Appreciation

Purpose: Compound capital. Build wealth over 5-10 years. Assets: Growth stocks, private equity, established businesses, long-term real estate Characteristics: Illiquid, moderate-to-high volatility, doubling potential Role: This is your muscle. It grows your system's capacity over time.

Allocation: 15-25% (higher when young, lower when autonomous)

Asymmetric Layer: Moonshots

Purpose: Capture outlier returns. Turn $10K into $100K+. Assets: Venture capital, angel investments, crypto, options strategies Characteristics: Highly illiquid, extreme risk, potential for 10-100x returns Role: This is your lottery ticket—except with skill, research, and calculated risk.

Allocation: 5-15% (maximum amount you can afford to lose entirely)

The System's Metabolic Rate

Every organism has a metabolism—the rate at which it converts inputs to energy.

Portfolios have metabolic rates determined by liquidity and turnover:

Slow metabolism (Turtle Portfolio):

- 60% foundation, 35% income, 5% growth
- Rebalances annually
- Minimal trading, tax-efficient
- Best for: Risk-averse individuals, those near autonomy, preservation-focused wealth

Medium metabolism (Architect Portfolio):

- 30% foundation, 35% income, 25% growth, 10% asymmetric
- Rebalances quarterly
- Moderate activity, strategic deployment
- Best for: Wealth builders, those 10-20 years from autonomy, balanced approach

Fast metabolism (Builder Portfolio):

- 20% foundation, 30% income, 30% growth, 20% asymmetric
- Rebalances monthly, actively deploys into opportunities
- Higher activity, tax considerations managed through structure
- Best for: High earners, long time horizons, sophisticated investors, builders under 45

Your portfolio's metabolism should match your season of life and risk capacity.

Compounding: The System's Superpower

Albert Einstein allegedly called compound interest "the eighth wonder of the world." Whether he said it or not, the principle stands.

But most people misunderstand compounding. They think it's just: money × time × interest rate.

True compounding has four dimensions:

1. Capital Compounding

Traditional: Your $100,000 grows to $107,000 at 7%, then $114,490, then $122,504...

This is good but limited. You're only compounding your initial capital plus gains.

2. Income Compounding

Advanced: Your $100,000 generates $7,000 income. You reinvest it, plus add $10,000 from earnings. Now $117,000 compounds.

This accelerates growth because you're adding fuel beyond market returns.

3. Knowledge Compounding

Mastery: With each investment, you learn. You improve due diligence. You build networks. You recognize patterns. Your decision quality improves, increasing your effective return.

Year 1: You might make a 6% return Year 5: Your improved skill generates 9% on the same strategy Year 10: Your expertise and network generate 12%

4. Optionality Compounding

Freedom: As passive income grows, you can take career risks—start businesses, consult, invest sweat equity in startups. These opportunities can 10x your wealth faster than passive compounding alone.

Example: Your portfolio generates $50,000/year. You can now angel invest time (not just money) into a startup, earning founder-level equity. That opportunity wasn't available when you needed every dollar of salary.

True compounding is multidimensional. The longer you're in the system, the more dimensions activate.

System Maintenance: Rebalancing and Pruning

Ecosystems need fires, floods, and predators to stay healthy. Without them, invasive species dominate and diversity collapses.

Portfolios need rebalancing and pruning.

Rebalancing: Restoring Equilibrium

As assets perform differently, allocations drift. Your 30% real estate position becomes 40% after appreciation. Your 10% asymmetric layer becomes 5% after a loss.

Rebalancing isn't just selling winners and buying losers—it's restoring your intended system design.

How often?

- Quarterly for active portfolios
- Annually for moderate portfolios
- Triggered by thresholds (when any allocation drifts 10%+ from target)

Pruning: Cutting Dead Weight

Not every investment works. Some theses break. Some managers underperform. Some markets shift permanently.

Architects prune without emotion:

- If a real estate syndication projected 7% returns but delivered 2% for three years, exit
- If a private fund charges 2% fees and returns less than index funds, exit
- If a startup you invested in has been "6 months from launch" for two years, write it off

Dead branches drain energy from healthy parts of the system. Cut them.

Case Study: The Portfolio That Evolved

Priya started at 29 with $60,000, entirely in a Vanguard Target Date Fund. Simple. Safe. Fine for beginnings.

Stage 1 (Ages 29-32): Foundation She kept 100% in index funds while learning about alternatives. She read, attended webinars, and joined investor communities. Her portfolio grew to $120,000.

Stage 2 (Ages 32-35): Diversification She began adding layers:

- 60% index funds (foundation)
- 30% real estate syndications (income)
- 10% private credit (income)

Her system now generated $6,800/year passive income. Portfolio: $180,000.

Stage 3 (Ages 35-38): Optimization She refined allocations based on learnings:

- 35% index funds
- 35% real estate

- 20% private credit
- 10% venture/PE through funds

Income: $14,200/year. Portfolio: $280,000.

Stage 4 (Ages 38-42): Acceleration Income compounding kicked in. She reinvested all distributions plus salary savings:

- 30% index funds
- 35% real estate
- 20% private credit/alternatives
- 10% direct venture investments
- 5% crypto/emerging tech

Income: $31,000/year (48% of expenses). Portfolio: $485,000.

Stage 5 (Age 42-present, age 45): Autonomy Her system now generates $42,000/year—covering 68% of expenses. By 48, she projects 100% coverage.

Her portfolio evolved like an organism: simple foundation → diversified structure → optimized metabolism → accelerating growth → approaching autonomy.

She didn't get lucky. She designed a living system and let it compound.

Your System Design Checklist

A healthy portfolio system exhibits:

- ✓ **Diversity across return drivers:** Not just different stocks, but different *types* of returns
- ✓ **Income generation:** At least 30-40% in cash-flowing assets
- ✓ **Asymmetric exposure:** Small allocations to high-upside opportunities
- ✓ **Liquidity layers:** Some money accessible within days, some locked for years
- ✓ **Rebalancing discipline:** Regular maintenance, not emotional reaction
- ✓ **Adaptation capacity:** Willingness to add new opportunities and prune failures
- ✓ **Tax efficiency:** Structured to minimize friction and maximize compounding
- ✓ **Alignment with values:** Investments you understand and believe in

If your portfolio lacks any of these, it's not a system—it's a collection.

The Living Portfolio Mindset

From today forward, stop asking: "What should I buy?"

Start asking:

- "What does my system need?"
- "Which layer is underdeveloped?"
- "What would make my portfolio more resilient?"
- "Does this investment strengthen my feedback loops?"

You're not a stock picker. You're a system architect.

You're not gambling on individual bets. You're designing an organism that generates freedom.

And like any living system, the magic isn't in the parts—it's in how they interact.

Key Takeaways:

- Portfolios are living systems, not mechanical collections
- Diversity creates resilience; feedback loops create acceleration
- The Portfolio Architecture Pyramid: Foundation → Income → Growth → Asymmetric
- True compounding is multidimensional: capital, income, knowledge, optionality
- Living systems require maintenance: rebalancing and pruning
- Evolution beats perfection—adapt as you learn

SECTION II

THE FOUNDATION

Principles of Portfolio Architecture

CHAPTER 5:

DESIGNING YOUR WEALTH BLUEPRINT

Before an architect draws a single line, they ask: What is this building for?

A hospital requires a different design than a concert hall. A family home serves different needs than a warehouse. Form follows function.

The same principle applies to wealth.

Most investors skip this step. They accumulate assets randomly, guided by what's popular or what some guru recommends, without ever defining what they're actually building toward.

Architects start with purpose.

The Purpose Question

Sit with this question for a moment:

What problem are you solving with money?

Not "How much do I want?" but "What do I want money to enable?"

Common answers I hear:

- "I want to quit my job" (seeking escape)
- "I want security" (seeking peace)
- "I want to travel" (seeking experience)
- "I want to provide for my family" (seeking contribution)
- "I want to start a business" (seeking creation)
- "I want to make an impact" (seeking meaning)

These aren't financial goals. They're life goals that money can facilitate.

Your portfolio blueprint must be designed for your specific purpose, not a generic template.

The Four Financial Stages

Most financial advice treats everyone identically. "Save 15%, retire at 65, withdraw 4%."

But you're not everyone. You're in a specific stage, with specific needs, requiring specific strategies.

Stage 1: Stability (Net Worth $0-$100K | Ages 20-35 typically)

Primary goal: Build foundation. Achieve financial security.

Defining characteristic: You're converting labor into capital for the first time. Every dollar saved is progress from zero.

Psychological state: Uncertainty, learning, building habits.

Portfolio focus:

- Emergency fund (3-6 months expenses)
- Tax-advantaged accounts (401k, IRA)
- Index funds (simple, low-cost, diversified)
- Debt elimination (high-interest first)

Success metric: Positive net worth, emergency fund established, consistent savings habit.

Common mistake: Trying to get rich quick. Jumping into complex investments before mastering basics. Lifestyle inflation that prevents saving.

Mindset: Foundation first. Boring beats broke.

Stage 2: Growth (Net Worth $100K-$500K | Ages 30-45 typically)

Primary goal: Accelerate wealth accumulation. Begin income engineering.

Defining characteristic: You have capital to deploy meaningfully. You're learning about alternatives. You're starting to see compounding.

Psychological state: Confidence growing, impatient for results, susceptible to FOMO.

Portfolio focus:

- Core/Satellite: 60% index funds, 40% alternatives
- First real estate or private investment exposures
- Beginning to generate passive income (even if small)
- Optimizing tax efficiency

Success metric: Net worth growing faster than salary. First meaningful passive income streams.

Common mistake: Over-diversifying into things you don't understand. Chasing yields without evaluating risk. Neglecting to build knowledge alongside wealth.

Mindset: Education is investment. Quality beats quantity.

Stage 3: Freedom (Net Worth $500K-$2M+ | Ages 40-60 typically)

Primary goal: Achieve financial autonomy. Passive income ≥ expenses.

Defining characteristic: You're optimizing the system you've built. You're shifting from accumulation to income generation. Freedom is visible on the horizon.

Psychological state: Strategic, focused, less swayed by market noise.

Portfolio focus:

- Income-weighted: 35% foundation, 40% income, 20% growth, 5% asymmetric
- Sophisticated alternatives (private credit, syndications, direct deals)
- Tax optimization becoming critical
- Potential career transitions enabled by passive income

Success metric: Freedom Index crossing 50%, then 75%, then 100%.

Common mistake: Getting conservative too early and missing growth. Or taking excessive risk because "I'm so close." Both extremes derail the plan.

Mindset: Discipline now creates optionality forever.

Stage 4: Legacy (Net Worth $2M+ | Ages 50+ typically, or earlier if autonomous)

Primary goal: Preserve wealth, create impact, transfer values.

Defining characteristic: You've achieved autonomy. Work is optional. You're thinking beyond yourself.

Psychological state: Abundance, contribution-focused, mentorship-oriented.

Portfolio focus:

- Preservation-weighted: 40% foundation, 35% income, 15% growth, 10% impact/asymmetric
- Trusts, estate planning, tax-efficient transfers
- Impact investing aligned with values
- Teaching others (family, community)

Success metric: Legacy defined and funded. Systems outlasting you. Others thriving from your wisdom.

Common mistake: Hoarding without purpose. Failing to enjoy the freedom earned. Not preparing heirs for wealth stewardship.

Mindset: Wealth is responsibility. Legacy is intentional.

The 4 Capital Pillars

Money is one form of capital. Architects understand that wealth rests on four pillars and neglecting any creates instability.

Pillar 1: Financial Capital

The measurable stuff: cash, investments, assets, income streams.

Build it through:

- Earning (labor, business, investments)
- Saving (spending discipline)
- Compounding (time + returns)

Protect it through:

- Diversification
- Insurance
- Legal structures

Most people focus exclusively here. It's necessary but insufficient.

Pillar 2: Intellectual Capital

Knowledge, skills, expertise, creativity, problem-solving ability.

Build it through:

- Formal education
- Self-directed learning
- Experience and experimentation
- Mentorship and coaching

Leverage it through:

- Career advancement
- Business creation
- Consulting and advisory
- Content and teaching

Why it matters: Intellectual capital generates financial capital. The more you know, the more you earn and the better you invest. Plus, it can't be taken from you.

Pillar 3: Social Capital

Relationships, networks, reputation, trust, access.

Build it through:

- Genuine relationship-building
- Providing value without expectation
- Joining communities of peers
- Reputation through integrity

Leverage it through:

- Deal flow (opportunities come through relationships)
- Partnerships and collaboration
- Mentorship (giving and receiving)
- Referrals and introductions

Why it matters: The best investments aren't advertised publicly. They're shared among trusted networks. Social capital grants access to opportunities others never see.

Pillar 4: Emotional Capital

Resilience, discipline, delayed gratification, stress tolerance, self-awareness.

Build it through:

- Adversity (experiencing and processing failure)
- Mindfulness and self-reflection
- Therapy and coaching
- Physical health (sleep, exercise, nutrition)

Leverage it through:

- Staying calm during market crashes
- Resisting FOMO and herd mentality
- Making rational decisions under uncertainty
- Maintaining long-term vision despite short-term noise

Why it matters: Emotional capital determines whether you keep your financial capital. Most wealth is lost through emotional decisions—panic selling, FOMO buying, lifestyle inflation, ego-driven bets.

The Wealth Blueprint Framework

Now let's design your specific blueprint. Grab paper or open a document. Answer honestly:

Part 1: Current State

1. What stage am I in? (Stability, Growth, Freedom, Legacy)
2. What's my net worth?
3. What's my annual income? (earned + passive)
4. What are my annual expenses?
5. What's my Freedom Index? (passive income ÷ expenses × 100)

Part 2: Purpose Definition

6. What does freedom mean to me specifically? (Not vague, concrete. "Freedom means working 20 hrs./week on projects I choose, traveling 3 months/year, and having time for family.")

7. What am I solving for? ☐ Time sovereignty ☐ Security and peace of mind ☐ Family support ☐ Creative pursuit ☐ Business building ☐ Impact and contribution ☐ Experience and adventure ☐ Legacy and continuity
8. What's my enough number? "I feel abundant when my lifestyle costs $____/year."
9. What's my Freedom Number? (Enough number ÷ conservative yield %)
10. What's my target timeline? "I want to achieve financial autonomy by age ____."

Part 3: Capital Assessment

Rate each pillar 1-10 (1=weak, 10=exceptional):

11. Financial Capital: ____/10. Do I have emergency savings? Multiple income streams? Growing net worth?
12. Intellectual Capital: ____/10. Do I have valuable skills? Am I continuously learning? Do I understand my investments?
13. Social Capital: ____/10. Do I have meaningful relationships? Access to opportunities? A reputation for integrity?
14. Emotional Capital: ____/10. Can I handle volatility? Do I make decisions rationally? Am I disciplined and patient?

Part 4: Gap Analysis

15. What's the biggest gap between current and desired state?
16. What's holding me back? ☐ Not enough capital yet ☐ Don't know what to invest in ☐ Fear of losing money ☐ Lack of time to research ☐ Don't have access to good opportunities ☐ Overwhelmed by options ☐ Income too low to save meaningfully
17. Which capital pillar needs the most development?
18. What's my next right action? (One specific, achievable step you can take this week)

Designing for Your Demographics

Your blueprint must account for your specific circumstances:

Age-Based Considerations

20s-30s (Time Abundance):

- Strengths: Long runway, compounding power, career growth ahead, risk capacity

- Challenges: Limited capital, student debt, temptation to lifestyle-inflate
- Strategy: Prioritize earning power and knowledge compounding. Take intelligent risks. Build foundation in index funds while learning alternatives. Accept illiquidity for higher returns.

40s-50s (Peak Earning):

- Strengths: Maximum income, established career, investment knowledge, deal access
- Challenges: Competing priorities (kids, aging parents, lifestyle), less time for recovery from mistakes
- Strategy: Aggressive income engineering. Transition from pure accumulation to cash flow. Leverage social capital for deal access. Optimize taxes ruthlessly.

60s+ (Preservation Mode):

- Strengths: Accumulated capital, wisdom, time flexibility, potential autonomy
- Challenges: Shorter time horizon, need for liquidity, sequence-of-returns risk
- Strategy: Income-focused with preservation. Avoid illiquid asymmetric bets. Simplify. Plan succession.

Income-Based Considerations

$40K-$80K (Constrained Capital):

- Reality: Saving is hard. Every dollar matters.
- Strategy: Master the foundation first (emergency fund, debt payoff, 401k match). Use fractional platforms (Fundrise, Arrived, DiversyFund) to access alternatives with $500-$5,000 minimums. Focus on knowledge compounding—your next raise might be worth more than investment returns.

$80K-$200K (Emerging Capacity):

- Reality: You can save meaningfully ($1,000-$3,000+/month) but still feel stretched.
- Strategy: Core/Satellite approach. 60-70% in tax-advantaged index funds, 30-40% exploring alternatives as you learn. Join investor communities. Start small in syndications ($10K-$25K). Build toward accredited investor status if not there yet.

$200K-$500K (Acceleration Zone):

- Reality: You have capital to deploy and possibly accredited status. Taxes hurt.
- Strategy: Sophisticated alternatives access opens up. Real estate syndications, private credit funds, direct venture/PE opportunities. Tax optimization becomes critical (entities, write-offs, deferrals). Potentially hire a fee-only financial advisor and CPA specializing in alternatives.

$500K+ (Full Access):

- Reality: Capital isn't the constraint—decision quality is.
- Strategy: Build a personal "family office" approach. Direct deal access. Fund commitments. Co-investments. Potentially hire a wealth advisor or build a team (CPA, attorney, advisor). Focus on legacy, impact, and teaching.

Life Situation Considerations

Single, No Dependents:

- Strengths: Maximum flexibility, can accept illiquidity and volatility
- Strategy: Aggressive growth and asymmetric exposure. Accept 5-10 year lockups for higher returns. Build the foundation of freedom before lifestyle inflates.

Married, No Kids:

- Strengths: Dual income potential, shared financial vision (if aligned)
- Strategy: Design combined strategy. Consider one partner covering expenses while other invests fully. Align on risk tolerance and timeline.

Parents with Young Children:

- Strengths: Motivated to build legacy, long time horizon
- Challenges: High current expenses, limited flexibility, need for security
- Strategy: Balance growth and security. Maintain liquidity for emergencies. Consider 529 plans and permanent life insurance as forced savings vehicles. Income generation enables career flexibility (part-time, sabbaticals).

Caring for Aging Parents:

- Challenges: Unexpected expenses, time constraints, emotional load

- Strategy: Maintain a higher emergency fund (9-12 months). Prioritize liquid investments. Consider long-term care insurance. Build passive income to create caregiving flexibility.

Values Alignment

Your blueprint isn't just numbers—it's the physical manifestation of your values.

If you value security, your portfolio should overweight stable income and preservation. If you value impact, your portfolio should include mission-driven investments, even at slightly lower returns. If you value growth, you'll accept volatility and illiquidity for asymmetric upside. If you value simplicity, you'll favor index funds and REITs over complex syndications.

There's no right answer. There's only your answer.

Exercise: Values Ranking

Rank these from 1 (most important) to 8 (least important):

___ Maximizing returns
___ Generating current income
___ Minimizing risk
___ Supporting businesses/causes I believe in
___ Simplicity and ease of management
___ Tax efficiency
___ Liquidity and access to capital
___ Learning and intellectual stimulation

Your rankings reveal your blueprint priorities.

Case Study: Three Blueprints for Three People

Blueprint A: Jasmine, 31, Teacher, $85K income, $95K net worth

Stage: Growth

Purpose: Financial security so she can teach without money stress. Eventually semi-retire at 50 to write a curriculum.

Freedom Number: $55,000/year (at 7% yield = $785K invested) Timeline: Financial autonomy by 50 (19 years)

Capital Assessment: Financial 6/10, Intellectual 8/10, Social 7/10, Emotional 9/10
Values: Security > Impact > Simplicity > Growth

Blueprint Design:

- Year 1-5: Build to $200K (max Roth IRA, 403b, aggressive saving)
    - 80% index funds, 20% learning (books, communities, small alternative pilots)
- Year 6-10: Expand to $400K
    - 60% index funds, 30% real estate syndications, 10% private credit
    - Target: $20K annual passive income
- Year 11-15: Accelerate to $650K
    - 45% index funds, 35% real estate, 15% private credit, 5% venture funds
    - Target: $40K annual passive income (73% coverage)
- Year 16-19: Achieve $800K
    - 40% index funds, 40% income assets, 15% growth, 5% asymmetric
    - Target: $56K annual passive income (102% coverage)

At 50, Jasmine can reduce teaching to part-time and pursue her curriculum work without financial stress.

Blueprint B: Marcus, 44, Tech Executive, $310K income, $1.8M net worth

Stage: Freedom (approaching)

Purpose: Leave corporate America by 50. Build businesses and advise startups. Travel extensively.

Freedom Number: $180,000/year (at 8% yield = $2.25M invested)

Timeline: Financial autonomy by 50 (6 years)

Capital Assessment: Financial 8/10, Intellectual 9/10, Social 9/10, Emotional 7/10
Values: Growth > Income > Impact > Simplicity

Blueprint Design:

- Current: $1.8M portfolio (70% stocks, 20% company stock, 10% cash)
- Year 1-2: Reposition
    - Diversify out of company stock (tax-efficiently, over time)
    - Deploy into: 30% index funds, 35% real estate, 20% private credit, 10% direct venture/PE, 5% cash
    - Target: $110K annual passive income

- Year 3-4: Accelerate
    - Portfolio: $2.2M (market growth + $300K contributions)
    - Income: $155K/year (86% coverage)
- Year 5-6: Achieve
    - Portfolio: $2.5M+
    - Income: $190K/year (106% coverage)

At 50, Marcus leaves his job to advise 3-5 startups for equity, build a coaching practice, and spend 4 months/year traveling with his family. He works because he wants to, not because he has to.

Blueprint C: Aisha, 28, Nurse, $72K income, $45K net worth

Stage: Stability → Growth transition

Purpose: Never feel financially trapped. Build to $3,000/month passive income by 45 so she can go per-diem (work when she wants, where she wants).

Freedom Number: $36,000/year (at 7% yield = $515K invested)

Timeline: Financial autonomy by 45 (17 years)

Capital Assessment: Financial 5/10, Intellectual 7/10, Social 6/10, Emotional 8/10
Values: Security > Simplicity > Income > Growth

Blueprint Design:

- Year 1-3: Foundation (to $100K)
    - Emergency fund: $15K (secured)
    - Roth IRA + 401k: $15K/year
    - 100% index funds while learning
- Year 4-7: Diversification (to $200K)
    - Add first real estate syndication ($25K)
    - Add private credit fund ($20K)
    - 65% index, 25% real estate, 10% private credit
    - Income: ~$8K/year
- Year 8-12: Acceleration (to $350K)
    - 50% index, 30% real estate, 15% private credit, 5% alternatives
    - Income: ~$20K/year (56% coverage)
- Year 13-17: Achievement (to $525K)
    - 40% index, 35% real estate, 20% private credit, 5% alternatives
    - Income: ~$37K/year (103% coverage)

At 45, Aisha transitions to per-diem nursing (working 15-20 hours/week, earning $25K/year), travels frequently, and volunteers with Doctors Without Borders for extended periods. Her passive income covers her modest lifestyle, and her part-time work funds extras.

The Blueprint is Not the Journey

A blueprint is a plan, not a prophecy. Life will intervene:

- Markets will crash (and recover)
- Opportunities will appear unexpectedly
- Your income will fluctuate
- Your priorities will evolve
- You'll make mistakes
- You'll learn and adapt

The blueprint gives you direction, not destination certainty. It's your North Star when you're lost in the fog of daily financial decisions.

When someone pitches you an investment, ask: "Does this align with my blueprint?" When markets crash, ask: "Does my blueprint still make sense?" When you get a raise, ask: "How does my blueprint accelerate?"

The blueprint is freedom from chaos. It's permission to ignore what doesn't serve your specific design.

Your Blueprint in One Page

Distill everything into a single-page document. Template:

MY WEALTH BLUEPRINT

<u>Core Purpose:</u> [One sentence. What is money enabling?]

Current State:

- Stage: [Stability/Growth/Freedom/Legacy]
- Net Worth: $______
- Passive Income: $______/year
- Freedom Index: _____%

Target State:

- Freedom Number: $______/year passive income
- Capital Required: $______
- Target Timeline: By age ____

Strategic Focus: [One quarter/year goals]

- This year: [Specific milestone]
- 1-3 years: [Specific milestone]
- 5-10 years: [Specific milestone]

Portfolio Design: [Current target allocation]

- Foundation: ____%
- Income: ____%
- Growth: ____%
- Asymmetric: ____%

Capital Development Priorities:

- Financial: [One action]
- Intellectual: [One action]
- Social: [One action]
- Emotional: [One action]

Decision Filter: Before any investment, I ask:

15. Does this move me toward my Freedom Number?
16. Does this fit my risk capacity and values?
17. Do I understand it well enough to own it?

Review Schedule: [Quarterly/Annually]

Print it. Put it somewhere visible. Reference it before every financial decision.

This is your blueprint. This is your system. This is your path to freedom.

Key Takeaways:

- Purpose precedes tactics—define what you're solving for
- Four financial stages: Stability → Growth → Freedom → Legacy
- Wealth rests on four pillars: Financial, Intellectual, Social, Emotional

- Your blueprint must account for your specific age, income, life situation, and values
- A one-page blueprint serves as your North Star for all decisions
- The blueprint evolves—review and adapt, but maintain strategic direction

CHAPTER 6:

THE CORE-SATELLITE MODEL 2.0

In 1952, Harry Markowitz published a paper that would earn him a Nobel Prize: Modern Portfolio Theory. His insight? Combining assets with different risk profiles could reduce overall portfolio volatility without sacrificing returns.

It revolutionized investing and gave birth to the 60/40 portfolio.

Seventy years later, we need a new model.

The Core-Satellite approach emerged in the 1990s as institutional investors sought to balance passive efficiency with active opportunity. Today, with democratized access to alternatives, individual investors can implement this strategy with sophistication previously reserved for endowments.

Welcome to Core-Satellite 2.0.

The Original Core-Satellite Model

The Core (70-80%): Passive index funds. Cheap, diversified, tax-efficient. The foundation that grinds out consistent market returns.

The Satellites (20-30%): Active managers, sector bets, international exposure. Attempts to beat the market and add alpha.

The Problem: Satellites were still just stocks and bonds. You had diversification within public markets but no exposure to private markets, real assets, or alternative return streams. Plus, actively managed mutual funds often underperformed after fees.

Core-Satellite 2.0: The Modern Framework

The new model keeps the core principle (stable foundation + opportunity satellites) but reimagines both components for the 2025 investment landscape.

The New Core (30-50%): Stabilized Cash Flow + Foundation

Purpose: Resilience, liquidity, income, ballast during storms

Components:

- Index Funds (15-25%): Total market exposure, foundation for growth
- Bonds/Fixed Income (5-15%): True diversification from equities, though less valuable than historically
- Cash/Money Market (5-10%): Liquidity for emergencies and opportunities
- Core Real Estate (5-10%): Stable, cash-flowing real assets (REITs, diversified funds)

Characteristics:

- Highly liquid (accessible within days)
- Low volatility
- Predictable behavior
- Tax-efficient (mostly long-term capital gains, qualified dividends)

Expected Returns: 4-8% annually

Role: This is your anchor. When markets crash, this protects you. When opportunities appear, this funds them. When you need cash, this provides it.

The New Satellites (50-70%): Diversified Alternatives + Growth

This is where Core-Satellite 2.0 diverges dramatically from the original model.

Instead of just active stock funds, satellites now include:

Income Satellites (25-35%):

- Real estate syndications (multifamily, storage, industrial)
- Private credit funds (direct lending, asset-based)
- Royalty investments (music, patents, revenue shares)
- Preferred equity and mezzanine debt

Purpose: Generate 7-12% cash yields, uncorrelated to stocks Liquidity: Low to medium (3-7 year holds typically) Risk: Moderate (contractual returns, asset-backed)

Growth Satellites (15-25%):

- Private equity funds (established businesses scaling)

- Growth-stage venture funds (Series A-C companies)
- Opportunistic real estate (value-add, development)
- Direct business investments

Purpose: 2-5x capital over 5-10 years Liquidity: Low (5-10 year lockups) Risk: Moderate to high (equity risk, execution risk)

Asymmetric Satellites (5-15%):

- Early-stage venture (angel, pre-seed, seed)
- Emerging technologies (crypto, AI, biotech)
- Direct startup investments
- Options strategies (when appropriate)

Purpose: 10-100x potential on small allocations Liquidity: Very low (7-10+ year holds, many total losses) Risk: Extreme (90% may go to zero, but winners cover losses)

The Wealth Orbit Diagram

Imagine your portfolio as a solar system

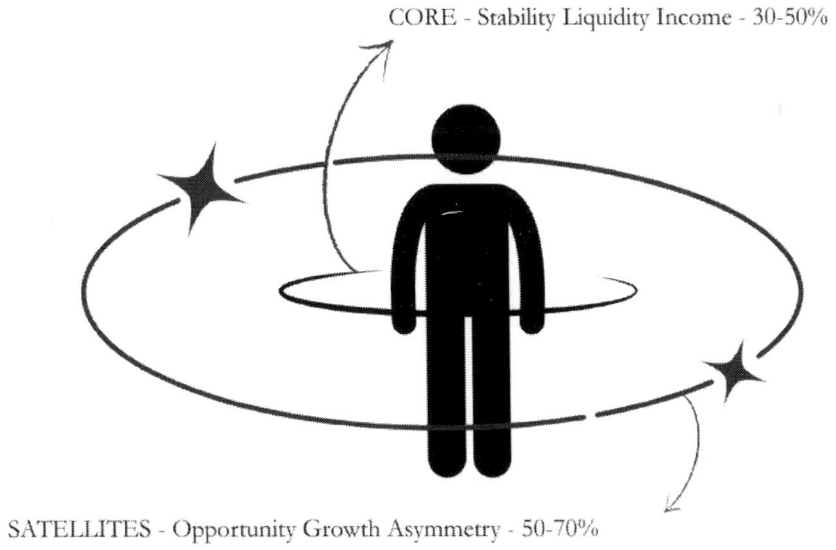

The core orbits close—stable, predictable, always accessible.

Satellites orbit at varying distances—income satellites closer (moderate risk, shorter duration), growth satellites mid-range (higher risk, medium duration), asymmetric satellites far out (extreme risk, long duration).

All orbiting around you—your purpose, your timeline, your blueprint.

Why This Model Works in 2025 and Beyond

1. True Diversification: You're not just diversified across stocks. You're diversified across:

- Return drivers (equity, debt, contractual, appreciation, asymmetric)
- Asset classes (public markets, private markets, real assets, alternatives)
- Liquidity profiles (instant access to 10-year lockups)
- Economic exposure (growth beneficiaries, inflation hedges, recession-resistant)

When public markets crash, your private credit fund still pays quarterly distributions. When real estate softens, your venture portfolio might have an exit. When everything feels uncertain, your cash core provides stability.

2. Income Engineering: The original model generated minimal income—maybe 2% dividend yield from stock index funds.

Core-Satellite 2.0 generates 6-9% income from satellites while the core continues compounding. This cash flow can:

- Fund your lifestyle (reducing dependence on salary)
- Reinvest for compounding acceleration
- Deploy into opportunities during downturns

3. Access to Superior Returns: Institutional investors (endowments, pensions, family offices) have long allocated 30-60% to alternatives. Why? Because private markets have historically outperformed public markets:

- Private equity: 14-15% annualized returns (vs. 10% for public equities)
- Venture capital: 20%+ annualized returns (vs. 10% for public equities)
- Private credit: 9-12% yields (vs. 4-5% for investment-grade bonds)
- Real estate: 12-18% IRRs (vs. 10% for REITs)

You now have access to these returns. The model gives you a framework to capture them.

4. Asymmetric Upside: The core protects your downside. The satellites capture unlimited upside.

A 10% allocation to early-stage ventures might lose half its value if only 1 in 5 investments succeeds. But if one succeeds 20x, your $50,000 becomes $100,000+, more than covering losses.

You can only capture asymmetry by: a) Taking positions in asymmetric opportunities b) Having a core that lets you stomach the volatility

Core-Satellite 2.0 enables both.

5. Lifecycle Adaptability: The beauty of the model: It scales across life stages.

In your 20s-30s (Stability → Growth):

- Core: 50% (building foundation)
- Satellites: 50% (learning alternatives while growing)

In your 30s-40s (Growth → Freedom):

- Core: 35% (established foundation)
- Satellites: 65% (aggressively building income and growth)

In your 50s-60s (Freedom → Legacy):

- Core: 45% (increased stability)
- Satellites: 55% (focus shifting to income and preservation)

The model adapts to your changing needs without requiring a complete rebuild.

Example Portfolios Across Demographics

Portfolio A: Age 28, $75K net worth, $90K income

Goal: Build foundation while learning alternatives

- Core (50% = $37,500):
  - 35% Index funds: $26,250
  - 10% Bonds: $7,500
  - 5% Cash: $3,750
- Satellites (50% = $37,500):
  - 30% Income (Real estate fund): $22,500

    - 15% Growth (None yet—learning): $0 → deployed gradually
    - 5% Asymmetric (Small crypto position): $3,750
    - 12.5% Cash (saving for first syndication): $11,250

Income Generated: ~$2,000/year (2.7% yield) Strategy: Build core, learn about alternatives, make first meaningful alternative investment within 12 months.

Portfolio B: Age 39, $425K net worth, $145K income

Goal: Accelerate toward financial autonomy

- Core (35% = $148,750):
    - 20% Index funds: $85,000
    - 8% Bonds: $34,000
    - 7% Cash: $29,750
- Satellites (65% = $276,250):
    - 35% Income: $148,750
        - $75,000 in real estate syndications
        - $50,000 in private credit funds
        - $23,750 in dividend-growth stocks
    - 20% Growth: $85,000
        - $60,000 in PE/VC funds
        - $25,000 in opportunistic real estate
    - 10% Asymmetric: $42,500
        - $30,000 in angel investments
        - $12,500 in emerging tech

Income Generated: ~$28,000/year (6.6% yield) Strategy: Income satellites producing meaningful cash flow. Growth and asymmetric exposure building. Targeting 100% expense coverage within 8-10 years.

Portfolio C: Age 52, $1.9M net worth, $185K income

Goal: Achieve full financial autonomy within 3 years

- Core (40% = $760,000):
    - 25% Index funds: $475,000
    - 10% Bonds: $190,000
    - 5% Cash: $95,000
- Satellites (60% = $1,140,000):
    - 35% Income: $665,000
        - $380,000 in real estate syndications (8-10 properties)
        - $190,000 in private credit funds
        - $95,000 in preferred equity and royalties
    - 18% Growth: $342,000

        - $250,000 in private equity funds
        - $92,000 in growth-stage venture
    - 7% Asymmetric: $133,000
        - $95,000 in direct startup investments
        - $38,000 in emerging opportunities

Income Generated: ~$105,000/year (5.5% yield on total, 9.2% on satellites) Freedom Index: 78% (expenses: $135K/year) Strategy: Three more years of contributions + compounding = $115K+ passive income = full autonomy. Can retire or work by choice.

The Rebalancing Dance

Core-Satellite 2.0 requires disciplined rebalancing, but not the traditional way.

Traditional rebalancing: Sell winners, buy losers to maintain percentages.

Core-Satellite 2.0 rebalancing:

1. Annual review: Check actual allocations vs. targets
2. New capital first: Deploy new contributions to underweight areas
3. Maturity harvesting: When satellites mature (real estate sale, fund distribution), redeploy according to current targets
4. Tax-aware adjustment: Only sell in taxable accounts when necessary; prioritize rebalancing in IRAs
5. Opportunistic shifts: During crashes, overweight satellites; during euphoria, overweight core

Example: Your target is 35% core, 65% satellites. A bull market runs for 3 years and your core grows to 45% of the portfolio.

Instead of selling stocks (triggering taxes), you:

- Deploy all new contributions to satellites for 2-3 years
- When a real estate syndication sells, reinvest proceeds into new satellites rather than core
- Gradually drift back to target without tax hits

The Capital Deployment Strategy

Core-Satellite 2.0 changes how you deploy new capital:

Step 1: Core Foundation First: Until you have 6 months emergency fund + $50K+ in liquid index funds, prioritize core. Don't jump into illiquid alternatives before your foundation is solid.

Step 2: Satellite Exploration: With foundation established, begin testing satellites with 10-20% of portfolio. Learn by doing. Make small bets ($5K-$25K) in different alternative types.

Step 3: Satellite Acceleration: As you gain conviction and see results, increase satellite allocation. Diversify across multiple syndications, funds, and opportunities—never concentrated in one deal or one manager.

Step 4: Mature Portfolio Management: Once at target allocations, new capital flows where you're underweight, according to opportunities available and market conditions.

Common Mistakes to Avoid

Mistake 1: Satellites Before Core: Putting $20K into a real estate syndication when you have $15K in emergency savings and $30K in index funds. You're building the roof before the foundation.

Fix: Core first, always. Even if satellites are exciting.

Mistake 2: Over-Concentration in One Satellite: Investing $100K into a single real estate deal because you love the sponsor. If that deal fails, you've devastated your portfolio.

Fix: Diversify within satellites. 10+ income positions, 5+ growth positions, 8+ asymmetric positions (if at scale).

Mistake 3: Illiquidity Overload: Locking up 80% of your portfolio in 5-10 years. Then needing cash and having to sell core at a loss.

Fix: Maintain 20-30% in liquid core, always. Life happens.

Mistake 4: Chasing Yield Without Understanding Risk: Seeing a 14% yield and deploying $50K without understanding the risk. High yield = high risk, usually.

Fix: Risk-adjusted thinking. A 9% return with moderate risk beats a 14% return with extreme risk.

Mistake 5: Paralysis by Analysis: Spending 3 years "researching" and never deploying capital beyond index funds because satellites feel overwhelming.

Fix: Start small. Learn by doing. $10K in a well-vetted syndication teaches more than 10 books.

Case Study: The System That Self-Balanced

Trevor, 43, implemented Core-Satellite 2.0 in 2019 with $650K.

Initial Allocation:

- Core 40%: $260K (stocks, bonds, cash)
- Satellites 60%: $390K (real estate, private credit, some PE)

2020-2021: Markets soared. His core grew to $380K. Satellites remained ~$420K (slower growth, but generating $32K income).

New allocation: Core 48%, Satellites 52%

Instead of selling stocks, he deployed all new capital ($80K over two years) entirely into satellites. By end of 2021: Core $400K (44%), Satellites $510K (56%).

2022: Market crashed. His core fell to $320K (-20%). Satellites held steady at $515K (private markets lag public).

New allocation: Core 38%, Satellites 62%

He deployed new savings into core (buying low). Simultaneously, two real estate investments sold, distributing $95K. He reinvested $70K into new real estate and $25K into core.

2023-2024: Recovery. Core rebounded. Satellites compounded.

Current allocation (2025): $1.1M portfolio—Core 40% ($440K), Satellites 60% ($660K).

He never panic-sold. Never made emotional decisions. The system self-balanced through disciplined deployment and patient harvesting.

His passive income: $68,000/year. His freedom index: 89% (expenses $76K). He's 2-3 years from full autonomy.

The model worked because he trusted the system.

Your Core-Satellite Design

Based on your blueprint from Chapter 5, determine your targets:

If in Stability Stage (Building Foundation):

- Core: 50-60%
- Satellites: 40-50%

If in Growth Stage (Accumulating):

- Core: 35-45%
- Satellites: 55-65%

If in Freedom Stage (Approaching Autonomy):

- Core: 30-40%
- Satellites: 60-70%

If in Legacy Stage (Preservation):

- Core: 45-55%
- Satellites: 45-55%

Within satellites, allocate based on risk tolerance and timeline:

- Conservative: 25% income, 15% growth, 5% asymmetric
- Moderate: 30% income, 20% growth, 10% asymmetric
- Aggressive: 35% income, 25% growth, 15% asymmetric

There's no perfect formula. There's only your formula, aligned with your blueprint, adapted as you evolve.

The core keeps you safe. The satellites make you free.

Key Takeaways:

- Core-Satellite 2.0 combines public market stability with private market opportunity
- Core (30-50%): Liquid, stable foundation generating baseline returns

- Satellites (50-70%): Income, growth, and asymmetric alternatives generating superior returns
- The model provides true diversification across asset classes and return drivers
- It scales across life stages through allocation adjustments
- Rebalance through new capital deployment and maturity harvesting, not forced selling
- Core protects downside; satellites capture upside

CHAPTER 7:

INTELLIGENT RISK ENGINEERING

On September 15, 2008, Lehman Brothers collapsed. The S&P 500 would eventually fall 57% from its peak.

Two investors watched their portfolios:

Investor A:

- $1M entirely in S&P 500 index fund
- September 2007: $1M
- March 2009: $430K
- Emotional state: Panic. Considered selling to "stop the bleeding."
- If he held: Recovered by 2013
- If he sold at bottom: Locked in 57% loss, missed recovery

Investor B:

- $1M diversified portfolio:
    - 30% S&P 500 ($300K)
    - 30% Real estate syndications ($300K)
    - 20% Private credit ($200K)
    - 15% Bonds ($150K)
    - 5% Cash ($50K)
- September 2007: $1M
- March 2009:
    - Stocks: $129K (-57%)
    - Real estate: $240K (-20%, slower private market repricing)
    - Private credit: $190K (-5%, continued payments)
    - Bonds: $165K (+10%, flight to safety)
    - Cash: $50K (unchanged)
    - Total: $774K (-23%)
- Emotional state: Concerned but calm. Portfolio generating $52K annual income despite crisis.
- Action: Deployed cash + income into crashed stocks at generational lows

Outcome: By 2013, Investor B had $1.4M and was generating $85K annual income. He experienced less than half the drawdown, maintained income throughout, and bought assets on sale.

This is intelligent risk engineering.

The Fundamental Misunderstanding of Risk

Ask most people "What is risk?" and they say: "Losing money" or "Volatility."

Both wrong—or at least incomplete.

Risk is not volatility. Risk is the probability of permanent capital impairment or failure to meet your goals.

A stock that fluctuates 30% isn't risky if:

- You don't need the money for 10+ years
- You have income from other sources
- You have conviction in the underlying asset

Meanwhile, a "safe" bond yielding 2% is extremely risky if:

- Inflation is running 4% (you're losing 2% purchasing power annually)
- You need growth to hit your Freedom Number
- Rising rates cause bond prices to fall

True risk engineering asks:

1. What's the probability this investment causes permanent loss?
2. What's the magnitude of potential loss?
3. How does this interact with my other holdings?
4. Does this move me toward or away from my goals?

The Risk-Return Spectrum Reimagined

Traditional finance teaches: Higher risk = higher return.

Reality is more nuanced: Higher uncertainty can generate higher returns, but not all risk is rewarded.

Rewarded risks:

Market risk (equities vs. bonds)

- Illiquidity risk (private markets vs. public)
- Complexity risk (structured deals vs. simple investments)
- Execution risk (startups vs. established businesses)
- Concentration risk (focused bets vs. diversification)

Unrewarded risks:

- Leverage risk (borrowing to invest without edge)
- Fraud risk (investing with unverified operators)
- Ignorance risk (buying what you don't understand)
- Timing risk (trying to predict short-term moves)
- Ego risk (overconfidence in your abilities)

Intelligent risk engineering means taking rewarded risks while eliminating unrewarded ones.

The Asymmetric Allocation Model™

This is the cornerstone of intelligent portfolio design:

80% Defense | 20% Offense

Defense (80%): The Unbreakable Base

Purpose: Survive anything. Generate income. Sleep well.

Allocation:

- 30-40%: Index funds, bonds, cash (liquid, stable)
- 40-50%: Income-producing alternatives (real estate, private credit)

Characteristics:

- Limited downside (contractual returns, asset-backed, diversified)
- Predictable cash flow (6-8% yields)
- Low correlation to stock market crashes
- Can withstand job loss, recessions, market collapses

Expected return: 6-9% annually

The Defense Test:_If markets crashed 50% tomorrow and stayed down for 5 years, would this portion:

- Still generate income? ✓
- Preserve most of its value? ✓
- Allow you to sleep at night? ✓

If yes to all three, it's defense.

Offense (20%): The Asymmetric Engine

Purpose: Capture outlier returns. Turn $100K into $500K+.

Allocation:

- 15%: Growth investments (private equity, growth venture, opportunistic real estate)
- 5%: Asymmetric bets (early-stage startups, emerging tech, calculated speculation)

Characteristics:

- Significant downside possible (could lose 50-100%)
- Unlimited upside potential (could return 5-50x)
- High volatility and illiquidity
- Concentrated positions in high-conviction opportunities

Expected return: Highly variable, but portfolio-level target of 15-30% annually (with significant losses offset by massive wins)

The Offense Test:_If this portion went to zero, would it:

- Devastate your financial plan? ✗ (If yes, it's too big)
- Prevent you from reaching autonomy? ✗ (If yes, it's too big)
- Teach you valuable lessons? ✓
- Potentially change your life if it works? ✓

If you answer correctly, it's a properly sized offense.

Why 80/20 Works

Psychological: You can stomach 20% of your portfolio being volatile because 80% is stable. This prevents panic-selling during drawdowns.

Mathematical: You need defense to compound reliably. You need offense to capture outliers. 80/20 optimizes both.

Historical: Endowments, family offices, and sophisticated investors naturally drift toward 70-85% stable/income and 15-30% growth/asymmetric.

Example: $500K portfolio using 80/20:

- Defense ($400K): Generates $28K annual income at 7% yield
- Offense ($100K):
    - 5 positions perform poorly: -$40K
    - 3 positions perform okay: +$15K
    - 2 positions perform great: +$85K
- Net offense return: +$60K (60% return on offense)

Total portfolio: $560K (+12% overall) + $28K income Even with half your offense positions failing, your total portfolio thrived.

Without the 80% defense, you'd have panic-sold during the losses.

Controlled Exposure: The Barbell Strategy

Nassim Taleb introduced the barbell strategy: Be extremely conservative with most capital, extremely aggressive with a small portion. Avoid the "risky middle."

Applied to portfolios:

The Barbell:

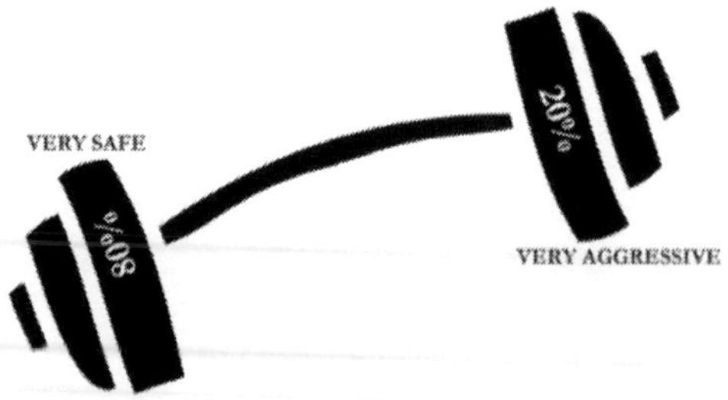

Avoid the risky middle:

- Leveraged ETFs
- Penny stocks
- High-fee active mutual funds
- Speculative options without strategy
- Concentrated sector bets

These have downsides like aggressive investments but lack the asymmetric upside. They're risks without reward potential.

The barbell protects and performs:

- If the aggressive 10% goes to zero, you lose 10% of portfolio
- If the aggressive 10% goes 10x, your portfolio gains 90%
- Meanwhile, the 60% safe portion grinds out reliable returns
- The 30% moderate portion generates income and moderate growth

You're never ruined. You're always positioned for miracles.

The Risk Layers Framework

Think of risk as layers you can stack, remove, or adjust:

Layer 1: Asset-Level Risk

Question: What are the risks inherent to this specific asset?

- Real estate syndication: Tenant turnover, market downturn, operator execution, refinancing
- Startup investment: Product failure, team issues, market timing, competitive dynamics
- Corporate bond: Company bankruptcy, credit downgrade, interest rate changes

Mitigation: Due diligence, understanding the business model, assessing management quality

Layer 2: Concentration Risk

Question: How much of my portfolio is in this single position?

- High concentration: 20%+ in one investment (high risk)
- Moderate concentration: 5-10% in one investment (moderate risk)
- Diversified: <5% in any single investment (low concentration risk)

Mitigation: Position sizing, diversification across multiple investments

Layer 3: Category Risk

Question: How much exposure do I have to this entire category?

- All real estate in one market (geographic concentration)
- All investments with one operator (manager concentration)
- All tech startups (sector concentration)
- All private equity funds in same vintage year (timing concentration)

Mitigation: Diversify across geographies, operators, sectors, vintages

Layer 4: Systemic Risk

Question: What macro events could impact my entire portfolio?

- Economic recession affecting all equities
- Rising interest rates affecting all real estate
- Regulatory changes affecting an entire industry
- Technological disruption making assets obsolete

Mitigation: True diversification across asset classes, income generation to weather storms, cash reserves

Layer 5: Liquidity Risk

Question: Can I access capital when needed?

- Portfolio 90% locked in 5-10 year investments = extreme liquidity risk
- Need cash for emergency but must sell at loss = liquidity crisis

Mitigation: Maintain 20-30% in liquid assets, ladder investment maturities

Layer 6: Personal Risk

Question: What happens to my plan if my circumstances change?

- Job loss with no passive income
- Health crisis with inadequate insurance
- Divorce affecting asset split
- Aging parents requiring financial support

Mitigation: Emergency fund, adequate insurance, income diversification, stress-testing the plan

Stress-Testing Your Portfolio

Architects stress-test buildings for earthquakes, hurricanes, fires. Portfolio architects stress-test for financial disasters.

The Stress Test Exercise:

For each scenario, calculate your portfolio's projected value and income generation:

Scenario 1: Stock Market Crash (-50% equities)

- Current portfolio: $______
- Projected portfolio: $______
- Projected income: $______ /year
- Can I survive? Yes / No

Action required: ____________

Scenario 2: Real Estate Depression (-30% real estate values)

- Projected portfolio: $______
- Projected income: $______ /year
- Can I survive? Yes / No

Scenario 3: Job Loss (6-12 months without salary)

- Emergency fund covers: ____ months
- Passive income covers: ____% of expenses
- Liquid assets available: $______
- Can I survive? Yes / No

Scenario 4: Inflation Surge (7% sustained inflation)

- Assets with inflation protection: ____%

- Real returns after inflation: ____%
- Income keeping pace with inflation? Yes / No

Scenario 5: Everything Crashes (Great Depression scenario)

- Stocks -50%, Real estate -30%, Private investments -20%, Some startups → $0
- Projected portfolio: $______
- Projected income: $______ /year
- Time to recovery: ____ years
- Can I survive? Yes / No

If you can survive scenarios 1-4 without major lifestyle changes, your portfolio is resilient.

If you can survive scenario 5 without devastation, your portfolio is antifragile.

The Antifragile Portfolio

Nassim Taleb's concept: Some things benefit from stress and volatility. They're not just resilient (survive), they're antifragile (thrive).

How portfolios become antifragile:

1. **Income Generation:** When markets crash, your dividends and distributions continue. You can reinvest at depressed prices. Every crash becomes a buying opportunity rather than a nightmare.

2. **Optionality:** Cash reserves + available credit + partnership opportunities = ability to capitalize when others panic. Financial flexibility is antifragile.

3. **Asymmetric Positions:** Small positions with unlimited upside and limited downside. The worse things get, the cheaper quality assets become, the higher your future returns.

4. **Skills and Networks (Human Capital):** Economic downturns can't erase your knowledge or relationships. In fact, crises often accelerate relationship depth and learning.

Example of Antifragile Positioning:

2008 Financial Crisis investor:

- Had $200K in cash and credit lines (optionality)
- Was generating $35K annual income from diversified sources (continued through crisis)
- Portfolio down 25% overall (vs. 50% for pure equity investors)
- Used cash + income to buy:
    - Foreclosed properties at 40% discounts
    - Blue-chip stocks at generational lows
    - Distressed debt at 50 cents on the dollar

By 2015, that investor had 3x'd their wealth while most were just recovering to breakeven.

They didn't just survive the crisis. They feasted during it.

Risk Budgeting: The Allocation Decision

You have a finite "risk budget"—the total amount of risk you can tolerate without derailing your plan or your psychology.

Traditional approach: Allocate by dollars

- 60% stocks, 40% bonds = done

Architect approach: Allocate by risk contribution

- How much risk does each holding contribute to the portfolio?

Example: $500K portfolio with two positions:

- $400K in index funds (high volatility: 20% annualized)
- $100K in private credit (low volatility: 5% annualized)

By dollars: 80% stocks, 20% credit

By risk contribution: Stocks contribute ~90% of total portfolio volatility

Insight: Small allocations to high-volatility assets can dominate your risk profile.

Application: If you want moderate overall risk, you can't just diversify by dollars. You must diversify by risk contribution:

- Index funds: 30% of capital, 40% of risk

- Real estate: 40% of capital, 30% of risk
- Private credit: 20% of capital, 15% of risk
- Venture capital: 10% of capital, 15% of risk

This creates balanced risk across the portfolio, not just balanced dollars.

The Due Diligence Checklist

Every investment must pass through filters before entering your portfolio:

Filter 1: Understanding

- ☐ Can I explain this investment to a 10-year-old?
- ☐ Do I understand how returns are generated?
- ☐ Do I know what could go wrong?

If not to any: Don't invest. Ignorance is an unrewarded risk.

Filter 2: Operator Quality

- ☐ Is the operator experienced in this specific strategy?
- ☐ Do they have a track record I can verify?
- ☐ Are incentives aligned (they invest their own capital)?
- ☐ Can I speak to references?

If not to any: Proceed with extreme caution or pass.

Filter 3: Risk/Return Alignment

Is the expected return commensurate with the risk?

- ☐ What's the downside scenario? Can I handle it?
- ☐ What's the upside scenario? Is it worth the risk?
- ☐ Are there structural protections (collateral, seniority, guarantees)?

If risk/return is unfavorable: Pass.

Filter 4: Portfolio Fit

- ☐ Does this fit my allocation targets?
- ☐ Am I over-concentrated in this category?
- ☐ Does this diversify or concentrate my existing holdings?
- ☐ What happens to my portfolio if this fails?

If it creates dangerous concentration: Size down or pass.

Filter 5: Exit and Liquidity

- ☐ How and when do I get my money back?
- ☐ Can I afford to have this locked up?
- ☐ What are the exit scenarios (sale, refinance, buyout, IPO)?
- ☐ Is there a secondary market if I need out early?

If liquidity doesn't match needs: Pass or size appropriately.

The Ultimate Filter: Would I be comfortable explaining this investment to my spouse/partner/parent? If you'd be embarrassed by the risk or complexity, don't do it.

Case Study: Two Portfolios, One Crisis

2020 COVID-19 Pandemic:

Portfolio A (Traditional): Jake, 41, $850K

- 70% stocks ($595K)
- 25% bonds ($212K)
- 5% cash ($43K)

February 2020: $850K March 2020: $638K (-25%)

Jake panics. Markets feel like they'll never recover. He sells $200K in stocks to "protect what's left." April 2020: Markets rebound. Jake is sitting in cash, missing the recovery. December 2020: Market fully recovered. Jake has $720K (stocks he kept + bonds + cash + the $200K he panic-sold) Loss due to poor risk engineering: $130K+ in missed gains

Portfolio B (Architected): Keisha, 43, $850K

- 30% stocks ($255K)
- 35% real estate syndications ($297K)
- 20% private credit ($170K)
- 10% PE/VC funds ($85K)
- 5% cash ($43K)

February 2020: $850K March 2020: $748K (-12%)

- Stocks: $178K (-30%)
- Real estate: $282K (-5%, slower private repricing)
- Private credit: $168K (-1%, continued payments)
- PE/VC: $82K (-3%)
- Cash: $43K
- Income continuing: $55K annual from real estate + credit

Keisha's response: Calm. Half the drawdown of Jake. Income is still flowing. Uses some cash to buy stocks at 30% discount.

December 2020: $980K

- Stocks recovered + her March purchases up 60%
- Real estate steady and distributing
- Private credit distributing
- PE/VC steady

Gain due to intelligent risk engineering: $130K portfolio growth + $55K income during crisis = $185K advantage over Jake

Same starting point. Different architecture. Massively different outcomes.

Your Risk Engineering Action Plan

Step 1: Calculate Current Risk Profile

What percentage of your portfolio would you lose in these scenarios?

- 50% stock crash: ____%
- 30% real estate decline: ____%
- 3 failed startup investments: ____%
- Total portfolio impact of worst year: ____%

Step 2: Assess Risk Capacity

Maximum loss you can tolerate without:

- Panic-selling: ____%
- Lifestyle changes: ____%
- Derailing long-term plan: ____%

Your risk capacity = the lowest of these three numbers.

Step 3: Identify Concentrations

Do you have >20% in:

- One single investment? ☐
- One operator/manager? ☐
- One geography? ☐
- One asset class? ☐
- One sector? ☐

Each "yes" is a risk to mitigate.

Step 4: Implement 80/20 Model

Current allocation:

- Defense: ____%
- Offense: ____%

Target allocation:

- Defense: 80%
- Offense: 20%

Gap: _____ (adjust gradually over 1-2 years)

Step 5: Build Stress-Test Protocol

Quarterly exercise:

1. Run through 5 stress scenarios
2. Calculate projected outcomes
3. Identify vulnerabilities
4. Adjust allocations or add hedges

Step 6: Create Decision Rules

"I will never:"

- Put more than __% in a single investment
- Invest in something I don't understand
- Lock up more than __% of my portfolio illiquid

- Take on leverage without cash flow to service it
- Invest with operators I haven't thoroughly vetted

These rules protect you from your future self.

The Risk Paradox

Here's the final insight on risk:

The riskiest portfolio isn't the one with volatile investments. It's the one that can't fund your life.

A $2M portfolio generating $0 income forces you to sell assets to live—exposing you to sequence-of-returns risk, market timing risk, and depletion risk.

A $800K portfolio generating $60K annual income lets you live indefinitely without selling—eliminating those risks entirely.

Traditional finance calls the first portfolio "safer" because it's in index funds.

Architects know the second portfolio is actually safer because it's *functional.*

Risk isn't about volatility. Risk is about failure to achieve your purpose.

Engineer accordingly.

Key Takeaways:

- Risk is permanent capital impairment or failure to meet goals, not volatility
- The Asymmetric Allocation Model: 80% Defense, 20% Offense
- Use the Barbell Strategy: Very safe + very aggressive, avoid risky middle
- Risk has six layers: asset, concentration, category, systemic, liquidity, personal
- Stress-test your portfolio across multiple disaster scenarios
- Antifragile portfolios benefit from volatility through optionality and income
- Risk-budgeting allocates by risk contribution, not just dollars
- The riskiest portfolio is the one that can't fund your life

CHAPTER 8:

THE CAPITAL STACK ADVANTAGE

In 2019, two investors each put $100,000 into the same apartment building.

Investor A bought common equity—ownership shares in the deal.

Investor B bought preferred equity—a senior position with contractual returns.

The deal thesis: Buy a 200-unit property, renovate units, raise rents, sell in 5 years.

What happened:

Years 1-3: Property performs as projected. Both investors receive distributions.

- Investor A (common equity): 8% annual distributions ($8,000/year)
- Investor B (preferred equity): 10% annual distributions ($10,000/year)

Year 4: Recession hits. Occupancy drops. Rents stagnate. Property struggles to cover debt service.

- Investor A: $0 distributions (common equity is last to be paid)
- Investor B: $10,000 distribution (preferred equity has payment priority)

Year 5: Sponsor decides to hold longer rather than sell in a weak market.

- Investor A: Still $0 distributions, uncertain timeline
- Investor B: Continues receiving $10,000 annually, has option to convert to common equity if property recovers

Year 7: Property finally sells after recovery.

- Investor A (common equity): $180,000 return ($80K gain) after 7 years = 80% total return
- Investor B (preferred equity): $170,000 return ($70K in distributions + return of capital) = 70% total return

But consider the risk-adjusted reality:

- Investor A went 3 years with no income and high uncertainty
- Investor B received income every single year and had downside protection

This is the capital stack advantage.

Understanding the Capital Stack

Every real estate deal, private equity investment, or business has a "capital stack"—the layers of capital that fund it, ranked by seniority (who gets paid first).

Think of it like a building:

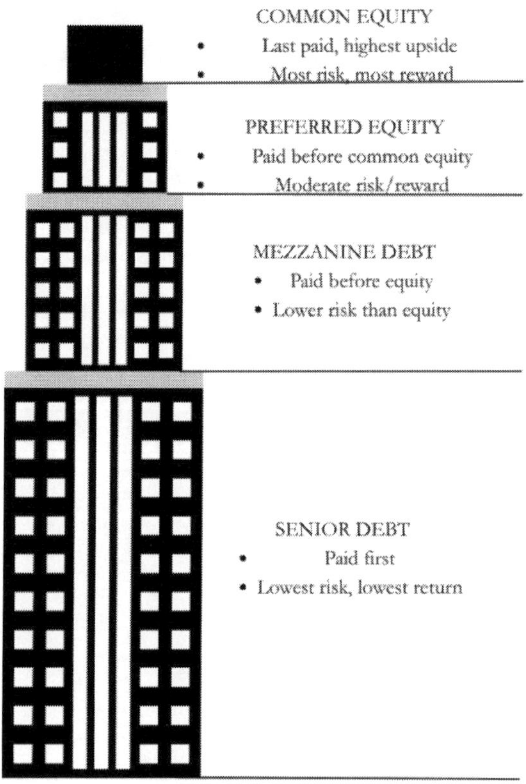

When cash flows in: It flows up from the bottom. Senior debt gets paid first, then mezzanine, then preferred equity, then common equity.

When things go bad: Losses hit from the top down. Common equity loses first, then preferred, then mezzanine, then senior debt (only if property value drops below loan amount).

The Four Capital Stack Positions

Position 1: Senior Debt (The Foundation)

What it is: A secured loan against the asset. First lien. First to be paid.

Example: A mortgage lender provides $15M to buy a $25M property (60% LTV - loan-to-value).

Returns: 5-8% interest (contractual, not variable) Risk: Very low—property would need to drop >40% before loan is at risk Upside: None beyond interest rate Downside protection: Strongest—secured by asset, first claim

Best for: Conservative investors prioritizing capital preservation and steady income

Position 2: Mezzanine Debt (The Middle Ground)

What it is: Subordinated debt, junior to senior debt but senior to equity. Often secured by equity interests rather than property itself.

Example: Mezzanine lender provides $3M (sits between the $15M senior loan and $7M equity).

Returns: 9-13% interest (contractual) Risk: Moderate—only at risk if property value drops AND senior debt isn't fully covered Upside: Limited to interest + possibly warrants (rights to buy equity) Downside protection: Strong—gets paid before any equity holders

Best for: Investors wanting equity-like returns with debt-like protection

Position 3: Preferred Equity (The Hybrid)

What it is: Equity ownership with preferential treatment—gets paid before common equity, often with a minimum return hurdle.

Example: Preferred equity investor provides $4M, entitled to 10% annual preferred return before common equity receives anything.

Returns: 8-12% preferred return + potential upside participation Risk: Moderate-to-high—no distributions if property underperforms Upside: Moderate—gets preferred return plus sometimes a share of profits Downside protection: Moderate—senior to common equity but junior to all debt

Best for: Investors wanting equity upside with some downside protection

Position 4: Common Equity (The Top)

What it is: Ownership in the asset. Last to be paid but unlimited upside.

Example: Sponsor puts in $3M of common equity to complete the $25M purchase

Returns: Variable—could be 0-30%+ annually depending on performance Risk: Highest—first to lose money if deal underperforms Upside: Unlimited—captures all appreciation after debt and preferred equity are satisfied Downside protection: None—absorbs first losses

Best for: Investors with high risk tolerance seeking maximum appreciation

Why This Matters for Individual Investors

Most individual investors only ever invest in common equity:

- Buy stocks = common equity in public companies
- Invest in real estate syndications = usually common equity
- Angel invest = common equity in startups

You're always at the top of the stack, taking maximum risk.

The Architect's approach: Diversify across the capital stack.

A $500K alternative investment portfolio could be:

- $150K (30%): Senior debt positions (private credit funds, real estate debt)
    - Target: 7-9% annual cash yield
    - Risk: Very low
    - Income: $10,500-$13,500/year
- $150K (30%): Mezzanine/Preferred equity positions
    - Target: 10-12% annual returns
    - Risk: Moderate
    - Income: $15,000-$18,000/year
- $150K (30%): Common equity positions (real estate syndications, PE funds)

    - Target: 15-20% IRR (mostly from appreciation at exit)
    - Risk: Higher
    - Income: $7,500-$12,000/year during hold
- $50K (10%): Asymmetric common equity (early-stage venture)
    - Target: 0-100x (binary outcomes)
    - Risk: Extreme
    - Income: $0 (growth only)

Total portfolio:

- Blended expected return: 12-16% annually
- Annual income: $33,000-$43,500 (6.6-8.7% yield)
- Risk: Balanced across stack—if common equity struggles, debt positions still pay

The LTV (Loan-to-Value) Concept

LTV determines safety margin in debt positions.

Formula: LTV = Loan Amount ÷ Property Value

Example:

- Property value: $10M
- Senior debt: $6M
- LTV = 60%

What this means: The property value could drop 40% (to $6M) and the lender would still be fully covered.

LTV by risk level:

- 0-50% LTV: Extremely safe (50% buffer)
- 50-65% LTV: Very safe (35-50% buffer)
- 65-75% LTV: Moderate (25-35% buffer)
- 75-85% LTV: Aggressive (15-25% buffer)
- 85%+ LTV: Risky (<15% buffer)

When evaluating debt investments, always ask: "What's the LTV?"

A 10% return on a 50% LTV loan is spectacular—you have a 50% safety margin. A 10% return on an 85% LTV loan is risky—you have only a 15% margin for error.

Leverage: The Double-Edged Sword

Leverage means using borrowed money to amplify returns—and risks.

Example without leverage:

- You invest $100K in property
- Property appreciates 20% to $120K
- Your return: 20% ($20K gain on $100K invcsted)

Example with leverage:

- You invest $25K
- Borrow $75K at 5% interest
- Buy $100K property
- Property appreciates 20% to $120K
- Loan payoff: $75K + $3,750 interest = $78,750
- Your equity: $120K - $78,750 = $41,250
- Your return: 65% ($16,250 gain on $25K invested)

Leverage amplified your 20% return into 65%. Amazing!

But what if property drops 20%?

- Property value: $80K
- Loan payoff: $78,750
- Your equity: $1,250
- Your return: -95% (nearly total loss on your $25K)

Leverage amplifies in both directions.

Guidelines for intelligent leverage:

- Never use leverage on assets you don't fully understand
- Never use leverage without cash flow to service the debt
- Conservative leverage (2:1 to 3:1 ratio) can enhance returns safely
- Aggressive leverage (5:1+) is speculation, not investment
- In personal portfolios, limit total leverage to 20-30% of net worth

Real-World Application: Evaluating Opportunities

Opportunity A: Real Estate Syndication (Common Equity)

- Property: 150-unit multifamily, $30M purchase
- Your investment: $50,000 minimum
- Position: Common equity (after $18M senior debt)
- Projected returns: 7% annual cash-on-cash, 18% IRR over 5 years
- Risk: Property value decline, occupancy loss, interest rate risk on refinance
- Capital stack protection: None—you're last in line

Opportunity B: Private Credit Fund (Senior Debt)

- Strategy: First-lien loans on commercial real estate
- Your investment: $50,000 minimum
- Position: Senior debt (typically 60-70% LTV)
- Projected returns: 9% annual cash yield
- Risk: Borrower default, but protected by asset collateral and seniority
- Capital stack protection: Strong—first in line, significant equity cushion below you

Opportunity C: Preferred Equity Deal

- Property: Industrial development, $50M project
- Your investment: $50,000 minimum
- Position: Preferred equity (10% preferred return, after $30M debt)
- Projected returns: 10% annual preferred + 20% profit participation
- Risk: Development delays, cost overruns, market softness
- Capital stack protection: Moderate—you get paid before common equity, but after debt

Which should you choose?

It depends on your portfolio needs:

If you need income and stability: Choose B (private credit)

- Highest current income (9%)
- Lowest risk (senior position)
- Most predictable
- If you want balanced risk/return: Choose C (preferred equity)
- Good income (10%)

- Some upside participation
- Moderate protection

If you want maximum appreciation: Choose A (common equity)

- Highest total return potential (18% IRR)
- Highest risk
- Lower current income

The Architect answer: All three, diversified.

- \$50K in each = \$150K deployed
- Blended return: ~12-15%
- Blended income: ~\$12,000/year (8% yield)
- Risk: Balanced across capital stack

The Wealth Stack Pyramid™

Your entire portfolio can be visualized as a capital stack:

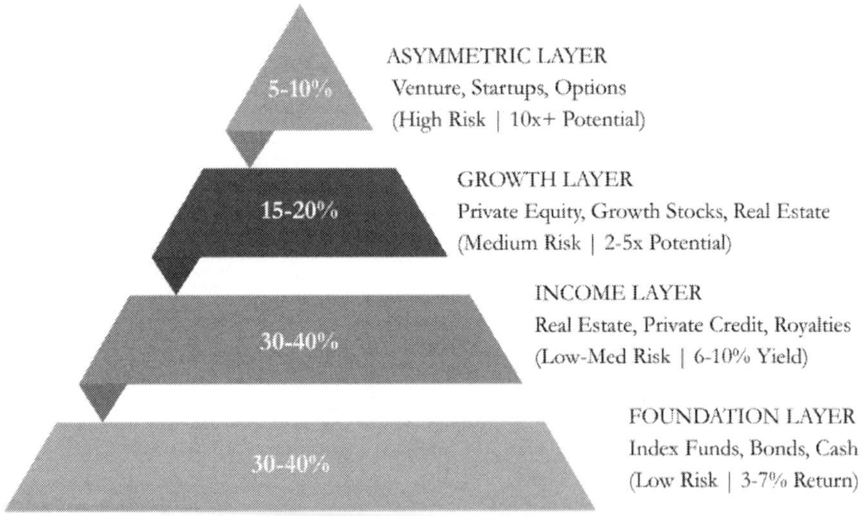

How capital earns differently across levels:

- Foundation: Market returns, compound growth, liquidity premium
- Income: Contractual returns, seniority premium, illiquidity premium
- Growth: Appreciation, operational improvements, market expansion
- Asymmetric: Outlier returns, winner-take-most dynamics, moonshots

Each level serves a different purpose in your wealth system.

Case Study: The Stack That Saved a Portfolio

2022 was brutal. Stocks fell 18%. Bonds fell 13%. Many "diversified" portfolios lost 15-20%.

Investor: Chen, 49, $1.2M portfolio

His stack allocation:

- 30% Foundation ($360K): Index funds + bonds
- 40% Income ($480K):
    - $200K in private credit (senior debt positions)
    - $180K in real estate syndications (mix of preferred and common equity)
    - $100K in dividend aristocrat stocks
- 20% Growth ($240K): Private equity and growth real estate
- 10% Asymmetric ($120K): Venture investments

2022 Results:

- Foundation: -15% = $54K loss (stocks and bonds both down)
- Income:
    - Private credit: +9% = $18K gain (continued payments despite market chaos)
    - Real estate: +5% = $9K gain (slower repricing + steady distributions)
    - Dividend stocks: -8% = -$8K loss
    - Income layer total: +$19K (+4%)
- Growth: -10% = -$24K loss (private markets lag but also fell)
- Asymmetric: -20% = -$24K loss (venture valuations down)

Total portfolio 2022: $1.15M (-4.2%) vs. Traditional 60/40: -16%

More importantly: Chen's income didn't stop. His portfolio generated $78,000 in distributions during 2022, funding his lifestyle while others panicked.

His senior debt positions (private credit) increased distributions as interest rates rose.

By diversifying across the capital stack, he weathered the storm and continued compounding.

Your Capital Stack Strategy

Step 1: Assess Current Stack Position

What percentage of your portfolio is in:

- Senior debt / credit: ____%
- Mezzanine / preferred equity: ____%
- Common equity: ____%

Most investors are 95%+ common equity. That's an unnecessary risk.

Step 2: Determine Target Allocation

Based on your risk tolerance:

Conservative:

- 40% Senior debt/credit
- 30% Preferred/mezzanine
- 20% Common equity (established)
- 10% Common equity (asymmetric)

Moderate:

- 30% Senior debt/credit
- 25% Preferred/mezzanine
- 30% Common equity (established)
- 15% Common equity (asymmetric)

Aggressive:

- 20% Senior debt/credit
- 20% Preferred/mezzanine

- 40% Common equity (established)
- 20% Common equity (asymmetric)

Step 3: Access Stack Positions

How to invest in different stack positions:

Senior Debt:

- Private credit funds (Cliffwater, PennantPark, etc.)
- Real estate debt funds (ArborCrowd, RealtyMogul Debt)
- P2P lending platforms for senior positions
- Interval funds specializing in first-lien loans

Mezzanine/Preferred:

- Specialty funds offering mezzanine strategies
- Individual syndications offering preferred equity tranches
- Some crowdfunding platforms offer preferred shares
- Family office co-investments

Common Equity:

- Real estate syndications (most are common equity)
- Private equity funds
- Venture capital funds
- Direct investments in businesses/startups

Step 4: Rebalance Over Time

Don't rush to reposition everything immediately. As investments mature and return capital, redeploy according to your target stack allocation.

Over 2-3 years, you'll have built a properly stacked portfolio.

The Seniority Mindset

The capital stack teaches a crucial lesson: You don't always want to be the owner.

Sometimes it's better to be the lender. Sometimes the hybrid position is optimal.

Ownership (common equity) gets glory. Seniority (senior debt) gets paid.

Architects want to get paid.

Key Takeaways:

- The capital stack ranks how different capital gets paid: senior debt → mezzanine → preferred equity → common equity
- Senior positions offer lower returns but higher safety and priority
- Common equity offers highest upside but maximum risk and last payment priority
- Diversifying across the stack reduces risk while maintaining strong returns
- LTV (loan-to-value) determines safety margin in debt positions
- Leverage amplifies both gains and losses—use conservatively
- Most investors are over-concentrated in common equity
- Target allocation: 30-40% senior positions, 20-30% mezzanine/preferred, 30-40% common equity
- The Wealth Stack Pyramid visualizes your entire portfolio by risk layer

SECTION III

THE MODERN INVESTMENT UNIVERSE

CHAPTER 9:

THE REAL ESTATE RENAISSANCE

Rachel walks into her kitchen on a Tuesday morning and makes coffee while checking her phone. Three notifications:

- Property A (Phoenix multifamily): $1,847 distribution deposited
- Property B (Atlanta self-storage): Quarterly report—occupancy up to 94%
- Property C (Austin mixed-use): Refinance completed, $8,200 capital distribution incoming

Rachel doesn't own these properties. She doesn't manage tenants, fix toilets, or negotiate leases. She invested $25,000 in each syndication 2-3 years ago and now receives passive income while operators handle everything.

Her total real estate portfolio: $175,000 invested across seven properties. Annual income: $14,500. Average return: 8.3% cash-on-cash, projected 16% IRR when properties sell.

She's a nurse. She lives in North Carolina. She's never met the property managers. And she's building wealth through real estate without being a landlord.

This is the real estate renaissance.

Why Real Estate Remains the Wealth Builder

For 5,000 years, real estate has been the most reliable path to wealth. The Romans built fortunes in land. The Medici family-controlled Florence through property. Rockefeller famously said, "The major fortunes in America have been made in land."

Why does real estate persistently work?

1. Scarcity: They're not making more land (in desirable locations)

2. Utility: People always need shelter, storage, workspaces, hospitality

3. Inflation hedge: Rents and property values typically rise with inflation

4. Leverage: Banks eagerly lend against real estate at low rates (60-80% LTV)

5. Tax advantages: Depreciation, 1031 exchanges, capital gains treatment

6. Cash flow + appreciation: Dual return streams (rent income + value growth)

7. Tangibility: You can see it, touch it, understand it

8. Asymmetric information: Local knowledge creates advantages unavailable in public markets

But for decades, real estate investing meant two paths:

Path A: Buy rental properties yourself (be a landlord)

- Pro: Full control, maximum returns
- Con: Significant capital, active management, concentrated risk, stress

Path B: Buy REITs (public real estate stocks)

- Pro: Liquidity, diversification, passive
- Con: Trade like stocks, dividend taxes, no control, no tax advantages of direct ownership

Path C (The New Way): Invest in private real estate syndications

- Pro: Passive ownership, professional management, tax advantages, diversification, direct asset ownership
- Con: Illiquid (5-7 year holds), accredited investor requirements (though changing), minimum investments ($25K-$50K typically)

Technology platforms have democratized Path C. What was once available only to institutions and ultra-wealthy investors is now accessible to individuals with $25,000-$50,000.

The Five Real Estate Segments

Not all real estate is created equal. Each segment has different economics, risk profiles, and return drivers.

Segment 1: Multifamily (Apartment Buildings)

What it is: Residential apartment complexes, typically 100-500 units

Investment thesis: Housing is non-discretionary. People always need a place to live. Multifamily offers diversification (loss of one tenant = 1-2% income loss, not 100%).

Return profile:

- Cash-on-cash: 6-9% annually
- Total IRR: 14-18% over 5-7 years
- Risk: Moderate (recession-resistant but sensitive to overbuilding)

Value-add strategy: Buy Class B/C properties, renovate units, raise rents, increase property value through operational improvements.

Example deal:

- 200-unit complex in Nashville
- Purchase price: $35M (60% debt, 40% equity)
- Investor equity raise: $14M
- Strategy: $3M in renovations over 2 years, increase rents from $1,100 to $1,450/unit
- Hold: 5 years
- Projected sale: $52M
- Investor returns: 7% annual distributions + 2.1x equity multiple = 16% IRR

Best for: Core income + appreciation, recession-resistant cash flow, first-time alternative investors

What to watch: Local employment growth, new supply in market, demographic trends, crime rates, school quality

Segment 2: Self-Storage

What it is: Climate-controlled storage units, typically 400-800 units per facility

Investment thesis: Storage is a unique asset class—people accumulate stuff and hate throwing it away. Low maintenance (no toilets, no tenants living on property), high margins (70-80% NOI margins), sticky customers (who wants to move their stuff?).

Return profile:

- Cash-on-cash: 7-10% annually
- Total IRR: 16-22% over 5-7 years
- Risk: Low-to-moderate (recession-resistant, people need storage in good and bad times)

Value-add strategy: Buy underperforming facilities, implement revenue management (dynamic pricing), add climate control, improve marketing, expand footprint.

Recession performance: Storage often performs well in recessions—people downsize homes, store belongings; businesses reduce office space, store inventory.

Example deal:

- 500-unit facility in Denver suburbs
- Purchase price: $12M
- Strategy: Increase occupancy from 72% to 90%, raise rates from $0.90/sq ft to $1.25/sq ft
- Hold: 6 years
- Projected sale: $18M
- Investor returns: 8% annual distributions + 2.3x equity multiple = 18% IRR

Best for: Stable cash flow, recession resilience, operators with revenue management expertise

What to watch: Population density (need 50K+ people within 3-5 mile radius), local competition, occupancy rates, pricing power

Segment 3: Industrial (Warehouses, Distribution)

What it is: Warehouses, distribution centers, flex spaces, last-mile logistics

Investment thesis: E-commerce growth requires massive distribution infrastructure. Amazon effect = insatiable demand for industrial space near population centers.

Return profile:

- Cash-on-cash: 5-8% annually (lower because it's institutional-grade)
- Total IRR: 12-16% over 7-10 years
- Risk: Low (long-term leases, credit tenants, structural demand)

Key trend: Last-mile distribution—warehouses within 30 miles of major metros where goods can be delivered same-day/next-day.

Example deal:

- 180,000 sq ft distribution center outside Atlanta
- Purchase price: $28M
- Tenant: Regional logistics company (7-year lease)
- Strategy: Buy and hold with lease escalators
- Hold: 8 years
- Projected sale: $38M
- Investor returns: 6% annual distributions + 1.7x equity multiple = 13% IRR

Best for: Conservative investors seeking stable, long-term cash flow with institutional-quality assets

What to watch: E-commerce growth, highway access, proximity to population centers, tenant credit quality

Segment 4: Hospitality (Hotels, Short-Term Rentals)

What it is: Hotels, motels, extended-stay, Airbnb portfolio plays

Investment thesis: Travel and tourism sector, high-occupancy markets, business travel, vacation destinations

Return profile:

- Cash-on-cash: 4-8% annually (volatile, depends on occupancy)
- Total IRR: 15-25% over 5-7 years (higher risk = higher potential return)
- Risk: High (economically sensitive, highly competitive, operational complexity)

The catch: Hospitality is pro-cyclical. Thrives in economic booms, suffers in recessions. Operational intensity is high.

Best for: Aggressive investors comfortable with volatility, strong operators with hospitality expertise

What to avoid: First-time syndication sponsors, overleveraged deals, markets dependent on single event/industry

Segment 5: Opportunistic (Land, Development, Redevelopment)

What it is: Raw land development, ground-up construction, major redevelopments, conversions (office → residential)

Investment thesis: Buy undervalued or underdeveloped assets, create value through development, sell or refinance at higher valuation.

Return profile:

- Cash-on-cash: 0-3% annually (most returns come at exit)
- Total IRR: 18-35% over 4-7 years
- Risk: Very high (construction risk, entitlement risk, market timing risk, cost overrun risk)

Example deal:

- 12-acre land parcel in Austin
- Purchase: $4M
- Strategy: Entitle for 80-unit townhome development, build over 3 years, sell units
- Total project cost: $18M
- Projected revenue: $28M
- Investor returns: Minimal distributions + 2.8x equity multiple = 25% IRR (if all goes well)

Risk factors: Permitting delays, construction cost overruns, market timing (what if demand softens before units sell?), contractor performance

Best for: Sophisticated investors with high risk tolerance, long time horizons, and capital they can afford to lose

What to watch: Sponsor experience (only invest with developers who've completed similar projects), market fundamentals, entitlement risk mitigation

The Five Return Drivers (CAETI Framework™)

Real estate generates returns through five distinct mechanisms. Understanding these helps you evaluate opportunities:

1. Cash Flow (C)

What it is: Net operating income (rent revenue minus operating expenses) distributed to investors

Importance: Immediate returns, funds your freedom, compounds when reinvested

How to evaluate: Cash-on-cash return (annual distributions ÷ invested capital)

- 5-6%: Lower but stable
- 7-9%: Strong cash flow
- 10%+: Aggressive (verify it's not too good to be true)

2. Appreciation (A)

What it is: Property value increasing over time due to market growth, rent growth, or forced appreciation through improvements

Types:

- Market appreciation: Rising tide lifts all boats (2-4% annually historically)
- Forced appreciation: Value-add improvements increase NOI, which increases property value (most syndication deals)

Formula: Property value = NOI ÷ Cap Rate

If you increase NOI from $2M to $3M and cap rate is 5%, value increases from $40M to $60M.

3. Equity (E)

What it is: Paying down debt with tenant rent payments, increasing your ownership percentage

The magic: Tenants pay the mortgage. Over 5-7 years, significant equity builds automatically.

Example: $20M property with $12M mortgage at 4% interest

- Year 1 principal paydown: ~$400K
- Year 5 principal paydown: ~$500K/year (as interest decreases)
- Total over 5 years: ~$2.2M equity gained from debt paydown

This return is often overlooked but significant.

4. Tax benefits (T)

What it is: Real estate offers unique tax advantages unavailable in stocks/bonds

Key benefits:

- Depreciation: Deduct property "wear and tear" against income, even though property may be appreciating
- Bonus depreciation: Accelerated depreciation in year 1 (cost segregation studies)
- 1031 exchange: Defer capital gains by rolling proceeds into new property
- Long-term capital gains: Lower tax rate on appreciation
- Passive loss treatment: May offset other passive income

Real example: You invest $50K in a syndication. Year 1, you receive $4,000 distribution but show $8,000 paper loss due to depreciation. You receive cash but owe no taxes (and may offset other passive income).

IRS views depreciation as income offset. You view it as cash flow plus tax benefit. Win-win.

5. Inflation hedge (I)

What it is: Real estate tends to appreciate with inflation, and rents typically rise with inflation

Why it matters: When inflation runs 4-5%, stocks and bonds struggle. Real estate often thrives because:

- Construction costs rise (making existing properties more valuable)
- Rents increase (passing inflation to tenants)
- Property values rise (capitalization rates may compress)

Historical evidence: From 1970-2020, commercial real estate returns correlated 0.72 with inflation. Stocks correlated -0.18. Real estate is one of the best inflation hedges.

The CAETI advantage: A great real estate investment delivers all five return drivers simultaneously.

How to Evaluate a Real Estate Syndication

You're presented with an investment opportunity. How do you evaluate it?

Due Diligence Checklist

Part 1: The Sponsor (Most Important)

- ☐ Track record: How many deals have they completed? What were actual returns vs. projections?
- ☐ Experience: How many years in this specific asset class and market?
- ☐ Skin in the game: Are they investing their own capital (typically 5-15% of equity)?
- ☐ Transparency: Do they provide detailed reporting? Are they responsive?
- ☐ References: Can you speak to past investors?
- ☐ Alignment: Is their compensation tied to investor returns (preferred return before sponsor profit)?

Red flags:

- First-time sponsor
- No personal capital invested
- Promises above-market returns
- Vague about track record
- High-pressure sales tactics

Part 2: The Market

- ☐ Economic fundamentals: Population growth, job growth, income growth.
- ☐ Supply/demand: Is new supply overwhelming demand?
- ☐ Diversification: Diverse economy or dependent on one industry?
- ☐ Location quality: Crime rates, school quality, amenities, access.

Strong markets (historically): Austin, Nashville, Dallas, Phoenix, Atlanta, Charlotte, Denver, Tampa, Raleigh

Avoid: Markets losing population, dominated by one employer, over-supplied, high crime

Part 3: The Deal Structure

- ☐ Purchase price: Is it fair market value or overpaying?
- ☐ Leverage: What's the LTV? (60-75% is standard; 80%+ is aggressive)
- ☐ Business plan: Is the value-add plan realistic?
- ☐ Projected returns: Are they reasonable? (7% cash-on-cash, 15-18% IRR is typical for multifamily)
- ☐ Hold period: Does 5-7 years work for your liquidity needs?
- ☐ Fees: What is the sponsor charging? (Acquisition, asset management, disposition fees—2-3% total is reasonable)

Red flags:

- Overly optimistic projections (10% cash-on-cash, 25% IRR)
- Short flip timeline (2-3 years = speculative)
- Excessive fees (5%+ total)
- High leverage (85%+ LTV)
- Unclear exit strategy

Part 4: The Offering Terms

- ☐ Preferred return: Do investors receive a hurdle before sponsor profits? (6-8% preferred is common)
- ☐ Profit split: How are profits divided after preferred return? (70/30 or 80/20 in favor of investors is typical)
- ☐ Minimum investment: Can you diversify at this level?
- ☐ Accreditation requirement: Do you qualify?
- ☐ K-1 tax forms: Are you prepared for tax complexity?

The Investment Decision Framework

After due diligence, apply this framework:

Question 1: Do I trust this sponsor with my capital?

- If no → Pass, regardless of deal quality

Question 2: Do I understand the investment thesis?

- If no → Pass or learn more before investing

Question 3: Are projected returns commensurate with risk?

- Higher risk should equal higher projected returns
- If conservative asset but aggressive projections → Red flag

Question 4: Does this fit my portfolio?

- Am I over-concentrated in real estate? In this market? With this sponsor?

Question 5: Can I afford the illiquidity?

- Will I need this capital in the next 5-7 years?

Question 6: How does this move me toward my Freedom Number?

- What annual income will this generate?
- What's the projected equity multiple at exit?

If you answer positively on all six, invest. If uncertain on any, pass or size down.

Building a Diversified Real Estate Portfolio

Avoid: Putting $150K into one syndication with one sponsor in one market.

Do: Build a portfolio across:

Geographic diversification:

- 3+ different markets
- Diverse regions (Southeast, Southwest, Mountain West)
- Mix of primary, secondary markets

Asset class diversification:

- 40-50% Multifamily (stable, liquid market)
- 20-30% Self-storage (recession-resistant)
- 15-20% Industrial (institutional-grade)
- 10-15% Opportunistic/specialty (higher risk/return)

Sponsor diversification:

- 4+ different sponsors
- Never more than 30% with one sponsor
- Verify track records independently

Vintage diversification:

- Don't deploy all capital in one year
- Spread across 2-3 years
- Protects against market timing risk

Example: $300K real estate allocation:

- 6 syndications at $50K each
- 3 different sponsors
- 4 different markets

- 3 multifamily, 2 self-storage, 1 industrial
- Deployed over 18 months (not all at once)

Projected returns:

- Annual income: $21,000 (7% yield)
- Projected 5-7 year exit: $480K-540K (16-18% IRR)

The Tax Advantages Explained

Real estate's tax benefits are powerful but complex. Here's what you need to know:

Depreciation: The Phantom Deduction

The concept: IRS assumes buildings "wear out" over 27.5 years (residential) or 39 years (commercial). You can deduct this theoretical depreciation against income.

The reality: Most properties appreciate, but you still get the deduction.

Example:

- $25M property: $20M building value (80%), $5M land (20%)
- Annual depreciation: $20M ÷ 27.5 years = $727K
- Your 5% ownership: $36,350 annual depreciation deduction
- Your actual distribution: $10,000
- Your taxable income: $10,000 - $36,350 = -$26,350 (paper loss)

Result: You received $10,000 cash but show a tax loss, potentially offsetting other passive income.

Cost Segregation: Accelerated Depreciation

What it is: Engineering study that separates property components into shorter depreciation schedules

Example:

- Normal: Entire $20M building over 27.5 years
- Cost seg: $5M in personal property (carpets, appliances, fixtures) over 5 years + $15M over 27.5 years

Effect: Massively front-loads depreciation, creating larger early-year tax benefits

Typical result: First-year paper losses of 40-80% of investment, providing immediate tax benefits

1031 Exchange: Infinite Deferral

What it is: When property sells, instead of paying capital gains taxes, roll proceeds into a new property within strict timeframes (45 days to identify, 180 days to close)

The power: Continuously defer taxes through multiple properties until death (step-up in basis for heirs)

Example:

- Property A sells, $200K gain
- Without 1031: Pay ~$40K in taxes (20% federal + state)
- With 1031: Roll full $200K into Property B, no taxes paid
- Property B eventually sells for $300K gain
- 1031 again into Property C...continue indefinitely

Syndication note: When syndications sell, sponsors often offer 1031 options into their next deal, allowing you to defer continuously

Qualified Opportunity Zones

What it is: Tax incentive to invest in economically distressed areas

Benefits:

- Defer capital gains taxes by investing gains in QOZ fund
- If held 10+ years, pay no taxes on QOZ appreciation

Use case: If you have large capital gains (from stock sale, business exit, property sale), QOZ investments can defer and potentially eliminate taxes on both the original gain and new appreciation

Caution: Must invest in designated zones, which may have higher risk. Don't let the tax tail wag investment dog.

Common Mistakes to Avoid

Mistake 1: Chasing yield without vetting sponsor High returns means nothing if sponsor loses your capital. Always prioritize sponsor quality.

Mistake 2: Investing in hot markets at peak When everyone wants Austin real estate, valuations are high and returns are compressed. Consider secondary markets with better fundamentals.

Mistake 3: Over-concentrating Three deals with the same sponsor in the same market = concentration risk. One market downturn devastates your portfolio.

Mistake 4: Ignoring liquidity needs Real estate is illiquid. Don't invest capital you'll need in 5 years. Maintain a 20-30% portfolio in liquid assets.

Mistake 5: Falling for "guaranteed returns" No real estate investment is guaranteed. If marketed as "guaranteed 10% returns," it's likely misrepresented or extremely risky.

Mistake 6: Analysis paralysis Waiting for the perfect deal means missing good deals. After proper due diligence, trust your process and deploy capital.

Mistake 7: Ignoring fees High fees erode returns. Calculate total sponsor compensation and compare to industry standards (2-3% total is reasonable, 5%+ is excessive).

Case Study: Building Freedom Through Real Estate

Investor: Marcus, 38, Project Manager, $165K income

Starting point (2018):

- Net worth: $220K (mostly 401k and home equity)
- Real estate experience: Zero
- Goal: Generate $60K annual passive income by age 50

Year 1 (2018): Education phase

- Read books, joined online communities, attended webinars
- Continued saving in 401k while learning
- Saved additional $35K for first investment

Year 2 (2019): First investment

- $50K into Phoenix multifamily syndication
- Sponsor: Established team, 15+ deals
- Projected: 7% cash-on-cash, 16% IRR
- Result: $3,500 annual distributions began

Year 3 (2020): Expansion

- COVID hit, but real estate fundamentals stayed strong
- Added $50K into Atlanta self-storage (different sponsor)
- Added $35K into Denver multifamily (third sponsor)
- Annual income: $9,800

Year 4 (2021): Diversification

- Markets hot, but he continued deploying
- Added $40K into Dallas industrial
- Added $45K into Nashville multifamily
- Total invested: $220K across 5 properties
- Annual income: $16,500 (7.5% average yield)

Year 5 (2022): First harvest

- Phoenix property sold: $50K → $78K ($28K gain + distributions)
- Rolled $78K into two new syndications
- Total portfolio: 6 active investments
- Annual income: $18,200

Year 6 (2023): Acceleration

- Added $50K from salary savings
- Added $30K from property distribution
- Total invested: $378K across 8 properties
- Annual income: $27,500

Year 7 (2024): Momentum

- Second property sold: $35K → $62K
- Reinvested + added new capital
- Total invested: $465K across 10 properties
- Annual income: $34,000

Current state (2025):

- Real estate portfolio: $525K invested
- Annual passive income: $38,500 (7.3% yield)
- Freedom Index: 64% (expenses: $60K/year)

- Projected by age 50 (2037): $1.2M invested, $75K+ annual income = 125% Freedom Index

Keys to Marcus's success:

- Started with education before deploying capital
- Diversified across sponsors, markets, asset classes
- Consistent deployment regardless of market conditions
- Reinvested distributions for compounding
- Stayed disciplined with due diligence

Marcus will reach financial autonomy through one asset class: real estate. No stock market brilliance. No business exists. Just systematic, intelligent allocation into cash-flowing assets managed by professionals.

Key Takeaways:

- Real estate remains the most reliable wealth-building asset: scarcity, utility, leverage, tax advantages, dual returns
- Five segments: Multifamily (core), Self-storage (stable), Industrial (institutional), Hospitality (cyclical), Opportunistic (aggressive)
- CAETI Framework: Cash flow, Appreciation, Equity (debt paydown), Tax benefits, Inflation hedge
- Sponsor quality is paramount—vet experience, track record, alignment, transparency
- Diversify across sponsors, markets, asset classes, vintages
- Real estate syndications offer passive ownership, professional management, and tax advantages
- Tax benefits (depreciation, 1031 exchanges) significantly enhance after-tax returns
- Build systematically over years, not all at once—dollar-cost average into real estate

CHAPTER 10:

THE PRIVATE EQUITY AND VENTURE ACCESS

In 1999, a teacher's pension fund in California made a $25 million investment in a small venture capital fund. That fund invested early in companies like Google, PayPal, and LinkedIn.

Twenty years later, that $25 million position was worth over $1 billion—a 40x return.

The teacher didn't invest. The pension fund did. And until recently, individual investors like you couldn't access the same opportunities.

That's changing.

The Private Markets Outperformance

Public markets (stocks) have delivered ~10% annual returns over the long term.

Private markets have consistently outperformed:

- Private Equity: 14-15% annualized returns (2000-2023)
- Venture Capital: 18-25% annualized returns for top quartile funds (2000-2023)
- Private Credit: 9-12% annualized returns with lower volatility

Why the premium?

1. **Illiquidity premium:** You lock up capital for 7-12 years; you're compensated for that constraint

2. **Information asymmetry:** Less efficient markets = more opportunities for skilled investors

3. **Operational improvement:** Private equity firms actively improve businesses (not passive ownership)

4. **Less volatility:** No daily mark-to-market, so less emotional decision-making

5. **Selection bias:** Only quality companies access institutional private capital

For decades, this "alternative" premium was reserved for institutions (endowments, pensions, sovereign wealth funds) and ultra-high-net-worth individuals.

Today, platforms like AngelList, EquityZen, Forge Global, and specialized fund-of-funds have opened access to individuals with $50K-$100K+ to invest.

Understanding Private Equity

What it is: Investment firms that buy established businesses, improve operations, and sell 5-7 years later for profit.

Types of PE:

Buyout Funds (Most Common)

Strategy: Acquire majority/full ownership of mature companies, optimize operations, exit at higher valuation

Example deal:

- PE firm acquires regional manufacturing company for $200M
- EBITDA (earnings): $25M (8x multiple)
- Strategy over 5 years:
    - Improve operations (reduce costs, increase efficiency)
    - Add bolt-on acquisitions (buy 3 smaller competitors)
    - Professionalize management

    - Grow revenue 40% and margins from 12% to 17%
- New EBITDA: $45M
- Exit at 10x multiple = $450M
- Return to investors: 2.25x equity, ~18% IRR

How they create value:

- Operational improvements (cost reduction, revenue optimization)
- Strategic repositioning (new markets, products, pricing)
- Add-on acquisitions (roll-up strategy)
- Financial engineering (optimize capital structure)

- Management incentivization

Growth Equity

Strategy: Minority investments in established, fast-growing companies that need capital to scale

Profile:

- Companies doing $10M-$100M revenue
- Already profitable or near profitability
- Proven product-market fit
- Need capital for expansion, not survival

Example:

- SaaS company doing $30M ARR, growing 80% annually
- Growth equity invests $20M for 25% ownership
- Company uses capital to expand sales team, enter new markets
- 4 years later: $150M ARR, acquired by strategic buyer
- Investor stake: $20M → $90M (4.5x, 45% IRR)

Lower risk than VC, higher than buyout—balanced risk/reward

Distressed/Special Situations

Strategy: Buy undervalued or distressed companies, turn them around

Higher risk, higher potential returns (20-30% IRR targets)

Best for: Sophisticated investors who understand business fundamentals and can evaluate turnaround plans

Understanding Venture Capital

What it is: Investment in early-stage companies with high growth potential and high failure risk

The math that makes VC work:

- 10 investments
- 5 go to zero (50% failure rate)

- 3 return 1-2x (break-even/small wins)
- 1 returns 10x
- 1 returns 50x

Portfolio result: 10x portfolio return despite 50% failure rate

This is power law distribution: Winners win so big they overcome all losses.

VC Stage Breakdown:

- Pre-Seed / Seed ($250K-$3M raise)
  - Stage: Idea to early product
  - Risk: Extreme (80%+ failure rate)
  - Potential: 100x+ if it works
  - Timeline: 10-12 years to exit (if successful)
- Series A ($5M-$15M raise)
  - Stage: Product-market fit established, scaling revenue
  - Risk: Very high (50-60% failure rate)
  - Potential: 20-50x
  - Timeline: 7-10 years to exit
- Series B-C ($20M-$100M+ raises)
  - Stage: Scaling rapidly, clear path to profitability
  - Risk: Moderate-high (30-40% failure rate)
  - Potential: 5-15x
  - Timeline: 4-7 years to exit
- Late-stage / Pre-IPO
  - Stage: Established, path to IPO or acquisition
  - Risk: Moderate (20-30% downside possible)
  - Potential: 2-5x
  - Timeline: 2-4 years to exit
- Individual investor access
  - Seed/Series A: Angel platforms (AngelList, SeedInvest)
  - Series B+: Secondary marketplaces (Forge, EquityZen)
  - All stages: VC funds (commit capital, they deploy across stages)

How to Access Private Markets

Option 1: Private Equity Funds

Minimum investment: $100K-$250K (sometimes lower through fund-of-funds)

Structure: Commit capital, fund calls it over 3-5 years, invested across 10-20 companies, distributions over 7-12 years

Returns: Target 15-20% net IRR

Pros: Professional management, diversification, institutional access

Cons: Illiquid (10-12 year lockup), high minimums, J-curve (losses early as fees charged before gains realized)

Platforms:

- Moonfare (European PE access)
- Proportion (PE fund marketplace)
- Fundrise Innovation Fund (Tech-focused, $10K min)
- Through wealth advisors (typically $250K+ min)

Option 2: Venture Capital Funds

Minimum investment: $50K-$100K (individual funds) or $10K-$25K (fund-of-funds)

Structure: Similar to PE funds; commit capital, deployed over 2-4 years, returns over 10-12 years

Returns: Top quartile 25%+ IRR; median 12-15% IRR; bottom quartile negative

Critical factor: Manager selection is everything in VC. The top quartile dramatically outperforms the median.

Pros: Access to venture portfolio, potential for outlier returns, participation in innovation economy

Cons: Extreme illiquidity (10-12 years), high variance (many funds lose money), manager selection difficult

Platforms:

- AngelList Rolling Funds (subscribe quarterly, $50K typical min)
- Screened and funded rolling funds ($1K-$5K minimums)
- Alumni funds (if you attended a target school—Stanford, Harvard, MIT have alumni VC funds)

Option 3: Direct Venture Investments

Minimum investment: $1K-$50K depending on platform and deal

Access: Angel platforms, equity crowdfunding, direct relationships

Returns: Binary outcomes—most go to zero, occasional moonshots

Pros: You choose specific companies, learn about sectors deeply, potential for massive returns

Cons: Extreme risk, requires significant due diligence, heavy time investment, diversification requires many investments

Platforms:

- AngelList (curated deals, often $5K-$25K mins)
- Republic (equity crowdfunding, $100-$10K)
- Wefunder (equity crowdfunding, $100-$5K)
- SeedInvest (vetted startups, $500-$5K)
- Direct networks (if you have access to deal flow)

Option 4: Secondary Markets

What it is: Buy shares in private companies from existing shareholders (employees, early investors) before IPO/acquisition

Minimum investment: $10K-$100K depending on company and platform

Access: EquityZen, Forge Global, Nasdaq Private Market

Returns: Lower than early-stage VC (2-5x typical) but also lower risk (companies more mature)

Pros: Later-stage companies with proven models, shorter time to liquidity (2-4 years typical), known companies (Stripe, SpaceX, Epic Games)

Cons: Valuations already elevated (no seed-stage pricing), still illiquid, shares may have restrictions

Best for: Investors who want venture exposure without extreme risk, shorter hold periods, or conviction in specific growth companies

Option 5: Interval Funds / BDCs

What it is: Business Development Companies or interval funds that invest in private markets but offer periodic liquidity

Minimum investment: $2,500-$10,000

Structure: Semi-liquid (quarterly or annual redemption windows), invest across private credit, PE, VC

Returns: Target 8-12% annually

Pros: Much lower minimums, periodic liquidity, diversification, professional management

Cons: Fees (2%+ typically), liquidity windows may be limited, may not capture full private market premium

Examples:

- ICONIQ Strategic Partners Access Fund
- Apollo Diversified Credit Fund
- FS Specialty Lending Fund

Fund Structure Basics: What You Need to Know

When you invest in a PE or VC fund, you're becoming a Limited Partner (LP). Understanding the structure protects you:

Key Terms

Capital Commitment: The amount you pledge to invest. You don't write a check immediately—the fund "calls" capital over time as they find investments.

Capital Call: When a fund needs money for an investment, they issue a call. You typically have 10-15 days to wire funds.

Management Fee: Annual fee (typically 2%) charged on committed capital (early years) or invested capital (later years). Covers fund operating costs.

Carry (Carried Interest): The profit share the fund managers receive. Typically 20% of profits above a "hurdle rate."

Hurdle Rate (Preferred Return): Minimum return threshold (typically 8%) that LPs receive before managers earn carry.

Example:

- You commit $100K to a fund
- Management fee: 2% = $2K/year for 10 years = $20K total
- Fund returns $250K total to all investors
- Net return: $150K profit
- First $80K profit (8% hurdle on $100K over 10 years) goes to LPs
- Remaining $70K profit split: 80% to LPs ($56K), 20% to managers ($14K as carry)
- Your total distributions: $100K (capital back) + $80K (preferred) + $56K (profit share) = $236K
- Your net return after fees: 2.36x multiple, ~14% IRR

Typical fund economics:

- "2 and 20": 2% management fee, 20% carry above hurdle
- "1.5 and 15": Lower fees (increasingly common for larger funds)
- Hurdle rates: 6-8% typical

Distribution Timing

Unlike stock dividends, private fund distributions are unpredictable:

The J-Curve:

- Years 1-3: Negative returns (fees charged, no exits yet)
- Years 4-7: Portfolio companies maturing, early exits begin
- Years 7-10: Major exits, distributions accelerate
- Years 10-12: Final portfolio liquidation

Cashflow pattern:

- Year 1: Call $25K (25% of commitment)
- Year 2: Call $40K (40% of commitment)
- Year 3: Call $35K (35% of commitment)
- Year 4: Distribution $15K (early exit)
- Year 5: Distribution $30K
- Year 6: Distribution $80K
- Years 7-10: Remaining distributions

Important: You must have liquid capital available for calls throughout the commitment period. Don't commit more than you can fund over 3-5 years.

Evaluating Private Market Funds

Not all funds are created equal. Due diligence is critical.

The Track Record Deep Dive

What to examine:

- DPI (Distributions to Paid-In Capital): Actually returned money vs. invested. 1.5x+ is good, 2.0x+ is excellent
- TVPI (Total Value to Paid-In Capital): Returned + unrealized value vs. invested. Includes paper gains not yet realized
- IRR: Time-weighted return. 15%+ is solid, 20%+ is top-tier
- Multiple vintages: Has the manager performed across different market cycles?

Red flags:

- Only showing TVPI without DPI (paper gains, not actual returns)
- Single vintage with outsized returns (could be luck)
- Inconsistent performance across funds
- Returns that are too good to be true (30%+ IRRs sustained)

The Manager Assessment

Questions to ask:

Experience: How many years has this team invested together?

- 5+ years together = good
- <3 years = higher risk

Strategy consistency: Do they stick to their stated strategy or chase trends?

- Specialized focus = better
- Generalist "we invest in everything" = concerning

Network and deal flow: How do they source investments?

- Proprietary deal flow (relationships, reputation) = valuable
- Reliant on brokers/publicly marketed deals = less differentiation

Value-add: What do they provide beyond capital?

- Board seats, operational expertise, network access = valuable
- Just capital = commodity

Alignment: Do GPs (managers) invest their own capital?

- 1-3% of fund size personally invested = aligned
- No personal capital = misaligned

The Portfolio Construction Check

Fund diversification:

- Number of investments: 10-15 is typical for VC, 15-25 for PE
- Concentration: Beware if >30% in a single investment
- Stage consistency: Seed funds should do seed deals, not suddenly late-stage
- Geographic focus: Stated focus should match actual deployment

Your diversification: If investing in multiple funds:

- Diversify across managers (no more than 30% with one manager)
- Diversify across vintages (spread commitments over 2-4 years)
- Diversify across strategies (VC + PE + growth equity)
- Diversify across stages (early + late)

The 4 M's Framework™ for Direct Investments

If you're considering direct startup investments (angel deals), evaluate using this framework:

M1: Market

Is this a large, growing market?

- TAM (Total Addressable Market): Is it a $10B+ market opportunity?
- Growth rate: Is the market expanding 15%+ annually?
- Timing: Are we early enough or already late?

Red flags:

- Tiny niche market with limited expansion
- Declining or stagnant market
- Already dominated by entrenched players with network effects

Questions:

- "How big is this market and how fast is it growing?"
- "What forces are driving growth?"
- "Who are the incumbents and what advantages do they have?"

M2: Model

Is the business model viable and scalable?

- Unit economics: Do they make money on each customer?
- LTV (lifetime value) should be 3x+ CAC (customer acquisition cost)
- Margins: Are gross margins 60%+ (software) or appropriate for the sector?
- Scalability: Can revenue grow without proportional cost growth?

Red flags:

- Unclear revenue model ("we'll monetize later")
- Negative unit economics with no path to profitability
- Capital-intensive model requiring endless fundraising

Questions:

- "What does a single customer cost to acquire and what revenue do they generate?"
- "At what scale does the business become profitable?"
- "What are the margin structures and how do they compare to successful competitors?"

M3: Momentum

Is the company gaining traction?

- Revenue growth: 100%+ YoY for early-stage, 50%+ for later-stage

- User/customer growth: Consistent acceleration or steady growth?
- Product development: Shipping features, iterating based on feedback?
- Team expansion: Hiring quality talent?

Red flags:

- Flat or declining metrics
- Constantly pivoting without clear learning
- Unable to retain customers (high churn)
- "Launching soon" for years

Questions:

- "What's your MoM or QoQ growth rate?"
- "What percentage of customers renew/remain active?"
- "What's changed in the last 6 months?"

M4: Management

Is the team capable of executing?

- Domain expertise: Have they worked in this industry?
- Technical chops: Can they build the product?
- Sales ability: Can they acquire customers?
- Prior success: Track record of building, scaling, or exiting companies?
- Coachability: Do they listen and adapt?
- Chemistry: Do they work well together? How long have they been working together?

Red flags:

- First-time founders with no domain expertise
- Solo founder (ideally 2-3 co-founders)
- Arrogant or defensive about feedback
- Misaligned co-founders (equity disputes, role confusion)

Questions:

- "Why are you uniquely positioned to solve this problem?"
- "What's been your biggest challenge and how did you overcome it?"
- "Tell me about a time you were wrong and had to pivot."

Investment decision:

- 4/4 M's strong = invest (appropriate amount)
- 3/4 M's strong = maybe (small position or pass)
- 2/4 or fewer = pass

Understanding IRR and Multiple (Return Metrics)

When evaluating returns, you'll see two primary metrics:

IRR (Internal Rate of Return)

What it is: The annualized rate of return accounting for timing of cash flows

Example:

- Invest $100K in 2020
- Receive $250K in 2027 (7 years later)
- IRR = ~14.9%

Why it matters: Time matters. Getting 2.5x in 5 years (20% IRR) is much better than 2.5x in 10 years (10% IRR).

Limitation: Can be manipulated by timing. Early distributions artificially inflate IRR.

Multiple (MOIC - Multiple on Invested Capital)

What it is: Total return divided by invested capital, regardless of time

Example:

- Invest $100K
- Receive $250K total
- Multiple = 2.5x

Why it matters: Simple, clear total return. Harder to manipulate than IRR.

Limitation: Ignore time. 2.5x in 5 years vs. 10 years look the same.

Use both together:

- Fund A: 2.0x, 25% IRR (fast returns, great)

- Fund B: 2.5x, 12% IRR (higher multiple but slow, mediocre)
- Fund C: 3.0x, 15% IRR (high multiple, reasonable time, excellent)

Good vs. Great Returns

Private Equity:

- Median: 1.5x, 12% IRR
- Good: 2.0x, 15% IRR
- Great: 3.0x+, 20%+ IRR

Venture Capital:

- Median: 1.2x, 8% IRR (yes, median VC barely beats index funds)
- Good: 2.0x, 15% IRR
- Great: 4.0x+, 25%+ IRR

Direct angel investments:

- Portfolio target: 3-5x blended (knowing 50%+ will go to zero)
- Individual winners: 10-50x

Risk Management in Private Markets

Private markets are illiquid and risky. Manage carefully:

Rule 1: Size Appropriately

Maximum allocation to private markets:

- Conservative: 15-20% of total portfolio
- Moderate: 25-35% of total portfolio
- Aggressive: 40-50% of total portfolio

Never go above 50%—you need liquidity.

Rule 2: Diversify Extensively

Within private markets, diversify across:

- Stages (seed, growth, late)

- Strategies (PE, VC, credit)
- Managers (5+ different funds)
- Vintages (2-4 year deployment window)
- Sectors (tech, healthcare, consumer, industrial)

Example $250K allocation:

- $75K: PE buyout fund
- $50K: Growth equity fund
- $50K: Early-stage VC fund
- $50K: Late-stage VC/secondary
- $25K: Direct angel investments (5 companies @ $5K each)

Rule 3: Maintain Liquidity Cushion

Capital call risk: If you commit $100K to a fund, you must have $100K+ in liquid assets to meet capital calls over 3-5 years.

Don't commit more than:

- Your liquid net worth minus 2 years of expenses
- What you can fund from income over the commitment period

Example:

- Liquid assets: $400K
- Annual expenses: $80K
- Available for commitments: $400K - $160K (2yr buffer) = $240K
- You could commit $240K across multiple funds over 2-3 years

Rule 4: Underwrite to Zero

Mental model: Assume every private investment could go to zero.

Question: "If this investment went to $0, would it derail my financial plan?"

If yes → position too large → size down or pass.

Apply this to direct investments especially: Angel investments in startups should be sized such that losing 100% is painful but not devastating.

Tax Considerations

Private investments have unique tax implications:

K-1 Tax Forms

What they are: Partnership tax forms detailing your share of income, gains, losses

The hassle:

- Arrive late (often mid-March or later, requiring extensions)
- Complex (may need CPA assistance)
- State filings (you may have tax obligations in states where properties/businesses operate)

Plan accordingly:

- Budget for CPA costs ($500-$2,000 additional for complex K-1s)
- File tax extensions
- Track basis carefully

Qualified Small Business Stock (QSBS)

What it is: IRS provision allowing $10M+ of gains from qualifying startup investments to be tax-free

Requirements:

- C-corporation (most startups)
- <$50M assets at time of investment
- Hold 5+ years
- Active business (not real estate, finance, etc.)

Value: If you angel invests $50K in a startup that becomes worth $10M+ in 5+ years, the entire gain could be tax-free federally.

This is a massive incentive for early-stage startup investing.

Carried Interest Treatment

What it is: Fund managers' carry (profit share) is taxed as long-term capital gains (20%) rather than ordinary income (37%+)

Relevance to you: As an LP, your returns are also primarily capital gains treatment, reducing tax burden vs. ordinary income

Loss Harvesting

Failed investments: Losses can offset other capital gains

Strategy: If a startup goes to zero, you can write off the loss against other investment gains, reducing taxes

Limitation: $3,000/year ordinary income offset (but unlimited capital gains offset)

Case Study: The Accidental VC

Investor: Priya, 36, Software Engineer, $180K income

Background: Working in tech, she had friends starting companies. In 2015, she started angel investing—$5K per company, mostly friends and former colleagues.

The Portfolio (2015-2019):

- 12 companies, $5K each = $60K invested
- Typical terms: $5K for 0.1-0.5% equity (depending on valuation)

Outcomes after 7-8 years:

Total failures (6 companies): $30K → $0

- Most startups fail. She expected this.

Struggling (2 companies): $10K → $10K (flat, still operating but unlikely exits)

- Zombie companies—neither dead nor thriving

Small wins (3 companies): $15K → $45K (3x)

- Acquired for modest amounts or growing steadily with small secondary sales

The moonshot (1 company): $5K → $285K (57x)

- B2B SaaS company, invested at $8M valuation pre-revenue

- Now valued at $450M, she owns 0.063% (after dilution from multiple rounds)
- She sold half her shares in secondary ($142.5K), holding rest for potential IPO/acquisition

Total outcome:

- Invested: $60K
- Current value: $340K ($142.5K cash + ~$197.5K remaining positions)
- Multiple: 5.7x
- IRR: ~28%

Lessons from Priya:

- Expect losses: 50% failure rate was expected and accepted
- Diversification: 12 investments allowed one huge winner to overcome losses
- Network advantage: Investing in people she knew and trusted improved hit rate
- Patience: 7-8 years from investment to meaningful returns
- Liquidity management: Selling half in secondary provided cash while maintaining upside

Priya now allocates $15K-20K annually to angel investments (3-4 companies), maintains a day job for income, and uses her growing angel portfolio for future financial freedom.

Private Markets in Your Portfolio

Appropriate allocations by stage:

Stability Stage ($0-$100K portfolio):

- 0-5% private markets (focus on building foundation)
- If any: Interval funds with low minimums

Growth Stage ($100K-$500K portfolio):

- 10-20% private markets
- Mix: Fund-of-funds, interval funds, potentially one direct fund commitment

Freedom Stage ($500K-$2M portfolio):

- 20-35% private markets
- Mix: 2-3 PE/VC funds, secondary investments, selective angel deals
- Blended allocation: 40% PE, 40% VC, 20% direct

Legacy Stage ($2M+ portfolio):

- 25-40% private markets
- Sophisticated portfolio: direct funds, co-investments, angel portfolio, secondary positions
- May have 5-10 active fund commitments

The progression: Start with funds (diversification, professional management) → Add secondaries (shorter duration) → Add direct investments (as knowledge and network develop)

The Future of Private Market Access

Democratization is accelerating. Emerging trends:

- Tokenization: Blockchain-based fractional ownership of private assets
- Rolling funds: Subscribe quarterly instead of 10-year lockups
- Secondary markets: More liquidity options for private positions
- Lower minimums: Competition driving minimums down from $250K to $10K-$25K
- Simplified structures: Interval funds and tender offer funds with periodic liquidity

Within 5-10 years: Private market access will look more like mutual fund access—lower minimums, more liquidity options, easier onboarding

For now: The illiquidity premium and minimum investments remain. But the doors are open wider than ever.

The question isn't whether you can access private markets. It's whether you should—and how much.

Key Takeaways:

- Private markets (PE, VC) have historically outperformed public markets: 14-15% for PE, 18-25% for top VC
- Illiquidity premium: You're compensated for locking up capital 7-12 years

- Access expanding: Funds, secondaries, direct investments, interval funds available to individuals
- Fund structure: Understand commitments, capital calls, management fees (2%), carry (20%), hurdles (8%)
- The 4 M's for startups: Market, Model, Momentum, Management
- Manager selection is critical: Track record (DPI, TVPI, IRR), experience, alignment
- Diversify extensively: Multiple managers, vintages, stages, strategies
- Size appropriately: 15-50% of portfolio max, maintain liquidity cushion for capital calls
- Tax benefits: QSBS can make startup gains tax-free, capital gains treatment reduces tax burden
- Expect losses: 40-60% of startups fail; diversification and occasional moonshots drive returns

CHAPTER 11:

THE STARTUP INVESTOR'S PLAYBOOK

David invested $10,000 in a friend's startup in 2012. The company made project management software for construction companies—nothing sexy, nothing that would ever make TechCrunch headlines.

By 2019, that $10,000 was worth $340,000. The company never went public. Never got acquired by Google. It just grew steadily, profitably, and bought out early investors at 34x.

Meanwhile, David's college roommate invested $25,000 in a hot AI startup that raised at a $100M valuation. It was featured in Wired. The founders were on podcasts. Five years later, it shut down. $25,000 → $0.

This chapter is about how to be David, not his roommate.

The Asymmetric Bet Philosophy

Startup investing is about asymmetry: limited downside, unlimited upside.

The math:

- Maximum loss: 100% (your investment goes to zero)
- Maximum gain: Theoretically infinite (but practically 10-100x)

This creates a powerful portfolio dynamic:

Invest $5,000 each in 10 startups ($50,000 total):

- 6 fail completely: -$30,000
- 2 return 1-2x: +$5,000
- 1 returns 10x: +$45,000
- 1 returns 50x: +$245,000

Portfolio result: $50,000 → $265,000 (5.3x return)

Even with a 60% failure rate, one massive winner transforms the portfolio.

This only works if:

- You size positions to afford total losses
- You diversify across enough startups (minimum 8-10)
- You have patience (7-10+ years)
- You have access to quality deal flow

Why Startups Fail (And How to Avoid Them)

Understanding failure modes helps you screen better.

CB Insights studied 110 startup failures. Top reasons:

1. No Market Need (42%)

Built something nobody wanted. Classic founder delusion: "If we build it, they will come."

How to avoid: Talk to potential customers. Ask: "How are they solving this problem today? How painful is it? Would they pay for a solution?"

Red flag: The founder can't name 10 potential customers who desperately need this product.

2. Ran Out of Cash (29%)

Burned through the runway before achieving sustainability. Often due to overbuilding, over-hiring, or slow sales cycles.

How to avoid: Examine burn rate and runway. Ask: "How many months of runway at current burn? What's the plan to reach profitability or the next fundraise?"

Red flag: <6 months runway with no clear path to revenue or fundraising.

3. Wrong Team (23%)

Incompetent execution, founder conflict, inability to adapt.

How to avoid: Assess team dynamics. Have they worked together before? Do they have complementary skills? Are they coachable?

Red flag: Solo founder, or co-founders who just met, or team with no domain expertise.

4. Got Outcompeted (19%)

Better-funded, faster-moving, or more established competitors crushed them.

How to avoid: Understand competitive landscape. Ask: "Who else is solving this? What's your unfair advantage?"

Red flag: "We have no competitors" (usually means no market) or "We'll execute better" (not a strategy).

5. Pricing/Cost Issues (18%)

Unit economics don't work. Can't acquire customers profitably.

How to avoid: Examine CAC (customer acquisition cost) and LTV (lifetime value). Ratio should be 3:1 or better.

Red flag: CAC > LTV or unclear path to profitable unit economics.

Other notable failures:

- Poor product (17%)
- Business model problems (17%)
- Bad marketing (14%)
- Ignored customers (14%)

The pattern: Most failures are avoidable through better diligence.

The Deal Flow Problem

The #1 challenge in angel investing: access to quality deals.

The harsh reality: Best deals don't need to advertise. They're oversubscribed through founder networks, tier-1 VC referrals, and insider channels.

If you see it on a crowdfunding platform, it's likely:

- Already been passed on by institutional investors
- Overpriced for the risk
- Founder-friendly terms that disadvantage small investors

This doesn't mean all public deals are bad—but the odds are worse.

How to Access Better Deal Flow

Strategy 1: Join Angel Networks

- Angel groups (Tech Coast Angels, Golden Seeds, Harvard Angels)
- Typically $2,500-10,000 annual membership
- Curated deal flow, group diligence, educational programs
- Better terms through syndicated investments

Strategy 2: Leverage Your Network

- Alumni networks (university-specific angel groups)
- Industry connections (invest in sectors where you have expertise)
- Former colleagues who became founders
- Referrals from trusted investors

Strategy 3: Build Reputation

- Write about your domain expertise
- Advise startups (even informally)
- Speak at events, host meetups
- Be genuinely helpful without expectation
- Founders will seek you out

Strategy 4: Invest Through Syndicates

- AngelList syndicates (follow experienced lead investors)
- Lead does diligence, negotiates terms, manages investment
- You piggyback at $1K-$10K minimums
- Learn from leads while accessing their deal flow

Strategy 5: Use Platforms Intelligently

- Republic, Wefunder, SeedInvest have occasional gems
- Look for: Strong founder credentials, existing revenue, clear product-market fit

- Avoid: First-time founders, pre-revenue, unclear business model

The compounding effect: Good investments lead to more deal flow. Founders talk to other founders. Success breeds access.

The Investment Process

Stage 1: Initial Screening (5 minutes)

Before spending hours on diligence, quick-screen using these filters:

Pass immediately if:

- [ ] Team has zero relevant experience
- [ ] Market is tiny or shrinking
- [ ] Business model unclear or non-existent
- [ ] Already raised $10M+ at high valuation (limited upside)
- [ ] Terms are predatory (discussed below)

Advance to deeper diligence if:

- [ ] Team has domain expertise
- [ ] Market is large and growing
- [ ] Clear revenue model
- [ ] Reasonable valuation
- [ ] Fair terms

This eliminates 70-80% of opportunities immediately.

Stage 2: Deep Diligence (2-4 hours)

For opportunities that pass screening:

A. Team Assessment (40% weight)

Founder backgrounds:

- Prior startup experience (success or instructive failure)?
- Domain expertise (worked in this industry)?
- Technical capability (can they build the product)?
- Sales ability (can they close customers)?

Team dynamics:

- Known each other for how long?
- Complementary skills?
- Clear role delineation?
- How do they handle disagreement?

Reference checks:

- Talk to past employers, co-workers, investors
- Ask: "Would you work with them again? Why/why not?"

Interview questions:

- "Tell me about a time you were completely wrong and had to pivot."
- "What's the hardest problem you've faced building this?"
- "If I gave you $10M tomorrow, what would you do with it?"
- "What keeps you up at night?"

B. Market Analysis (25% weight)

Market sizing:

- TAM (Total Addressable Market): Total market size
- SAM (Serviceable Addressable Market): Portion you can reach
- SOM (Serviceable Obtainable Market): Realistic capture

Example:

- TAM: $50B (all project management software)
- SAM: $8B (construction-specific PM software)
- SOM: $400M (realistic 5% market share in 10 years)

If SOM < $100M, it's probably too small for venture returns.

Market trends:

- Growing 15%+ annually?
- Tailwinds (regulation, technology shifts, demographic changes)?
- Headwinds (potential disruption, commoditization)?

C. Product & Traction (25% weight)

Product status:

- Working product or still building?
- Customer testimonials?
- NPS (Net Promoter Score) if available

Traction metrics:

- Revenue: Growing 10%+ monthly?
- Users: Active and engaged?
- Retention: >90% monthly (consumer) or >95% annually (B2B)?
- Unit economics: Positive contribution margin?

The traction hierarchy (best to worst):

- Revenue growing consistently
- Users growing + clear monetization path
- Product built + early user validation
- Product in development + Letters of Intent from potential customers
- Idea only (highest risk)

Invest in #1-2. Be cautious with #3. Avoid #4-5 unless you have unique insight.

D. Business Model Validation (10% weight)

Revenue model:

- How do they make money?
- Is it recurring (subscription) or transactional?
- Proven at scale elsewhere?

Unit economics:

- CAC (Customer Acquisition Cost): What does it cost to acquire a customer?
- LTV (Lifetime Value): What revenue does a customer generate?
- LTV:CAC ratio should be 3:1 or better
- Payback period should be <12 months

Example:

- CAC: $1,000 (marketing + sales)
- Monthly subscription: $200
- Average customer lifespan: 24 months
- LTV: $200 × 24 = $4,800

- LTV:CAC = 4.8:1 ✓ (good)
- Payback: 5 months ✓ (excellent)

If they don't know these metrics, that's a red flag.

Stage 3: Terms Review (Critical)

Not all startup investments are created equal. Terms matter enormously.

Key terms to understand:

Valuation (Pre-money vs. Post-money):

- Pre-money: Company value before your investment
- Post-money: Company value after your investment
- Your ownership: Your Investment ÷ Post-money Valuation

Example:

- Pre-money valuation: $8M
- You invest: $100K
- Post-money: $8.1M
- Your ownership: $100K ÷ $8.1M = 1.23%

Dilution protection:

- Future fundraises will dilute your ownership
- Pro-rata rights: Ability to maintain percentage by investing more
- Without pro-rata, you might go from 1% to 0.3% after Series A

Liquidation preference:

- Who gets paid first if company sells
- 1x non-participating (standard): You get your money back first, then share in remaining proceeds
- 1x participating: You get money back AND share in proceeds (better for investors)
- 2x or higher: Red flag (too investor-favorable, misaligns incentives)

Valuation caps (for SAFEs/Convertibles):

- SAFE: Simple Agreement for Future Equity

- Converts to equity at next priced round
- Valuation cap: Maximum valuation at which your SAFE converts

Example:

- You invest $50K via SAFE with $8M cap
- Company raises Series A at $20M valuation
- Your SAFE converts as if company valued at $8M (not $20M)
- You own 2.5x more equity than if you invested at Series A pricing

Good vs. Bad terms:

Good (investor-friendly but fair):

- Reasonable valuation (not 10x revenue pre-revenue)
- 1x liquidation preference
- Pro-rata rights
- Information rights (quarterly updates)
- Standard vesting for founders (4 years, 1-year cliff)

Bad (avoid):

- Sky-high valuation ($50M pre-revenue)
- No pro-rata rights (you'll be diluted to nothing)
- Participating preference >1x
- No information rights (you'll never know how investment is doing)
- Founders fully vested (if they leave, they keep all equity—misaligned)

Stage 4: The Investment Decision

After diligence, use a scorecard:

Scoring (1-10 scale):

- Team: ___/10
- Market: ___/10
- Product/Traction: ___/10
- Business Model: ___/10
- Terms: ___/10
- Total: ___/50

Decision framework:

- 40-50 points: Strong yes (invest full allocation)
- 30-39 points: Qualified yes (invest 50% of allocation)
- 20-29 points: Pass
- <20 points: Hard pass

Also ask:

- "Would I be excited to tell friends about this investment?"
- "Do I understand this well enough to explain it simply?"
- "Am I investing because of FOMO or genuine conviction?"

Portfolio Construction

Position Sizing

Conservative approach:

- $2,500-$5,000 per investment
- 15-20 investments = $37,500-$100,000 total
- Broad diversification, lower risk of ruin

Moderate approach:

- $5,000-$10,000 per investment
- 10-15 investments = $50,000-$150,000 total
- Balance between diversification and meaningful positions

Aggressive approach:

- $10,000-$25,000 per investment
- 8-12 investments = $80,000-$300,000 total
- Concentrated, higher potential but higher risk

Never invest:

- More than 5% of net worth in a single startup
- More than 25% of net worth in all startups combined
- Money you'll need in the next 10 years

Diversification Strategy

Across stages:

- 40% Seed/Pre-Seed (highest risk, highest return potential)
- 40% Series A-B (proven traction, moderate risk)
- 20% Later-stage (Series C+, lower risk, lower returns)

Across sectors:

- Don't put everything in one industry
- Diversify across 3-4 sectors
- Consider: SaaS, fintech, healthcare, consumer, deep tech

Across vintages:

- Don't deploy all capital in one year
- Spread across 2-3 years
- Market timing protection

The Follow-On Strategy

The dilemma: Your best investments will raise future rounds. You'll have the opportunity (pro-rata rights) to invest more and maintain ownership percentage.

The strategy:

- Reserve 50-100% of initial investment for follow-ons
- Only follow into companies showing strong traction
- Don't follow-on just because you can (good money after bad)

Example:

- $100K angel portfolio budget
- Initial: $50K across 10 companies ($5K each)
- Reserve: $50K for follow-ons
- After 18 months, 3 companies doing very well
- Follow-on: $15K-$20K into each of the 3 winners

This concentrates capital into winners while letting losers die naturally.

Managing Your Angel Portfolio

Expectations

Timeline reality:

- Years 1-3: No liquidity, mostly bad news
- Years 4-7: Some companies start showing exits
- Years 7-10+: Meaningful liquidity events

Outcome distribution (typical):

- 40-60% complete failures ($0 return)
- 20-30% zombies (break-even or small losses)
- 10-20% small wins (2-5x)
- 5-10% meaningful wins (10-30x)
- 1-5% home runs (50x+)

Don't expect:

- Quick flips (this isn't house flipping)
- All winners (most will fail)
- Regular updates (many founders go dark)

Do expect:

- Long holding periods (7-10+ years)
- Emotional rollercoaster
- Learning opportunity (you'll become better at evaluating businesses)

Staying Engaged (Without Being Annoying)

Good investor behavior:

- Respond promptly to founder questions
- Make introductions to potential customers/partners
- Share relevant articles or insights
- Attend annual meetings or calls
- Be supportive during tough times

Bad investor behavior:

- Demanding weekly updates
- Micromanaging decisions
- Constantly asking "what's my investment worth?"
- Complaining to other investors
- Threatening legal action over minor issues

Remember: You're a tiny investor. You have almost no power. Be helpful or be quiet.

Secondaries: Getting Liquidity Early

As companies mature, secondary markets (Forge, EquityZen) may allow you to sell shares before IPO/acquisition.

When to consider selling:

- You need the liquidity
- Valuation seems high relative to fundamentals
- You want to lock in gains and reduce risk
- Company is taking much longer than expected to exit

When to hold:

- Company trajectory is strong
- You believe in 2-5x more upside
- You don't need the liquidity
- Tax benefits of waiting (QSBS requires 5-year hold)

Typical haircut: Secondary buyers want 20-40% discount to last round valuation. Weigh the certainty of some gain vs. uncertainty of potential larger gain.

Tax Strategy for Angels

Qualified Small Business Stock (QSBS)

The benefit: Exclude up to $10M in gains from federal taxes if you hold 5+ years

Requirements:

- C-corporation
- <$50M in assets when you invested
- Original issuance (not secondary purchase)
- Active business (not real estate, financial services, etc.)

- Hold 5+ years

Strategy:

- Prioritize C-corps over LLCs for this benefit
- Track your 5-year holding periods carefully
- This can save $2M+ in taxes on a successful exit

Loss Harvesting

Failed investments:

- Can offset capital gains from other investments
- $3,000/year offset against ordinary income
- Carry forward unused losses indefinitely

Strategy:

- When companies officially shut down, claim the loss
- Use to offset gains from real estate, stocks, or other angels

Entity Structuring

Options:

- Individual (simplest, full QSBS benefit)
- LLC (liability protection, pass-through taxation)
- Self-directed IRA (tax-free growth but no QSBS, complex rules)

Most angels invest as individuals to preserve QSBS eligibility.

Case Study: The $5K That Became $380K

Investor: Jason, early employee at a mid-size tech company

2013: Friend from college starts SaaS company for property management. Pre-revenue, just an MVP.

Jason's diligence:

- Team: Founder had been a property manager for 10 years (domain expertise ✓)
- Market: $20B property management software market, but fragmented (opportunity ✓)
- Product: Simple but functional MVP, 5 beta customers loving it (validation ✓)
- Traction: $15K MRR after 4 months (early momentum ✓)
- Terms: $4M valuation, $500K round, SAFE with pro-rata rights (reasonable ✓)

Investment: $5,000 (1.25% of round, 0.125% of company post-money)

2014-2016: Company grows steadily

- Not flashy, but consistent 15-20% MoM revenue growth
- Bootstrapped mentality, profitable by end of 2015
- Jason receives quarterly updates

2017: Series A offer

- $12M valuation, $3M round
- Jason exercises pro-rata: Invests additional $3,000 to maintain ownership
- Total invested: $8,000

2018-2019: Continued growth

- Revenue hits $10M ARR
- Approached by private equity firms

2020: Acquisition offer

- Acquired by larger property management company for $95M
- Jason's ownership (after dilution): 0.4%
- Jason's payout: $380,000

Return: $8,000 → $380,000 (47.5x return over 7 years)

Why it worked:

- Strong founder with domain expertise
- Real problem being solved for underserved market

- Sustainable business model (not VC-dependent growth-at-all-costs)
- Jason supported with follow-on capital
- Patience through 7-year holding period

Jason's reflection: "It wasn't the sexiest investment. No press coverage. But it was the best investment I've ever made because the fundamentals were rock-solid."

Common Mistakes to Avoid

Mistake 1: Investing in ideas, not traction: Pre-revenue, pre-product companies fail 90%+ of the time. Wait for evidence of product-market fit.

Mistake 2: Following FOMO into hot deals: Everyone wants in = overvalued = limited upside. The best returns come from contrarian bets with strong fundamentals.

Mistake 3: Insufficient diversification: Putting $50K into 2 startups is speculation. Putting $50K into 10 startups is a portfolio.

Mistake 4: Ignoring terms: A great company at bad terms can be a bad investment. Always read and understand the term sheet.

Mistake 5: No follow-on capital: Your best investments will offer you the chance to invest more. If you're fully deployed, you'll miss it.

Mistake 6: Investing outside your expertise: You won't recognize red flags in biotech if you're a marketer. Stay in domains where you have insight.

Mistake 7: Mixing friendship and investment: Investing in friends often ends badly—either the investment fails (strain), or it succeeds and they resent your return. Tread carefully.

The Startup Investor's Mindset

Principle 1: Be a learning investor: Every investment—win or loss—teaches you something. Pay attention. Get better over time.

Principle 2: Support don't interfere: You're a minor investor. Be helpful when asked. Don't be a burden.

Principle 3: Celebrating founders: Building companies is brutally hard. Even failed founders deserve respect for trying.

Principle 4: Accept losses: Most startups fail. If you can't accept 50-60% of your portfolio going to zero, don't angel invest.

Principle 5: Be patient: This is a 7-10+ year asset class. Checking valuations quarterly will drive you crazy.

Principle 6: Stay humble: Even experienced VCs have 70% failure rates. You're not smarter than them. Luck plays a massive role.

The best angel investors aren't the smartest. They're the most disciplined—systematic diligence, appropriate position sizing, broad diversification, and infinite patience.

Key Takeaways:

- Startup investing is about asymmetry: Limited downside (100% loss), unlimited upside (10-100x returns)
- Portfolio approach essential: Expect 40-60% failures, diversify across 10+ investments
- Deal flow is the challenge: Build networks, join syndicates, leverage domain expertise
- Diligence framework: Team (40%), Market (25%), Traction (25%), Business Model (10%)
- Terms matter: Understand valuation, liquidation preferences, pro-rata rights, SAFE structures
- Position sizing: Never more than 5% of net worth per startup, 25% total in all startups
- Tax benefits: QSBS can eliminate federal taxes on $10M+ gains if held 5+ years
- Timeline: 7-10+ years from investment to meaningful liquidity, patience is essential
- Learn from every investment, support founders without interfering, accept that most will fail

CHAPTER 12:

BEYOND STOCKS AND BONDS

"I put $15,000 into a Banksy print in 2008. Sold it in 2019 for $120,000."

"I invested $25,000 in a whiskey cask fund. Annual returns: 12%. Plus I get whiskey."

"My music royalty portfolio generates $800/month. I own tiny pieces of 40 songs."

The modern investment universe extends far beyond stocks, bonds, and real estate. Welcome to the frontier.

The Alternative Asset Explosion

For centuries, alternative investments were the domain of the ultra-wealthy. Today, fractional ownership platforms have democratized access to:

- Fine art and collectibles
- Music and intellectual property royalties
- Farmland and timberland
- Commodities and precious metals
- Litigation finance
- Equipment leasing
- Revenue-based financing
- Cryptocurrency and digital assets
- Domain names and digital real estate

Why alternatives matter:

1. **Uncorrelated returns:** When stocks fall, art may hold value or appreciate

2. **Inflation hedges:** Real assets (commodities, farmland) often rise with inflation
3. Yield diversification: Different income streams beyond dividends

4. **Passion + profit:** Invest in what you know and enjoy

5. **Inefficient markets:** More opportunity for skilled investors

The caution: Many alternatives are illiquid, opaque, and risky. They belong in the 5-15% "experimental" allocation, not your core portfolio.

Asset Class #1: Collectibles and Passion Assets

Fine Art

What it is: Investing in paintings, sculptures, and works by established or emerging artists

Historical returns: 8-10% annually (Artprice Global Index, 2000-2023), but highly variable

Platforms enabling access:

- Masterworks: Fractional ownership of blue-chip art ($10K minimum)
- Rally: Collectibles including art ($5-$50 per share)
- Otis: Cultural assets including art ($10-$100 per share)

How it works (Masterworks example):

1. Masterworks acquires Banksy painting for $2M
2. Files SEC offering to securitize painting into shares
3. Investors buy shares ($10K-$50K typical investment)
4. Masterworks holds 3-10 years, then sells
5. Net proceeds distributed to shareholders

Returns: Target 10-15% annual appreciation, but no income during holding period

Risks:

- Illiquidity (3-10 year holds, limited secondary markets)
- Authentication and provenance issues
- Fashion/taste changes (what's hot today may not be tomorrow)
- Storage and insurance costs
- Platform fees (1-2% annual, 20% of profits)

Best for: Investors with long time horizons, interest in art, seeking non-correlated assets

Due diligence:

- Research the artist (established vs. emerging, auction history, museum placements)
- Understand the platform's track record
- Consider this entertainment as much as investment

Classic Cars

What it is: Collectible automobiles, typically 25+ years old

Historical returns: 10-12% annually for select marques (Hagerty Index), but top 10% of cars drive most returns

Access:

- Direct purchase ($50K-$500K+ for investable classics)
- Rally, Otis (fractional ownership, $50-$500 investments)
- Classic car funds (rare, high minimums)

The winners: Ferrari, Porsche, Mercedes, historically rare/iconic models

The trap: Most classic cars are money pits. Maintenance, storage, insurance can exceed appreciation.

Best for: Car enthusiasts with significant capital and interest in the hobby, not pure investors

Wine and Whiskey

What it is: Investing in fine wine bottles or whiskey casks that appreciate as they age

Historical returns:

- Fine wine: 10-13% annually (Liv-ex Fine Wine Index)
- Whiskey casks: 8-12% annually

Platforms:

- Vinovest: Automated wine portfolio ($1,000 minimum)
- CultWines: Wine investment ($5,000 minimum)
- Whisky Invest Direct: Own whiskey casks (£1,000 minimum)

How it works:

- Platform purchases bottles/casks on your behalf
- Stores in bonded warehouse (temperature-controlled, insured)
- As wine/whiskey ages and becomes scarce, value increases
- Sell through platform or take physical delivery

Returns: Combination of appreciation and scarcity premium

Risks:

- Market taste changes
- Counterfeiting (especially wine)
- Storage costs
- Platform fees (2-3% annual management)

Best for: Enthusiasts who enjoy the asset class and want non-correlated returns

Trading Cards and Memorabilia

What it is: Sports cards, comic books, video game memorabilia, sneakers

The boom: Pandemic drove explosive prices (Michael Jordan rookie card: $1M+)

The bust: 2022-2023 saw 40-60% corrections in many categories

Platforms:

- Alt: Diversified collectibles fund ($5K minimum)
- Rally, Otis: Fractional ownership of cards, memorabilia
- Direct purchase: eBay, Heritage Auctions, specialty dealers

The reality: Extremely speculative. Most collectibles lose value. A few exceptional items appreciate dramatically.

Best for: Collectors first, investors second. If you love it regardless of value, consider it.

Asset Class #2: Intellectual Property Royalties

Music Royalties

What it is: Owning rights to songs, earning royalties every time they're played, streamed, or licensed

How songs generate income:

- Streaming (Spotify, Apple Music)
- Radio airplay
- TV/film licensing
- Cover versions
- Public performance (venues, businesses)

Platforms:

- Royalty Exchange: Auction marketplace for royalty rights ($1K-$100K+)
- SongVest: Fractional ownership of song catalogs ($500-$5K)
- ANote Music: European platform (€100+ investments)

How it works:

- Songwriter/artist sells future royalties for upfront cash
- You purchase those rights
- Receive quarterly/annual royalty payments for duration of rights

Returns: 8-14% annual yield typical, varies by catalog quality

Example:

- Purchase 10% of a song catalog for $10,000
- Catalog generates $20,000 annually in royalties
- Your share: $2,000/year (20% yield)
- If catalog value grows to $150,000, your stake worth $15,000

The magic: Established songs have predictable income streams. Streaming era increased royalty flows.

Risks:

- Streaming rates could be cut (Spotify reducing payouts)

- Song popularity fades over time
- Copyright term limits (songs eventually become public domain)
- Platform viability

Best for: Income-focused investors seeking uncorrelated cash flow

Patent and Technology Royalties

What it is: Licensing intellectual property—patents, software, technology—to companies that use it

Returns: 10-20%+ if successful patents, but binary outcomes (worthless or valuable)

Access: Mostly through specialized funds or direct deals (high minimums, sophisticated)

Best for: Sophisticated investors with technical expertise to evaluate patents

Asset Class #3: Real Assets

Farmland

What it is: Owning agricultural land that produces crops and generates rental income

Historical returns: 11-12% annually (NCREIF Farmland Index, 2000-2023)

Return drivers:

- Land appreciation (2-5% annually)
- Crop income (5-7% annual yield)
- Inflation protection (food prices rise with inflation)

Platforms:

- FarmTogether: Institutional farmland investments ($15K minimum)
- AcreTrader: Fractional farmland ownership ($10K minimum)
- Farmland LP: Fund structure ($100K minimum)

How it works:

- Platform acquires farmland (row crops, permanent crops like almonds/wine grapes)

- Leases to farmers or operates farms
- Distributes income to investors
- Holds 5-10+ years, sells appreciated land

Risks:

- Weather/climate (droughts, floods)
- Commodity price fluctuations
- Long hold periods (5-10+ years)
- Illiquidity

Best for: Long-term investors seeking inflation protection and portfolio diversification

Timberland

What it is: Owning forests that produce timber

Historical returns: 9-11% annually (NCREIF Timberland Index)

Return drivers:

- Biological growth (trees get bigger automatically, 2-4% annual)
- Timber price appreciation (1-3% annually)
- Land appreciation (1-2% annually)

Access:

- Timber REITs (Weyerhaeuser, Rayonier - publicly traded)
- Institutional timber funds ($250K+ minimums)

Best for: Very long-term investors (20+ years), inflation hedge, biological growth independent of economic cycles

Commodities and Precious Metals

What it is: Physical assets like gold, silver, oil, agricultural products

Purpose: Inflation hedge, portfolio diversification, crisis hedge

Access:

- Physical metals (gold/silver coins, bars)

- ETFs (GLD for gold, SLV for silver)
- Commodity futures (sophisticated, high risk)
- Mining stocks (equity exposure to commodities)

Historical returns: Highly variable, gold ~7% annually (2000-2023), but volatile

Role in portfolio: 5-10% allocation for inflation protection and crisis insurance

Best for: Conservative allocation (5-10%) as portfolio insurance against inflation and market crashes

Asset Class #4: Structured Alternatives

Private Credit (Beyond Traditional Loans)

What it is: Lending strategies beyond conventional mortgages and corporate bonds

Types:

Asset-Based Lending:

- Loans secured by inventory, equipment, accounts receivable
- Returns: 10-14% annually
- Risk: Moderate (asset collateral provides protection)

Consumer Credit:

- Personal loans, consumer debt portfolios
- Returns: 8-12% annually
- Risk: Moderate-high (default risk, economic sensitivity)

Litigation Finance:

- Funding lawsuits in exchange for portion of settlement/award
- Returns: 15-30% if successful
- Risk: High (cases can be lost, long duration 3-7 years)

Platforms:

- Yieldstreet (diverse private credit, $5K-$10K minimums)
- CrowdStreet (real estate debt, $25K minimums)
- LendingClub, Prosper (consumer credit, $1K minimums)

Best for: Income-focused investors seeking higher yields than bonds with moderate risk

Revenue-Based Financing (RBF)

What it is: Providing capital to businesses in exchange for percentage of future revenue

Structure:

- Invest $100K in a business
- Receive 5% of monthly revenue until you've received $150K back (1.5x return)
- No equity ownership, just revenue share

Returns: 12-20% IRR typical

Advantages over equity:

- Faster returns (3-5 years vs. 7-10 years)
- No dilution in future rounds
- More predictable than equity

Risks:

- Revenue decline = reduced/delayed payments
- Business failure = loss
- No upside beyond agreed multiple

Access:

- Lighter Capital (direct RBF provider)
- Clearbanc (now Clearco - RBF for e-commerce)
- Some crowdfunding platforms offer RBF deals

Best for: Investors wanting business exposure without long illiquidity of equity

Equipment Leasing

What it is: Purchasing equipment (construction, medical, transportation) and leasing to businesses

Returns: 8-12% annually

How it works:

- Fund purchases equipment
- Leases to businesses at monthly rate
- After lease term, sells equipment (residual value)
- Returns = lease income + residual

Platforms:

- Specialized interval funds
- Private placement funds (high minimums $100K+)

Risks:

- Equipment obsolescence (technology depreciates fast)
- Lessee default
- Residual value risk (equipment worth less than projected)

Best for: Diversification within alternatives, investors seeking contractual income

Asset Class #5: Digital and Emerging

Cryptocurrency and Digital Assets

What it is: Bitcoin, Ethereum, and other blockchain-based assets

The debate:

- Bulls say: New asset class, store of value, inflation hedge, revolutionary technology
- Bears say: Speculative bubble, no intrinsic value, regulatory risk, environmental concerns

Historical returns: Extremely volatile

- Bitcoin: +100,000% (2010-2021), -70% (2021-2022), +150% (2023-2024)
- Most altcoins: Go to zero

Access:

- Direct purchase (Coinbase, Kraken, Gemini)
- Bitcoin ETFs (IBIT, FBTC - spot Bitcoin ETFs approved 2024)
- Crypto funds (accredited investor only, many)

Role in portfolio (if any): 1-5% speculative allocation

The architect's view:

- Treat as a speculative bet, not core holding
- Only invest what you can afford to lose completely
- Bitcoin more established than altcoins
- Understand technology before investing
- Beware of hype cycles and FOMO

Best for: Risk-tolerant investors comfortable with 50-90% drawdowns, long time horizons (5-10+ years)

Domain Names and Digital Real Estate

What it is: Owning valuable domain names (URLs) and virtual property in metaverses/games

Domain names:

- Premium domains (Hotels.com sold for $11M) can be highly valuable
- Most domains are worthless
- Returns: Highly speculative, binary outcomes

Virtual real estate:

- Metaverse land (Decentraland, The Sandbox)
- In-game assets (NFTs, virtual property)
- Extremely speculative, dependent on platform adoption

Best for: Tech-savvy speculators only, tiny allocation (<1% portfolio)

NFTs (Non-Fungible Tokens)

What it is: Unique digital assets representing ownership of art, collectibles, media

The 2021 boom: Digital art NFTs selling for millions (Beeple's "Everydays" for $69M)

The 2022-2023 bust: Market collapsed 90%+, most NFTs worthless

Current state: Niche use cases (digital collectibles, gaming assets, ticketing) surviving

Investment thesis: Too early, too speculative, mostly worthless

Best for: Nobody, unless you're a digital art collector accepting total loss

The Modern 100™ Allocation Framework

How should alternatives fit into your portfolio? Here's a framework for a $1M portfolio across asset classes:

Foundation (35%):

- 25% Index Funds (S&P 500, Total Market)
- 5% Bonds (Investment-grade, treasuries)
- 5% Cash (Emergency fund, opportunities)

Real Estate (25%):

- 20% Private Real Estate Syndications
- 5% REITs (liquid real estate exposure)

Private Markets (20%):

- 10% Private Equity Funds
- 7% Venture Capital Funds
- 3% Direct Angel Investments

Alternatives - Income (12%):

- 5% Private Credit Funds
- 4% Music/IP Royalties
- 3% Farmland

Alternatives - Growth (5%):

- 2% Collectibles (Art, wine, etc.)
- 2% Commodities/Precious Metals
- 1% Cryptocurrency

Alternatives - Experimental (3%):

- Emerging opportunities, speculative bets, learning investments

This allocation provides:

- True diversification across 10+ return drivers
- Income generation: 6-8% portfolio yield
- Growth potential: 10-14% blended annual return
- Inflation protection: Real assets, commodities
- Risk management: Uncorrelated assets
- Optionality: Cash + alternatives create flexibility

Evaluating Alternative Investments

Before committing to any alternative:

The Comprehension Test

- [ ] Can I explain this investment to a 10-year-old?
- [ ] Do I understand how returns are generated?
- [ ] Do I know what could go wrong?

If no, don't invest.

The Liquidity Test

- [ ] Can I afford to lock up this capital for X years?
- [ ] Do I have adequate liquid reserves (6-12 months expenses)?
- [ ] Am I over-allocated to illiquid investments (>50% of portfolio)?

If liquidity is a concern, pass.

The Fee Test

- [ ] What are total fees (management, performance, transaction)?
- [ ] Are fees competitive with similar investments?
- [ ] Do fees leave adequate returns after costs?

If fees exceed 3% total annually, scrutinize carefully.

The Platform Test

- ☐ Is the platform established (3+ years operating)?
- ☐ Do they have a track record I can verify?
- ☐ Are they regulated (SEC registration, audited financials)?
- ☐ What happens if platform shuts down?

If platform is sketchy, pass regardless of opportunity.

The Diversification Test

- ☐ Does this diversify my portfolio or concentrate risk?
- ☐ Am I over-allocated to this asset class or strategy?
- ☐ What percentage of net worth is this single investment?

If this creates concentration risk, size down or pass.

Common Alternative Investment Mistakes

Mistake 1: Chasing Returns Without Understanding Risk: Seeing "15% annual returns" on farmland and investing without understanding weather risk, commodity volatility, or long hold periods.

Fix: Risk-adjusted thinking. A 10% return with low correlation and moderate risk may beat a 15% return with high risk and correlation to your other holdings.

Mistake 2: Over-Allocating to Illiquid Assets: Locking up 70% of portfolio in 7-10 year investments, then needing cash and being forced to sell liquid holdings at a loss.

Fix: Never exceed 50% of the portfolio in illiquid alternatives. Maintain 20-30% in highly liquid holdings.

Mistake 3: Paying Excessive Fees: Investing in a wine fund with 3% annual management fees + 20% performance fees that leave you with 6% net returns (barely beating index funds).

Fix: Calculate net returns after all fees. Compared to alternatives. Walk away if fees are unreasonable.

Mistake 4: Confusing Passion with Investment: Buying expensive watches, cars, or art at retail prices, calling it "investing," while they depreciate 30-50%.

Fix: If you love it, buy it for enjoyment. Don't justify purchases as investments unless you're buying at wholesale and can prove historical appreciation.

Mistake 5: Platform Risk: Investing $50K in a new crowdfunding platform that shuts down 18 months later, leaving your investment in limbo.

Fix: Stick with established platforms (3+ years, thousands of investors, regulatory compliance). Diversify across platforms—don't concentrate with one.

Mistake 6: Ignoring Tax Complexity: Investing in 15 different alternative investments, each generating K-1 tax forms from multiple states, creating a tax nightmare.

Fix: Consider tax complexity when diversifying. Limit K-1-generating investments to manageable numbers (5-8 max). Budget for CPA costs.

Mistake 7: FOMO-Driven Decisions: Hearing about NFTs or crypto gains and jumping in at the peak without understanding the asset or your thesis.

Fix: Never invest based on FOMO. If you don't understand it deeply, pass—regardless of how much others are making.

Tax Treatment of Alternatives

Ordinary income (taxed at highest rates):

- Music royalties
- Rental income from some structures
- Interest from private credit
- Revenue share agreements

Capital gains (lower rates):

- Sale of collectibles (28% max rate—higher than stocks)
- Sale of real estate (20% + potential depreciation recapture)
- Sale of businesses/startups (20%, or 0% with QSBS)

Tax-advantaged structures:

- Holding alternatives in self-directed IRA (tax-deferred/free, but complex)
- 1031 exchanges for real estate
- Opportunity Zones for long-term holds

The tax impact can significantly affect returns. Always calculate after-tax returns.

Building Your Alternatives Portfolio

Phase 1: Foundation First (Net Worth $0-$100K) Focus: Build emergency fund, max tax-advantaged accounts, simple index funds Alternatives: 0-5% (only if you're learning; use low-minimum platforms)

Phase 2: Cautious Exploration ($100K-$500K) Focus: Core-Satellite 2.0, mostly traditional alternatives (real estate, private credit) Alternatives: 10-20% of portfolio Allocation: 70% real estate/private credit, 20% PE/VC funds, 10% experimental

Phase 3: Sophisticated Diversification ($500K-$2M) Focus: True alternative diversification across multiple asset classes Alternatives: 25-35% of portfolio Allocation: 40% real estate, 30% private markets, 20% income alternatives (royalties, credit), 10% experimental

Phase 4: Advanced Architecture ($2M+) Focus: Family office approach, direct deals, broader alternative access Alternatives: 30-50% of portfolio

Allocation: 30% real estate, 25% private markets, 20% income alternatives, 15% real assets (farmland, commodities), 10% speculative/emerging

The progression: Start conservative and proven (real estate, private credit), expand to sophisticated alternatives (IP royalties, farmland), finally add speculative bets (crypto, collectibles) in small doses.

The Reality Check

Most alternatives won't beat index funds on a risk-adjusted basis.

The S&P 500 has delivered 10% annually for 100 years. It's liquid, transparent, low-cost, tax-efficient, and requires zero specialized knowledge.

Why bother with alternatives?

1. **Diversification:** Uncorrelated assets reduce portfolio volatility

2. **Income generation:** Many alternatives provide cash flow, not just appreciation

3. **Inflation protection:** Real assets often outperform during inflation

4. **Access to skill:** Great managers in private markets can generate alpha

5. **Personal interest:** Investing in what you understand and enjoy creates engagement

But recognize: You're making your life more complex. You're sacrificing liquidity. You're paying higher fees. You're taking on additional risk.

Do it intentionally, not reactively.

Case Study: The Alternative Allocation That Worked

Investor: Chen, 44, $750K portfolio, software executive

2018 Starting Allocation:

- 60% Index funds
- 30% Real estate (syndications)
- 10% Cash

2019: First Alternative Additions

- Added 5% ($37.5K) to private credit fund
- Added 3% ($22.5K) to music royalties (SongVest)
- Income generation increased: Portfolio now yielding 4.5%

2020-2021: Expanding Alternatives

- Added 5% to farmland (FarmTogether)
- Added 3% to VC fund (AngelList)
- 2% in commodities (gold/silver ETFs)
- Portfolio: 45% index funds, 25% real estate, 10% private credit/royalties, 8% farmland/VC, 2% commodities, 10% cash

2022: The Test

- Stocks fell 18%
- Bonds fell 13%
- His portfolio fell only 6%
  - Index funds: -18%
  - Real estate: -3% (slower repricing)
  - Private credit: +8% (rising rates increased yields)
  - Music royalties: +7% (uncorrelated)
  - Farmland: +5% (inflation hedge)
  - VC: -15% (marked down)
  - Commodities: +12% (inflation surge)

2023-2024: Recovery and Growth

- Portfolio recovered faster than pure equity portfolios
- Income generation: $48,000 annually (6.4% yield)
- Total portfolio value: $980K (growth + contributions)

2025 Current:

- Portfolio: $1.1M
- Income: $58,000/year
- Freedom Index: 73% (expenses $80K/year)

Chen's reflection: "Alternatives made 2022 tolerable. While friends panicked about their 401(k)s down 20-25%, I was down 6% and still receiving $48K in distributions. The diversification worked exactly as designed."

Keys to success:

- Started simple (real estate), expanded gradually
- Never exceeded 50% in illiquid alternatives
- Diversified across 6-7 different alternative types
- Focused on income-generating alternatives
- Stayed disciplined during 2021 euphoria (didn't chase NFTs/crypto hype)

The Alternative Asset Decision Framework

Before allocating to any alternative:

Question 1: Why does this exist? What inefficiency or advantage does this create? If it's just "new and exciting," be skeptical.

Question 2: What's my edge? Do I understand this better than average? Do I have specialized knowledge? If no edge, index funds likely beat it.

Question 3: What problem does this solve in my portfolio? Does it provide diversification, income, inflation protection, or growth? If it doesn't clearly solve a problem, skip it.

Question 4: What's the worst case? Can I afford total loss? Does it create liquidity issues? If worst case is unacceptable, don't do it.

Question 5: How does this compare to doing nothing? Would my portfolio be meaningfully worse without this? If the marginal benefit is small, complexity isn't worth it.

If you can't answer these five questions confidently, pass.

The Alternatives Allocation Summary

Tier 1 (Core Alternatives - Proven, Lower Risk):

- Real estate syndications
- Private credit funds
- Index-based commodity exposure

Tier 2 (Expanded Alternatives - Moderate Risk, Established):

- Private equity funds
- Venture capital funds
- Farmland
- Music/IP royalties

Tier 3 (Speculative Alternatives - High Risk, Emerging):

- Direct angel investments
- Fine art and collectibles
- Cryptocurrency (1-5% max)
- Revenue-based financing

Tier 4 (Experimental - Very High Risk):

- NFTs
- Virtual real estate
- Emerging technologies
- Domain speculation

Recommended allocation:

- 60-80% Tier 1 (including traditional assets)
- 15-25% Tier 2
- 5-10% Tier 3
- 0-5% Tier 4

Never invert this pyramid. Your core should be stable and proven. Your edges should be experimental and small.

The goal isn't to own everything. It's to own what makes sense for your blueprint, enhances your returns, and helps you sleep at night.

Key Takeaways:

- Alternative assets extend beyond stocks/bonds: collectibles, royalties, farmland, commodities, digital assets
- Purpose: Diversification, uncorrelated returns, inflation protection, income generation
- Most alternatives are illiquid, opaque, and risky—belong in 5-15% experimental allocation
- Collectibles (art, wine, cars) provide passion + potential profit but high fees and illiquidity
- IP royalties (music, patents) offer uncorrelated income streams (8-14% yields)
- Real assets (farmland, timberland, commodities) provide inflation protection
- Private credit and structured alternatives offer higher yields (10-14%) than bonds
- Cryptocurrency remains highly speculative; if included, limit to 1-5% of portfolio
- Evaluation framework: Comprehension, liquidity, fees, platform quality, diversification
- Progressive approach: Start with proven alternatives (real estate, private credit), expand cautiously
- Most alternatives won't beat index funds; allocate intentionally for specific portfolio benefits

SECTION IV

THE DESIGN

Constructing a Freedom Portfolio

CHAPTER 13:

THE CASH FLOW ENGINE

Two investors, both age 50, both with $1.5 million portfolios, both planning to stop working.

Investor A (Traditional):

- 100% in index funds
- Portfolio value fluctuates with markets
- Plans to sell 4% annually ($60K) to fund life
- Terrified of sequence-of-returns risk (what if markets crash right when he retires?)
- Net worth: $1.5M → may decline over time through withdrawals

Investor B (Architect):

- 30% index funds, 40% income-producing real estate/credit, 20% PE/VC, 10% cash
- Portfolio generates $85K annually in distributions
- Never needs to sell appreciated assets
- Market volatility is irrelevant—income continues regardless
- Net worth: $1.5M → likely to grow over time even while "retired"

Who sleeps better? Who has more freedom? Who has built an actual wealth *system*?

This chapter is about building cash flow engines that fund your life indefinitely.

The Traditional Withdrawal Strategy (And Why It's Broken)

The 4% Rule: Conventional wisdom says you can safely withdraw 4% of your portfolio annually in retirement without running out of money.

The logic:

- $1M portfolio × 4% = $40K/year
- Historical analysis (1926-1995) showed 4% withdrawals survived all 30-year periods
- Adjust for inflation annually

Why it fails in practice:

Problem 1: Sequence-of-Returns Risk: If markets crash early in retirement, you're selling low to fund life, permanently impairing portfolio.

Example:

- Year 1: $1M portfolio, withdraw $40K, market drops 30% → $660K
- Year 2: Withdraw $41K (inflation-adjusted), market drops 15% → $520K
- Year 3: Even if markets recover, you've sold so much during the crash you never recover

Problem 2: Low Bond Yields: The 4% rule assumes bonds yielding 5-7%. Today's bonds yield 3-5%, reducing portfolio income.

Problem 3: Longer Lifespans: Rule designed for 30-year retirements (age 65-95). Many people now need 35-40 years or are retiring early (age 50).

Problem 4: Psychological Burden: Watching your portfolio decline every year as you withdraw creates anxiety, even if math says it's sustainable.

Problem 5: Market Dependency: Your lifestyle is entirely dependent on market performance. Bad decade = reduced spending or running out.

The Architect's Solution: Build an income engine that never requires selling appreciated assets.

The Cash Flow Engine Principles

Principle 1: Income ≠ Appreciation

Traditional thinking: Wealth = buying assets that appreciate, selling them when needed

Architect thinking: Wealth = owning assets that pay you indefinitely while also appreciating

The difference:

Appreciation-only portfolio:

- $1M in growth stocks
- No dividends
- Must sell shares to generate income
- Selling = permanent reduction in portfolio size

Cash-flowing portfolio:

- $1M in diversified income assets
- Generates $70K annually
- Never sell principal
- Portfolio continues compounding

30 years later:

Appreciation portfolio (4% withdrawal):

- If markets average 8% and you withdraw 4%, you have ~$1.3M
- But you're still withdrawing annually, still market-dependent

Cash flow portfolio (no withdrawals):

- $70K annual income continues (likely growing with inflation)
- Principal could be $2.5M+ (compounded at 8% without withdrawals)
- Or you've been reinvesting income, accelerating growth

The cash flow engine lets you live on investment income while principal compounds.

Principle 2: Diversify Income Sources

Don't depend on one income stream. Build multiple.

Target: 5-10 different income sources

Example income streams:

1. Dividends from index funds
2. Distributions from real estate syndication A
3. Distributions from real estate syndication B
4. Distributions from real estate syndication C
5. Private credit fund payments

6. Music royalty payments
7. Preferred equity distributions
8. Part-time consulting (active, but optional)
9. Rental income from a property
10. Distributions from PE fund

Why multiple streams matter:

- If one stops (property sells, fund matures), others continue
- Different cycles (real estate, private equity, public markets)
- Risk mitigation (no single point of failure)

The goal: No single income source represents >20% of total income.

Principle 3: Contractual > Discretionary

Contractual income: Obligatory payments based on agreements

- Bond interest
- Private credit payments
- Preferred equity returns
- Lease payments

Discretionary income: Optional payments based on performance

- Common stock dividends (can be cut)
- Real estate distributions (can pause during renovations)
- Bonus income from work

Priority hierarchy:

1. Contractual income (most reliable)
2. Preferred distributions (moderate reliability)
3. Common equity distributions (least reliable but higher potential)

Target allocation of income sources:

- 40-50% Contractual
- 30-40% Preferred/hybrid
- 20-30% Discretionary

This creates stable baseline income with upside potential.

Principle 4: Yield + Growth

Yield: Current income as percentage of investment Growth: Appreciation of principal over time

The mistake: Chasing yield without growth

- 12% yielding asset that loses 8% value annually = bad investment
- Net return: 4%, but you're being eaten alive

The goal: Assets that provide both meaningful yield AND principal growth

Examples:

Good yield + growth:

- Real estate syndication: 7% annual distributions + 15% IRR = great
- Growth stocks with 2% dividends + 10% annual growth = great
- Private credit: 10% annual yield + potential upside from equity kickers = great

Bad yield without growth:

- High-yield bond (junk bonds) at 12% but high default risk = risky
- Business in decline paying unsustainable dividend = value trap
- REIT with 10% yield but property values falling = losing money in real terms

Minimum thresholds:

- Yield: 4-5% minimum (below this, hard to fund life)
- Total return: 8-10% minimum (yield + growth)

Principle 5: Reinvestment Optionality

The power of choice: In wealth accumulation phase: Reinvest all income for maximum compounding In transition phase: Reinvest 50-75%, use 25-50% for life In freedom phase: Use 100% of income, let principal compound separately

Your income engine should provide options, not obligations.

Example:

- Income generated: $75K/year
- Expenses: $60K/year
- Options:
  - Reinvest $15K surplus for acceleration
  - Increase lifestyle ($15K travel budget)
  - Save for next opportunity
  - Gift to family/charity
  - Hybrid approach

The freedom to choose what to do with surplus income is wealth.

Building Your Cash Flow Engine

Step 1: Calculate Your Income Target

Formula: Annual Expenses ÷ 0.85 = Income Target

Why 0.85? Taxes. If you need $60K after taxes and your effective tax rate is 15%, you need $70,588 in income.

Example:

- Annual expenses: $75,000
- Estimated tax rate: 20%
- Income target: $75,000 ÷ 0.80 = $93,750

Your target might be higher if:

- You want lifestyle margin (15-25% surplus)
- You plan to travel extensively
- You have dependents or family obligations

Conservative approach: Target 125% of minimum expenses for comfort and flexibility.

Step 2: Audit Current Income

What passive income do you currently generate?

Worksheet:

- Dividends from stocks/funds: $______

- Interest from bonds/savings: $______
- Real estate distributions: $______
- Private fund distributions: $______
- Royalties/IP income: $______
- Business/partnership income: $______
- Other passive sources: $______
- Total current passive income: $______

Your Freedom Index = Current Passive Income ÷ Annual Expenses × 100

Example:

- Current passive income: $32,000
- Annual expenses: $70,000
- Freedom Index: 45.7%

You're 45.7% financially free. You need to build income streams to cover the other 54.3%.

Step 3: Design Your Income Mix

Based on your target income and risk tolerance, design your income allocation.

Conservative Income Engine (Lower risk, 5-7% target yield):

- 30% Dividend-growth stocks/funds (2-3% yield)
- 30% Private credit/senior debt (8-10% yield)
- 25% Core real estate (6-8% yield)
- 10% Preferred equity (8-10% yield)
- 5% Cash/bonds (3-5% yield)
- Blended yield: ~6%

Moderate Income Engine (Balanced, 6-8% target yield):

- 20% Dividend stocks/funds (2-3% yield)
- 25% Private credit (9-11% yield)
- 30% Real estate mix (6-9% yield)
- 15% Preferred/mezzanine (9-12% yield)
- 5% Royalties/alternatives (8-12% yield)
- 5% Cash (3-5% yield)
- Blended yield: ~7.5%

Aggressive Income Engine (Higher risk, 8-10% target yield):

- 15% Dividend stocks (2-3% yield)
- 20% Private credit (10-12% yield)
- 35% Real estate (heavy value-add) (7-10% yield)
- 20% Mezzanine/preferred (10-14% yield)
- 10% Alternatives (royalties, revenue share) (10-15% yield)
- Blended yield: ~9%

Your choice depends on:

- Risk tolerance
- Time horizon
- Current age and income needs
- Portfolio size

Step 4: Calculate Required Capital

Formula: Income Target ÷ Target Yield = Required Capital

Example:

- Income target: $80,000/year
- Target blended yield: 7%
- Required capital: $80,000 ÷ 0.07 = $1,142,857

This is your Freedom Number—the capital required in income-producing assets to generate your target income.

Current capital in income assets: $______ Required capital: $______ Gap: $______

Years to close gap = Gap ÷ (Annual Savings + Expected Compounding)

Step 5: Build Systematically

Don't rush to reposition everything overnight.

Year 1-2 Plan:

- Deploy new capital into income-focused investments
- As existing positions mature, reallocate toward income
- Target: Increase income by 20-30%

Year 3-5 Plan:

- Continue systematic deployment
- Rebalance annually
- Target: Reach 60-75% of income goal

Year 5-7 Plan:

- Fine-tune allocations
- Optimize tax efficiency
- Target: Reach 90-100%+ of income goal

Example transition (starting with $500K, target $1.2M):

Year 1:

- Current: $500K (mostly growth-focused)
- Add: $75K new capital + reposition $100K
- New income allocation: $175K generating $11,000/year

Year 3:

- Portfolio: $650K (growth + contributions)
- Income allocation: $350K generating $25,000/year

Year 5:

- Portfolio: $850K
- Income allocation: $550K generating $40,000/year

Year 7:

- Portfolio: $1.1M
- Income allocation: $800K generating $58,000/year
- Goal nearly achieved

The key: Systematic, patient, disciplined deployment over years, not panic repositioning overnight.

The Freedom Flow Matrix™

Visualize your cash flow engine:

INCOME SOURCES		INCOME POOL		ALLOCATION
Dividends: $8K				
RE Dist: $22K				Expenses: $70K
Credit: $12K	→	$85K/year	→	Reinvest: $15K
Royalties: $5K				Taxes: $12K (estimate)
PE Dist: $8K				Discretionary: $3K
Consulting: $30K (optional)				
TOTAL: $85K				**After-tax: ~$73K**

The matrix shows:

- **Income sources:** Where money comes from
- **Income pool:** Total annual cash flow
- **Allocation:** Where money goes

Health indicators:

✓ Multiple income sources (not dependent on one)
✓ Income exceeds expenses (positive cash flow)
✓ Surplus for reinvestment or lifestyle
✓ Tax-efficient structure

Warning signs:

✗ Single income source (concentration risk)
✗ Income < expenses (unsustainable)
✗ No surplus (fragile, no margin for error)
✗ High tax burden (inefficient structure)

Tax Optimization for Cash Flow

Income types are taxed differently. Optimize your cash flow tax treatment:

Ordinary income (highest tax rates, up to 37% federal):

- Interest from bonds

- Most royalty income
- Short-term capital gains
- Active business income

Qualified dividends (15-20% federal):

- Dividends from US corporations held >60 days

Long-term capital gains (15-20% federal):

- Assets sold after holding >1 year
- Real estate sale proceeds (may get additional benefits)

Tax-advantaged:

- Roth IRA distributions (tax-free)
- Municipal bond interest (federal tax-free)
- Return of capital distributions (tax-deferred)

Strategy:

- Hold high-yield ordinary income assets in IRAs (tax-deferred/free)
- Hold dividend-paying stocks in taxable accounts (lower rates)
- Use tax-loss harvesting to offset gains
- Time capital gains realization strategically

Example optimization:

- Traditional IRA: Private credit (10% ordinary income) → Tax-deferred
- Roth IRA: Growth stocks → Tax-free gains
- Taxable account: Dividend aristocrats, real estate → Qualified dividends, depreciation benefits

Tax savings can add 1-3% to your effective return.

Case Study: The $72K Cash Flow Engine

Investor: Maria, 42, Teacher, $580K portfolio

Goal: Generate $72K annual passive income by age 55 (13 years)

Starting point (age 42):

- Portfolio: $580K
- Current passive income: $18,500/year (3.2% yield)
- Allocation: 70% index funds, 20% real estate, 10% cash

Year 1-3: Foundation building

- Repositioned $150K from index funds into income assets:
    - $75K into 3 real estate syndications (7-8% cash-on-cash)
    - $50K into private credit fund (9% yield)
    - $25K into dividend growth stocks
- Added $45K/year from salary savings
- New allocation: 45% index funds, 35% income real estate, 10% private credit, 5% dividends, 5% cash
- Year 3 passive income: $32,000/year (4.8% blended yield)

Year 4-7: Acceleration

- Continued $45K annual contributions
- Reinvested all distributions
- One real estate investment exited (2.1x return), redeployed into 2 new income properties
- Added music royalty investment ($15K)
- Portfolio growth to $920K
- Income allocation now 65% of portfolio
- Year 7 passive income: $54,000/year (5.9% yield)

Year 8-13: Final push to goal

- Salary increased, savings rose to $55K/year
- Distributions + new capital deployed systematically
- Private credit and real estate positions maturing and redeploying
- Portfolio reached $1.35M by year 13
- Income allocation: $1.1M (81% of portfolio)
- Year 13 passive income: $76,000/year (6.9% yield)

Maria at age 55:

- Passive income: $76,000/year
- Living expenses: $72,000/year
- Freedom Index: 105%

- She retired from full-time teaching, now substitute teaches 2 days/week for enjoyment

Income sources breakdown:

- Real estate syndications (7 properties): $38,000
- Private credit funds: $18,500
- Dividend stocks: $8,500
- Music royalties: $4,200
- Preferred equity positions: $6,800
- Total: $76,000

Keys to success:

- Systematic deployment over 13 years
- Reinvested all distributions until goal achieved
- Increased savings rate as income grew
- Diversified across income sources
- Patient, disciplined execution

Income Stability vs. Income Growth

The tradeoff:

- High-yield assets (8-12%): May not grow principal much, or may even decline
- Lower-yield assets (2-5%): Often provide better principal appreciation

The solution: Blend both

Stability allocation (60% of income engine):

- Private credit, senior debt, core real estate
- High current yield (7-10%)
- Modest principal growth (2-4% annually)
- Purpose: Reliable income today

Growth allocation (40% of income engine):

- Dividend growth stocks, value-add real estate, preferred equity
- Moderate current yield (3-6%)

- Strong principal growth (6-12% annually)
- Purpose: Income growth over time, inflation protection

Example $1M income engine:

Stability ($600K):

- $250K private credit @ 9% yield = $22,500/year
- $250K core real estate @ 7% yield = $17,500/year
- $100K preferred equity @ 10% yield = $10,000/year
- Total: $50,000/year from $600K

Growth ($400K):

- $200K dividend growth stocks @ 3% yield = $6,000/year
- $200K value-add real estate @ 5% yield = $10,000/year
- Total: $16,000/year from $400K

Combined: $66,000/year (6.6% current yield)

But 5 years later:

- Stability principal: $660K (grew 2%/year) → $51,000 income
- Growth principal: $540K (grew 6%/year) → $25,000 income
- Total: $76,000/year (6.7% yield on original $1M, but portfolio now $1.2M)

The blend provides current income AND growing income over time.

The Reinvestment Decision

Once your engine generates surplus income beyond expenses, you face a choice:

Option 1: Increase lifestyle

- Travel more
- Upgrade housing
- Pursue expensive hobbies
- Financial margin for life enjoyment

Option 2: Reinvest for acceleration

- Compound surplus back into portfolio
- Reach higher Freedom Index (150-200%)
- Build wealth for legacy
- Create even greater optionality

Option 3: Give it away

- Support family
- Charitable giving
- Impact investing
- Align wealth with values

Most architects choose a blend:

- 50% lifestyle enhancement
- 30% reinvestment
- 20% giving

Example with $15K annual surplus:

- $7,500 → annual travel fund (enriches life)
- $4,500 → reinvest into next investment opportunity
- $3,000 → causes you care about

There's no right answer—only your answer, aligned with your values and goals.

Sequence of Returns and the Income Advantage

The biggest risk in traditional retirement: Sequence of returns

Scenario A: Bad early returns, good late returns

- Year 1-5: Portfolio returns -3%, 5%, -8%, 12%, 6% (volatile, flat overall)
- Withdraw 4% annually ($40K from $1M)
- After 5 years: $890K (despite positive overall market—withdrawals during down years devastated portfolio)

Scenario B: Good early returns, bad late returns

- Year 1-5: Portfolio returns 12%, 8%, 15%, -5%, -2%
- Withdraw 4% annually ($40K from $1M)
- After 5 years: $1.18M (strong early returns protected against later dips)

Same average returns, different sequences, massively different outcomes.

The income portfolio eliminates this risk:

- Receive distributions regardless of market performance
- Never forced to sell during downturns
- Principal continues compounding even during withdrawals
- Sequence of returns becomes irrelevant

This is the single biggest advantage of the cash flow engine approach.

Building Ladders for Liquidity

While income engines reduce the need to sell, you still want liquidity access.

The ladder strategy: Stagger maturities

Example $500K income allocation:

- Year 1 maturity: $50K (short-term bond, private credit fund)
- Year 2 maturity: $50K (another position)
- Year 3 maturity: $100K (real estate syndication projected exit)
- Year 4 maturity: $75K (preferred equity)
- Year 5+ maturity: $225K (longer-term positions)

This creates:

- Regular capital return for redeployment or needs
- Optionality to increase liquidity if needed
- Continuous opportunity to reallocate based on market conditions

Never have >30% maturing in the same year (concentration risk).

The Psychology of Income

Why cash flow engines succeed psychologically:

1. Tangible progress You see deposits hitting your account monthly/quarterly. Progress is visible and reinforcing.

2. Market detachment When your lifestyle is funded by distributions, market volatility becomes background noise, not existential threat.

3. Permanent vs. temporary Selling assets feels like losing something. Receiving distributions feels like gaining something, even though mathematically they can be similar.

4. Compounding without sacrifice Your principal continues growing while you live well. Win-win rather than zero-sum.

5. Abundance mindset Surplus income creates psychological safety and generosity. Scarcity creates anxiety and hoarding.

The emotional benefits of a cash flow engine often exceed the financial benefits.

Your Cash Flow Engine Blueprint

Action Steps:

Step 1: Define your income target

- Annual expenses: $______
- Desired surplus (15-25%): $______
- Tax adjustment: $______
- Total income target: $______

Step 2: Audit current income

- Current passive income: $______
- Current Freedom Index: ______%
- Income gap to close: $______

Step 3: Choose your yield target

- Conservative (5-6%): Lower risk, longer timeline

- Moderate (6-8%): Balanced approach
- Aggressive (8-10%): Higher risk, faster timeline
- Your target yield: ______%

Step 4: Calculate required capital

- Income target ÷ yield target = $______
- Current income-producing capital: $______
- Capital gap: $______

Step 5: Create deployment plan

- Annual savings available: $______
- Expected investment returns: ______%
- Estimated years to goal: ______

Step 6: Build your income mix

- % in contractual income (credit, debt): ____%
- % in preferred/hybrid: ____%
- % in common equity distributions: ____%
- % in dividends: ____%

Step 7: Execute systematically

- Quarter 1: Deploy $______ into ____________
- Quarter 2: Deploy $______ into ____________
- Quarter 3: Deploy $______ into ____________
- Quarter 4: Deploy $______ into ____________

Review quarterly. Adjust as needed. Stay disciplined.

The Ultimate Goal: Infinite Runway

Traditional retirement planning asks: "How long will my money last?"

Cash flow engineering asks: "How long until my income exceeds my expenses forever?"

One question creates anxiety. The other creates freedom.

When your cash flow engine generates more income than you need, compounding indefinitely while you live comfortably, you've achieved what Silicon Valley calls "infinite runway."

Your wealth isn't depleting. It's compounding. Your income isn't shrinking. It's growing. Your options aren't narrowing. They're expanding.

This is financial architecture at its finest.

Key Takeaways:

- Traditional 4% withdrawal strategy is fragile and psychologically burdensome
- Cash flow engines generate income without selling appreciated assets
- Target 5-10 diverse income sources for stability and risk mitigation
- Blend contractual (40-50%), preferred (30-40%), and discretionary (20-30%) income
- Calculate Freedom Number: Income Target ÷ Target Yield = Required Capital
- Build systematically over years through disciplined deployment
- Optimize for both current yield and income growth over time
- Sequence-of-returns risk eliminated when living on distributions
- Freedom Index of 100%+ provides true financial autonomy
- Cash flow engines provide psychological benefits beyond financial returns

CHAPTER 14:

COMPOUNDING THROUGH SYSTEMS

"Compound interest is the eighth wonder of the world. He who understands it, earns it; he who doesn't, pays it." —Attributed to Einstein (probably apocryphal, but true regardless)

Warren Buffett's net worth at age 50: $376 million Warren Buffett's net worth at age 90: $118 billion

He earned 99.7% of his wealth after age 50. Not because he became a better investor, but because he let compounding work for decades.

This chapter is about building systems that compound automatically—without constant intervention, without brilliance, without luck.

The Compounding Misconception

Most people think compounding is simple: Money × Time × Return Rate = Wealth

$10,000 × 10% annual return × 30 years = $174,494

That's compounding. But it's not *systematic* compounding.

Systematic compounding includes:

- Capital compounding (your initial investment growing)
- Income compounding (reinvesting distributions)
- Contribution compounding (adding new capital regularly)
- Tax-efficiency compounding (minimizing friction)
- Knowledge compounding (improving returns through learning)
- Network compounding (accessing better opportunities over time)

When all six work together, magic happens.

The Four Stages of Compounding

Stage 1: The Grind (Years 1-5)

Characteristics:

- Portfolio small ($0-$150K typically)
- Returns feel insignificant (10% of $50K = $5K—barely noticeable)
- Progress seems slow
- Temptation to chase higher returns
- Most people quit here

The psychology: "This isn't working. I need to get rich faster."

The reality: You're building the foundation. Compounding is happening, just invisibly.

Example:

- Start: $20K
- Add $1,000/month ($12K/year)
- 8% annual return
- Year 1: $33,920 (feels like grinding)
- Year 2: $49,154 (still grinding)
- Year 3: $65,766 (starting to see it)
- Year 4: $83,855 (momentum building)
- Year 5: $103,530 (crossed $100K!)

The first five years build the machine. Don't quit.

Stage 2: The Acceleration (Years 5-15)

Characteristics:

- Portfolio mid-size ($150K-$500K)
- Returns become noticeable (10% of $300K = $30K—meaningful)
- Confidence grows
- System is working
- Temptation to get clever

The psychology: "I'm figuring this out. Maybe I should try something riskier."

The reality: Don't sabotage yourself. The system is working. Stay disciplined.

Example (continuing from year 5):

- Year 5: $103,530
- Continue $1,000/month contributions
- 8% annual return
- Year 10: $235,000 (more than doubled)
- Year 15: $410,000 (returns now generating $32K/year—more than your contributions)

Years 5-15 are where compounding accelerates visibly. Trust the process.

Stage 3: The Inflection (Years 15-25)

Characteristics:

- Portfolio large ($500K-$2M+)
- Annual returns exceed your salary
- Financial autonomy approaching or achieved
- System runs itself
- Temptation to stop contributing or get conservative

The psychology: "I've made it. Time to protect it."

The reality: The best compounding is ahead. Don't coast.

Example (continuing from year 15):

- Year 15: $410,000
- Continue $1,000/month (now easier with higher income)
- 8% annual return
- Year 20: $720,000 (annual returns = $57K, more than most salaries)
- Year 25: $1.18M (returns = $94K annually)

The inflection point: When investment returns exceed earned income, you've crossed into a new reality.

Stage 4: The Autonomy (Years 25+)

Characteristics:

- Portfolio massive ($2M-$10M+)
- Returns far exceed lifestyle needs

- Work is optional
- Legacy considerations
- Temptation to overcomplicate

The psychology: "I should do something sophisticated with all this wealth."

The reality: Simplicity got you here. Don't mess it up with complexity.

Example (continuing from year 25):

- Year 25: $1.18M
- Can reduce/eliminate contributions (living on passive income)
- 8% annual return with 0 contributions
- Year 30: $1.73M
- Year 35: $2.54M
- Year 40: $3.73M

At this stage, the system is self-sustaining. Your job is not to break it.

The Automatic Wealth System (Wealth OS™)

Great architects design buildings that function without constant intervention. Lights turn on automatically. Temperature regulates itself. Systems maintain themselves.

Your wealth should work the same way.

Component 1: Automatic Contributions

Manual approach: Decide each month whether to invest, how much, where
Automatic approach: Pre-set transfers that happen without decision

How to automate:

- Direct deposit split: 15-25% of paycheck → investment account
- Auto-transfer: Monthly transfer from checking to investment accounts
- Auto-invest: Funds automatically deployed into preset allocations

Example automation:

- Paycheck: $7,500 bi-weekly
- Auto-transfer: $1,200 to taxable investment account
- Auto-transfer: $750 to Roth IRA

- Auto-invest: Funds deployed into target allocation automatically

Result: $46,800/year invested without thinking about it.

The power: Removes decision fatigue, emotion, and procrastination. You can't spend what you don't see.

Component 2: Automatic Rebalancing

Manual approach: Quarterly review, calculate drift, make trades Automatic approach: System rebalances when thresholds hit

How to set up:

1. Define target allocation (e.g., 30% core, 40% income, 20% growth, 10% asymmetric)
2. Set rebalance triggers (when any allocation drifts >10% from target)
3. Automate: Many platforms offer auto-rebalancing

Example:

- Target: 30% index funds
- Current: 38% (due to stock market rally)
- Trigger hit: Rebalance
- Action: Sell 8%, deploy into underweight positions (real estate, private credit)

The power: Enforces "buy low, sell high" discipline without emotion.

Component 3: Automatic Reinvestment

Manual approach: Receive dividend/distribution, decide what to do with it Automatic approach: All income automatically reinvested

Settings:

- Dividend reinvestment (DRIP): Auto-purchase more shares
- Distribution reinvestment: Syndication/fund distributions auto-deploy
- Cash sweep: Any cash balance above $X auto-invests

Example:

- Receive $2,000 dividend

- Auto-reinvest into same funds
- Compounding accelerates without thinking

Exception: When you've achieved financial autonomy and need income for living, turn off auto-reinvestment.

Component 4: Automatic Tax Optimization

Manual approach: Realize gains/losses randomly, pay unnecessary taxes Automatic approach: System harvests losses, defers gains, optimizes timing

Strategies:

- Tax-loss harvesting: Automatically sell losing positions to offset gains
- Asset location: System places high-tax investments in IRAs, low-tax in taxable
- Gain deferral: Avoid selling appreciated assets until necessary

Many robo-advisors (Wealthfront, Betterment) do this automatically. Worth the fees for large portfolios.

Component 5: Automatic Opportunity Deployment

The challenge: Great opportunities appear randomly. You need dry powder ready to deploy.

The system:

- Maintain 5-10% cash allocation always
- Auto-contribute to "opportunity fund"
- When compelling investment appears, capital is ready
- Deploy immediately without needing to sell other positions

Example:

- Maintain $50K cash (5% of $1M portfolio)
- Auto-contribute $500/month to opportunity fund
- December 2022: Market crash, stocks down 25%
- Deploy $30K immediately into quality stocks at discount
- Replenish opportunity fund over next 12 months

The advantage: Never miss opportunities due to lack of liquidity. Never forced to sell during downturns.

The Reinvestment Decision Framework

Not all distributions should be reinvested. Use this framework:

Question 1: Have I achieved my Freedom Number?

If NO → Reinvest 100% Your goal is reaching financial autonomy. Every dollar reinvested accelerates that goal.

If YES → Consider using income You've achieved the goal. You can start living on income.

Question 2: Is this income taxable or tax-deferred?

If taxable account → Consider partial reinvestment You'll owe taxes on distributions whether you reinvest or not. Using some for lifestyle doesn't create additional tax burden.

If IRA/401k → Reinvest 100% No tax due on reinvestment. Maximize tax-advantaged compounding.

Question 3: Is my lifestyle already sufficient?

If YES → Reinvest surplus If you're living comfortably and income exceeds expenses, keep compounding the surplus for faster progress.

If NO → Use income to enhance lifestyle If you're sacrificing enjoyment or quality of life, use some income to improve it. Wealth should enhance life, not be delayed indefinitely.

Question 4: Do I have better opportunities?

If YES → Deploy there If you have a compelling new investment opportunity, redirect reinvestment there rather than automatically back into the same assets.

If NO → Auto-reinvest If no better opportunities, reinvesting into what's already working compounds efficiently.

The Rebalancing Rhythm

How often should you rebalance?

Too frequent (monthly): Transaction costs, taxes, whipsaw risk Too infrequent (every 5 years): Massive drift, concentration risk

The optimal rhythm: Quarterly review, threshold-based action

Quarterly review (15 minutes):

- Check current allocations vs. targets
- Calculate drift percentages
- Note if any position >10% off target
- Decide: Rebalance now or wait

Threshold-based rebalancing:

- If any position >10% off target → rebalance
- If all positions within 10% → do nothing
- If new capital available → deploy to underweight positions

Example:

- Target: 35% core, 35% income, 20% growth, 10% asymmetric
- Actual: 30% core, 38% income, 22% growth, 10% asymmetric
- Drift: Core -5%, Income +3%, Growth +2%, Asymmetric 0%
- Decision: No rebalancing needed (all within 10% threshold)

Tax-aware rebalancing:

- In taxable accounts: Rebalance with new contributions first (avoid selling winners)
- In IRAs: Rebalance freely (no tax consequences)
- Consider: Taking gains in low-income years, losses in high-income years

The Capital Deployment Algorithm

When you have new capital to deploy (salary savings, distribution, windfall), use this decision tree:

Step 1: Emergency fund sufficient?

- If <6 months expenses → add to emergency fund
- If ≥6 months → proceed to step 2

Step 2: Tax-advantaged space available?

- If not maxed 401k/IRA → max those first
- If maxed → proceed to step 3

Step 3: Any positions severely underweight?

- If any position >15% below target → deploy there
- If all positions within 15% → proceed to step 4

Step 4: Compelling opportunity available?

- If yes and fits portfolio → deploy there
- If no → proceed to step 5

Step 5: Systematic allocation

- Deploy proportionally to target allocation
- Or deploy to highest-conviction underweight position

Example:

- New capital: $15,000
- Emergency fund: ✓ (covered)
- 401k/IRA: ✓ (maxed)
- Position check: Income allocation 28% vs. 35% target (-7% underweight)
- Decision: Deploy $10K to income positions (real estate/credit), $5K to maintain other allocations

This removes emotion and ensures systematic, disciplined deployment.

The Tax Alpha Loop™

Every dollar saved in taxes is a dollar that compounds.

The loop:

- Minimize taxes → More capital retained
- More capital retained → More compounding
- More compounding → Greater wealth
- Greater wealth → More tax planning opportunities

- Return to step 1

Tax efficiency strategies:

Strategy 1: Asset Location Optimization

Highest-tax assets (ordinary income) → IRAs:

- Private credit (10-12% ordinary income)
- REITs (ordinary dividend income)
- High-yield bonds

Lowest-tax assets (qualified dividends, long-term gains) → Taxable:

- Index funds (mostly qualified dividends)
- Real estate syndications (depreciation benefits)
- Long-term growth stocks

Tax-free assets → Roth IRAs:

- Highest growth potential
- Assets you never want to sell

Annual tax savings: 1-2% of portfolio value (on $1M portfolio = $10-20K/year)

Strategy 2: Tax-Loss Harvesting

How it works:

1. Investment declines in value
2. Sell it to realize loss
3. Immediately buy similar (but not identical) asset
4. Use loss to offset gains or $3,000 ordinary income
5. Carry forward unused losses indefinitely

Example:

- Own VTSAX (Vanguard Total Market Index), down $10K
- Sell VTSAX, realize $10K loss
- Immediately buy ITOT (iShares Total Market Index)—similar but not identical
- Use $10K loss to offset $10K gain elsewhere

- Net result: Maintained market exposure, reduced taxes

Annual benefit: $2,000-$5,000+ in tax savings for active harvesters

Strategy 3: Gain Timing

Simple rule: Realize gains in low-income years, defer in high-income years

Example:

- Year 1: $200K income (high bracket)
- Year 2: $80K income (job change/sabbatical)
- Strategy: Realize capital gains in Year 2 when bracket is lower
- Tax savings: Potentially 10-15% of gains

Strategy 4: Qualified Small Business Stock (QSBS)

For startup investors:

- Hold C-corp stock 5+ years
- Exempt up to $10M+ in gains from federal taxes
- Plan accordingly: Don't sell before 5-year mark unless necessary

Strategy 5: Charitable Giving of Appreciated Assets

Instead of:

- Sell stock, pay capital gains tax, donate cash

Do this:

- Donate stock directly to charity
- Charity gets full value
- You get deduction for full value
- No capital gains tax paid

Example:

- Stock worth $10K, cost basis $2K (gain = $8K)
- Donate stock directly
- Charity gets $10K
- You get $10K deduction

- You avoid $1,600 capital gains tax (20% rate)
- Net benefit: $1,600 vs. donating cash

The cumulative effect of all tax strategies: 2-3% annual return boost

On $1M compounding at 10% vs. 12% (after tax optimization) over 30 years:

- 10%: $17.4M
- 12%: $30.0M
- Tax optimization added $12.6M over 30 years

The Knowledge Compounding Advantage

Year 1 investor: Knows index funds exist, invests conservatively, 7% returns

Year 5 investor: Understands alternatives, diversifies, 9% returns

Year 10 investor: Can evaluate syndications, has network, 11% returns

Year 20 investor: Expert, gets access to best deals, 13% returns

Knowledge compounds your returns.

How to accelerate knowledge compounding:

1. Allocate 5-10 hours monthly to learning

- Books (2-3 annually on investing/business)
- Podcasts (weekly, during commute)
- Courses/webinars (quarterly)
- Communities (regular participation)

2. Learn by doing

- Small pilot investments (<$5K) in new asset classes
- Attend investment committee meetings
- Join angel groups or investment clubs
- Interview successful investors

3. Track and review

- Quarterly investment review
- Annual deep dive on performance
- Document lessons learned from wins and losses
- Iterate on strategy

4. Find mentors

- Identify investors 5-10 years ahead of you
- Offer value in exchange for guidance
- Learn from their mistakes

Example: Maria's knowledge compounding:

- Age 30 (Year 1): Only knew 401k, invested blindly, 6% returns
- Age 35 (Year 5): Discovered real estate, made first syndication investment, 8% returns
- Age 40 (Year 10): Sophisticated RE portfolio, added private credit, 10% returns
- Age 45 (Year 15): Deal access through network, direct investments, 12% returns

Same person, improved returns by 6% annually through knowledge. On $500K, that's $30K more per year.

The Network Compounding Effect

"Your network is your net worth."

How networks compound:

Year 1-3: Building

- Join communities (online forums, local meetups)
- Attend events (conferences, webinars)
- Provide value (answer questions, share insights)

Year 4-7: Leveraging

- Network provides deal flow (opportunities shared privately)
- Introductions to operators and fund managers
- Co-investment opportunities with experienced investors

Year 8+: Multiplying

- You become the source of deal flow for others
- Fund managers seek you out
- First access to oversubscribed deals
- Ability to bring others into opportunities (carry/fees)

Example:

- 2018: Maria joins online real estate syndication community
- 2019: Learns from experienced members, makes first investment through community
- 2020: Invited to private deal from sponsor she met through network
- 2021: Sponsor offers her co-GP opportunity (she brings investors, earns promote)
- 2023: She's now source of capital for sponsors, gets first look at all deals
- 2025: Her network provides 80% of her investment opportunities

The best deals never hit the open market. They're shared through networks.

The System Maintenance Schedule

Weekly (5 minutes):

- Review account balances
- Confirm auto-transfers executed
- Note any unusual activity

Monthly (15 minutes):

- Review cash flow (income received, expenses paid)
- Confirm investment contributions executed
- Check for new opportunities

Quarterly (1 hour):

- Full portfolio review (allocations, performance)
- Rebalancing check (any positions >10% off target?)
- Tax-loss harvesting opportunities
- Freedom Index calculation

Annually (4 hours):

- Deep performance review (vs. goals, vs. benchmarks)
- Strategy adjustment (change allocations? New asset classes?)
- Tax planning (year-end moves, next year strategy)
- Goal setting (update blueprint, adjust targets)

The system runs itself 99% of the time. Your job is 1% maintenance, 99% letting it work.

Case Study: The System That Ran Itself

Investor: David, 35, Software Engineer, $185K income

2015 (Starting point):

- Portfolio: $85K (all in 401k, target-date fund)
- System: None (random contributions, no strategy)

2016 (Building the system):

- Automated: 15% paycheck → 401k, $500/month → Roth IRA, $1,000/month → taxable
- Total automated contributions: $41,000/year
- Created target allocation: 60% stocks, 30% real estate, 10% alternatives
- Set up quarterly rebalancing

2017-2020 (System running):

- Contributions automatic, never thought about it
- Rebalanced quarterly (5 minutes each time)
- Portfolio grew from $85K → $310K
- Added real estate syndications as opportunities appeared
- System required <2 hours/year of active management

2021-2023 (System maturing):

- Increased contributions (salary growth): Now $55K/year automated
- Portfolio: $575K
- Passive income from real estate: $22K/year
- Still only 2 hours/year active management

2024-2025 (System thriving):

- Portfolio: $780K
- Passive income: $38K/year
- Freedom Index: 48%
- Projected financial autonomy: Age 48 (13 years from start)

David's reflection: "I set up the system in 2016 and basically forgot about it. It runs itself. I check quarterly, make minor adjustments, and it just... works. Best decision I ever made was automating everything."

Total active time invested: ~30 hours over 10 years (3 hours/year average) Wealth generated: $695K net growth + $100K+ in passive income

That's $23,166 per hour of effort. The system did the work.

Your Compounding System Checklist

- ☐ **Automatic contributions set up** (% of paycheck, monthly transfers)
- ☐ **Target allocation defined** (%, not just vague "diversified")
- ☐ **Rebalancing triggers set** (threshold-based, not emotional)
- ☐ Reinvestment defaulted to automatic (until Freedom Number achieved)
- ☐ **Tax optimization implemented** (asset location, loss harvesting)
- ☐ **Quarterly review scheduled** (calendar reminder, 1 hour)
- ☐ **Annual deep dive planned** (review goals, adjust strategy)
- ☐ **Knowledge plan created** (books, podcasts, courses, communities)
- ☐ **Network building active** (joined communities, attending events)
- ☐ **Opportunity fund maintained** (5-10% cash for deployment)

If you've checked 8+ boxes, you have a functioning system. If fewer than 8, start building.

The wealth you build isn't just from great investment selection. It's from letting compounding work uninterrupted for decades through systematic automation.

Key Takeaways:

- Compounding has four stages: Grind (1-5 years), Acceleration (5-15), Inflection (15-25), Autonomy (25+)
- Systematic compounding includes: capital, income, contributions, tax efficiency, knowledge, and network
- Build Wealth OS: Automate contributions, rebalancing, reinvestment, tax optimization, opportunity deployment
- Quarterly reviews with threshold-based rebalancing (>10% drift) optimize without overtrading

- Tax Alpha Loop: Optimization adds 2-3% annual returns through asset location, loss harvesting, gain timing
- Knowledge compounding can add 2-4% annual returns through improved decision-making
- Network compounding provides access to better deals, co-investment opportunities, and private deal flow
- System maintenance requires <3 hours annually once built; the system does the rest
- Best investors aren't the smartest—they're the most systematic

CHAPTER 15:

TAX-EFFICIENT WEALTH DESIGN

Two investors, same income, same returns, different tax strategies.

Investor A (Tax-unaware):

- $1M portfolio, 10% annual returns
- Pays 35% effective tax rate on gains
- After 30 years: $8.7M

Investor B (Tax-optimized):

- $1M portfolio, 10% annual returns
- Pays 18% effective tax rate through strategic planning
- After 30 years: $12.6M

Same starting point. Same returns. $3.9M difference through tax strategy alone.

This chapter is about keeping more of what you earn.

The Tax Drag Reality

Everything you own gets taxed:

- Wages: 25-37% federal + state
- Interest: 25-37% as ordinary income
- Dividends: 15-20% (qualified) or 25-37% (ordinary)
- Capital gains: 15-20% (long-term) or 25-37% (short-term)
- Real estate: Depreciation recapture, capital gains, but many benefits
- Inheritance: 0-40% estate tax (above exemption)

The average investor loses 2-3% annually to taxes.

On a 10% gross return, taxes reduce it to 7-8% net. Over 30 years, that 2-3% difference compounds to millions.

The architect's job: Minimize tax drag legally and systematically.

The Three Tax Optimization Layers

Layer 1: Tax-Advantaged Accounts (Foundation)

The power of tax deferral/exemption:

Traditional 401(k)/IRA:

- Contributions reduce current taxable income
- Growth is tax-deferred (no taxes until withdrawal)
- Withdrawals taxed as ordinary income

Roth IRA/Roth 401(k):

- Contributions are after-tax (no immediate deduction)
- Growth is tax-free forever
- Withdrawals are tax-free in retirement

HSA (Health Savings Account):

- Triple tax advantage: Deduction on contribution, tax-free growth, tax-free withdrawal for medical
- Can invest HSA funds (don't just keep as cash)
- After age 65, can withdraw for non-medical purposes (taxed as ordinary income, like IRA)

The math:

$10,000 invested in taxable account:

- 10% annual return
- 20% taxes paid annually on gains
- After 30 years: $44,677

$10,000 invested in Roth IRA:

- 10% annual return
- 0% taxes (ever)
- After 30 years: $174,494

Difference: $129,817 from tax-free compounding

Priority order:

1. Employer 401(k) match (free money, always max this first)
2. HSA (if eligible, triple tax advantage)
3. Roth IRA (if income-eligible, $6,500-$7,500 annually)
4. Max 401(k) ($22,500-$30,000 annually depending on age)
5. Backdoor Roth (if over income limits, convert traditional to Roth)
6. Mega Backdoor Roth (if plan allows, up to $66,000 total annual contributions)

Example maxing all tax-advantaged space:

- 401(k): $23,000
- Employer match: $11,500 (50% match on 6% of $200K salary)
- HSA: $4,150 (family coverage)
- Backdoor Roth (if eligible): $7,000
- Total: $45,650/year in tax-advantaged contributions

On $200K income, this saves $12,000-15,000 in current taxes plus decades of tax-free/deferred growth.

Layer 2: Asset Location Strategy (Intermediate)

Not all investments belong in the same account types.

The strategy: Place investments in accounts that maximize after-tax returns

Tax-inefficient assets → Tax-advantaged accounts:

- High-yield bonds (ordinary income, 37% tax)
- REITs (ordinary dividends, 37% tax)
- Actively-managed funds (frequent capital gains distributions)
- Private credit funds (ordinary income)
- Commodities and futures (special tax treatment)

Tax-efficient assets → Taxable accounts:

- Index funds (minimal distributions, mostly qualified dividends)
- Municipal bonds (tax-free interest)
- Real estate syndications (depreciation benefits)
- Long-term growth stocks (control when gains realized)

- Qualified Small Business Stock (potential tax-free gains)

Highest growth potential → Roth IRA:

- Venture capital
- Small-cap growth stocks
- Whatever you believe will have the highest long-term returns
- You'll never pay taxes on gains, so maximize gains here

Example optimization:

Before (suboptimal):

- Taxable account: REIT fund (8% yield, ordinary income)
- Traditional IRA: Total stock market index fund
- Roth IRA: Treasury bonds

After (optimized):

- Taxable account: Total stock market index fund (tax-efficient)
- Traditional IRA: REIT fund (ordinary income sheltered)
- Roth IRA: Small-cap growth/VC (highest growth potential, never taxed)

Annual tax savings: $1,200-2,000 on a $500K portfolio

Layer 3: Strategic Tax Management (Advanced)

Technique 1: Tax-Loss Harvesting

How it works:

1. Investment declines below cost basis
2. Sell to realize loss
3. Buy substantially similar (but not identical) investment immediately
4. Use loss to offset gains or $3,000 ordinary income
5. Carry forward unlimited losses to future years

Example:

- Own Vanguard Total Stock Market Index (VTI), cost $50K, now worth $42K
- Sell VTI, realize $8,000 loss

- Immediately buy Schwab Total Stock Market Index (SWTSX)—similar but not identical
- Use $8,000 loss to offset $8,000 gains from elsewhere
- Save ~$1,600 in taxes (20% capital gains rate)
- Remain fully invested in market

Rules to avoid:

- Wash sale rule: Can't buy "substantially identical" security within 30 days before or after sale
- Definition of "substantially identical": Same specific fund/stock. Different provider = usually OK.

Automated tax-loss harvesting:

- Wealthfront, Betterment, others do this automatically
- Worth 0.5-1% annual benefit through systematic harvesting

Technique 2: Capital Gains Management

The strategy: Control when and how much capital gains you realize

Tactics:

- Harvest losses in high-income years to offset gains
- Realize gains in low-income years (sabbaticals, job transitions, retirement)
- Donate appreciated stock instead of selling (avoid capital gains, get full deduction)
- Hold until death for step-up in basis (heirs inherit at current value, no capital gains)

Example:

- Stock worth $100K, cost basis $20K (gain = $80K)
- Option A: Sell now, pay $16K tax (20%)
- Option B: Hold until low-income year (0% capital gains bracket), pay $0
- Option C: Donate to charity, avoid $16K tax + get $100K deduction (worth $37K in tax savings if 37% bracket)
- Option D: Hold until death, heirs get step-up basis, $0 tax ever

The power of optionality to gain realization.

Technique 3: Qualified Opportunity Zones (QOZ)

What it is: Invest capital gains in designated economically-distressed areas, get tax benefits

Benefits:

- Defer capital gains taxes until 2026 or when QOZ investment sold
- 10% exclusion if held 5+ years
- 15% exclusion if held 7+ years (too late now for existing capital gains)
- Complete exclusion of QOZ investment gains if held 10+ years

Example:

- Sell business for $2M, $1.5M is capital gain ($300K tax due)
- Invest $1.5M gain into QOZ fund
- Hold 10+ years
- Original gain: Deferred until 2026, then pay tax
- QOZ investment appreciation: Tax-free forever

If QOZ investment 2x's to $3M, you pay $0 tax on $1.5M gain

Caution: Must invest in designated zones, which may have higher risk. Don't let the tax tail wag investment dog.

Technique 4: 1031 Exchange (Real Estate)

What it is: Defer capital gains on real estate by rolling proceeds into new property

Rules:

- Must be "like-kind" property (investment to investment)
- Must identify replacement within 45 days
- Must close within 180 days
- Must use qualified intermediary
- Can't touch money in between

Example:

- Sell rental property for $800K, cost basis $300K (gain = $500K)
- Without 1031: Pay $100K+ in taxes (federal + state + depreciation recapture)

- With 1031: Defer all taxes, roll full $800K into new property
- Repeat: Can continue indefinitely, never paying taxes
- Death: Heirs get step-up, avoid all accumulated gains

This is how real estate dynasties are built—infinite deferral.

Technique 5: Roth Conversion Ladder

The strategy: Convert traditional IRA to Roth in low-income years, pay taxes at lower rate

How it works:

- In low-income year (job loss, sabbatical, retirement), convert $X from Traditional IRA to Roth
- Pay taxes on conversion at current bracket (potentially 12-22% instead of 32-37%)
- Wait 5 years (conversion seasoning period)
- Withdraw converted amounts tax-free

Example:

- Age 55, early retirement, income drops from $200K to $50K
- Convert $75K from Traditional IRA to Roth
- Pay ~$10K in taxes (low bracket)
- After 5 years (age 60), can withdraw that $75K tax-free (before age 59.5 normally triggers penalties)
- Saved $15-20K vs. converting in high-income years

Strategic use case: Bridge early retirement before age 59.5 without penalties.

Entity Structure Strategy

How you hold investments affects taxes dramatically.

Individual/Joint Ownership (Simplest)

Pros:

- Simple tax reporting
- Step-up in basis at death
- Access to QSBS benefits

- Qualified dividends at lower rates

Cons:

- No asset protection
- All income taxed at personal rates
- Limited estate planning tools

Best for: Small portfolios (<$500K), W-2 earners, simple situations

LLC (Flow-Through Entity)

Pros:

- Asset protection (liability shield)
- Pass-through taxation (avoid double taxation)
- Can elect S-corp status for payroll tax savings
- Estate planning flexibility

Cons:

- State filing requirements
- Annual costs ($500-2,000)
- More complex tax returns
- K-1s for all members

Best for: Real estate holdings, side businesses, investors with $500K-5M

S-Corporation (Active Business)

Pros:

- Payroll tax savings (pay yourself salary + distributions)
- Can flow passive investment income through
- Asset protection

Cons:

- Requires "reasonable salary" (IRS scrutiny)
- State registration and compliance
- More complex (payroll, corporate formalities)

Best for: Active businesses with $150K+ net income

Trust Structures

Revocable Living Trust:

- Avoids probate
- Maintains control during life
- No tax benefits (same as individual)
- Simple estate transfer

Irrevocable Trust:

- Removes assets from estate (estate tax planning)
- Asset protection
- Potential income tax planning
- Can't change once created

Dynasty Trust:

- Multigenerational wealth transfer
- Avoids estate taxes across generations
- Complex but powerful

Best for: High net worth ($5M+), estate tax concerns, multigenerational planning

Self-Directed IRA/Solo 401(k)

What it is: Retirement account that can invest in alternatives (real estate, private equity, notes)

Pros:

- Tax-deferred or tax-free growth
- Access to alternative investments
- Can use leverage (UDFI rules apply)

Cons:

- Complex rules (prohibited transactions)
- UBIT/UDFI taxes on leveraged investments
- Distributions taxed as ordinary income (even capital gains)

- High setup and maintenance costs

Best for: Sophisticated investors with large retirement accounts wanting alternatives

Real Estate Tax Advantages

Real estate offers unique tax benefits beyond other investments.

Depreciation

The concept: IRS assumes buildings "wear out" over 27.5 years (residential) or 39 years (commercial)

The reality: Most buildings appreciate, but you still get the deduction

Example:

- $1M property: $800K building, $200K land (only building depreciates)
- Annual depreciation: $800K ÷ 27.5 years = $29,091
- This reduces taxable income by $29,091 despite property potentially appreciating

Impact:

- Property generates $40K rental income
- Depreciation: -$29K
- Taxable income: $11K
- You receive $40K but only pay taxes on $11K

Passive income from syndications often shows paper losses due to depreciation, offsetting other passive income.

Cost Segregation

What it is: Engineering study that reclassifies building components into shorter depreciation schedules

Standard depreciation:

- Entire building: 27.5-39 years

Cost segregation:

- Land improvements: 15 years (parking, landscaping)
- Personal property: 5-7 years (appliances, carpets, fixtures)
- Building shell: 27.5-39 years

Impact: Front-loads depreciation massively

Example:

- $5M commercial building
- Standard: $128K annual depreciation
- After cost seg: $300K+ first-year depreciation (60%+ of building reclassified)

Result: Creates large paper losses in early years, potentially eliminating taxes on distributions**

Bonus Depreciation

Current law (subject to change): 100% bonus depreciation on qualified assets (2023), phasing down

Combined with cost segregation: Take 100% of reclassified assets (appliances, fixtures, etc.) as immediate deduction

This can create 40-80% paper losses in year 1 of investment

Real Estate Professional Status (REPS)

For active real estate investors:

- Spend 750+ hours annually in real estate activities
- More than 50% of working time
- Material participation in rentals

Benefit: Passive loss limitations don't apply—can offset W-2 income with real estate losses

This is how some high-income earners (doctors, lawyers, tech executives) reduce taxes to near-zero through real estate

Caution: IRS scrutinizes REPS claims. Document everything.

The Tax-Efficient Withdrawal Strategy

When you've achieved autonomy and start living on portfolio income:

The Tax-Bracket Management Approach

Goal: Fill lower tax brackets efficiently, avoid jumping into high brackets unnecessarily

Federal 2024 brackets (married filing jointly):

- 10%: $0-$23,200
- 12%: $23,200-$94,300
- 22%: $94,300-$201,050
- 24%: $201,050-$383,900
- 32%: $383,900-$487,450
- 35%: $487,450-$731,200
- 37%: $731,200+

Strategy:

- Live on Roth IRA withdrawals + qualified dividends + capital gains (taxed at 0-20%)
- Fill up 10-12% brackets with traditional IRA withdrawals or realized gains
- Avoid pushing into 22%+ brackets unnecessarily
- Use standard deduction ($29,200 for couples) to shelter some income

Example:

- Need $100K for living
- Take $70K from Roth IRA (tax-free)
- Take $30K as long-term capital gains (0% rate if income under ~$94K)
- Total tax: $0-$2,000
- Effective rate: 0-2%

vs. taking $100K from traditional 401(k):

- Total tax: $12,000-15,000
- Effective rate: 12-15%

Choice of withdrawal source can save $10-13K annually

The ACA (Healthcare) Consideration

For early retirees (age <65, pre-Medicare):

Modified Adjusted Gross Income (MAGI) determines ACA subsidies:

- Keep MAGI between 100-400% of federal poverty level for max subsidies
- 2024: $15,060-$60,240 for individual, $20,440-$81,760 for couple

Strategy:

- Live on Roth IRA withdrawals (don't count as MAGI)
- Realize capital gains carefully to stay in subsidy range
- Can get $1,000-$2,000/month health insurance subsidized

Example:

- Early retiree couple, age 55
- Need $80K for living
- Take $60K from Roth (doesn't count for MAGI)
- Take $20K capital gains (long-term)
- MAGI: $20K (far below $81K threshold)
- Qualify for maximum ACA subsidies (~$20K+/year)

Healthcare savings alone can be worth $20-30K annually through strategic income management

The Charitable Giving Tax Strategy

If you're charitably inclined, strategic giving multiplies impact:

Donor-Advised Fund (DAF)

What it is: Charitable savings account—contribute now, grant to charities later

Benefits:

- Immediate tax deduction (up to 60% of AGI for cash, 30% for appreciated assets)
- Tax-free growth inside DAF
- Grant to charities over time

- Simplifies record-keeping

Strategic use:

- High-income year? "Bunch" multiple years of giving into one year
- Take large deduction when it provides most benefit
- Deploy to charities over 5-10 years

Example:

- Income: $400K (high bracket)
- Normally donate $10K/year to charity
- Strategy: Donate $50K (5 years' worth) to DAF in one year
- Tax savings: ~$18,500 (37% bracket)
- Grant $10K/year from DAF to charities

vs. donating $10K annually:

- Tax savings: $3,700/year × 5 years = $18,500 total
- Same economic outcome, but immediate tax benefit + growth inside DAF

Qualified Charitable Distribution (QCD)

For age 70.5+:

- Donate directly from IRA to charity (up to $105,000 annually as of 2024)
- Donation doesn't count as income
- Counts toward Required Minimum Distribution (RMD)

This is often better than standard deduction:

Example:

- Age 75, RMD = $50K
- Donate $30K to charity via QCD
- Only $20K counts as income
- vs. taking $50K distribution + donating $30K → pay taxes on $50K, then deduct $30K (less beneficial)

QCD saves $6,000-11,000 in taxes depending on bracket

Estate Tax Planning

Current exemption (2024): $13.61M per individual, $27.22M per couple

If estate exceeds exemption, 40% tax applies to excess

Strategies for high net worth ($10M+):

Spousal Lifetime Access Trust (SLAT)

- Transfer assets to irrevocable trust for spouse's benefit
- Removes from your estate (no estate tax)
- Spouse can access during life
- After spouse's death, passes to children tax-free

Grantor Retained Annuity Trust (GRAT)

- Transfer appreciating assets to trust
- Receive annuity payments for term
- Remaining assets pass to heirs tax-free
- Works best with rapidly appreciating assets

Family Limited Partnership (FLP)

- Create partnership holding investments
- Gift partnership interests to children (with discounts)
- Retain control as general partner
- Reduces estate value through valuation discounts (20-40%)

These are advanced strategies requiring estate attorneys. For estates >$15M, can save millions in taxes.

The Tax Optimization Scorecard

Rate your current tax efficiency:

1. Maxing all tax-advantaged accounts (401k, IRA, HSA)

    - Savings: $5,000-15,000/year

2. Asset location optimized (tax-inefficient in IRAs, efficient in taxable)

    - Savings: $1,000-3,000/year

3. Tax-loss harvesting systematically
    - Savings: $500-2,000/year
4. Strategic capital gains realization (timing gains in low-income years)
    - Savings: $2,000-10,000/year
5. Using 1031 exchanges for real estate
    - Savings: $20,000-100,000+ per property
6. Charitable giving optimized (DAF, QCD, donating appreciated stock)
    - Savings: $3,000-10,000/year
7. Entity structures appropriate (LLC, trust, etc.)
    - Savings: $2,000-10,000/year
8. Estate plan in place (for $5M+ estates)
    - Savings: $500,000-5,000,000+ for heirs

Total potential annual tax savings for $1-2M portfolio: $15,000-50,000/year

Over 30 years, tax optimization can add $1-3M+ to wealth

Case Study: The $42,000 Annual Tax Savings

Investor: James, 52, $2.1M portfolio, $175K income

Before tax optimization (2020):

- All investments in taxable account
- No tax-loss harvesting
- Paid full capital gains on rebalancing
- Charitable giving: Cash donations
- Annual tax bill: $56,000

After working with CPA + implementing strategies (2021-2024):

Changes:

1. Maxed 401(k) + HSA ($27,500 annually)
    - Tax savings: $9,600
2. Repositioned assets:
    - Moved REITs, private credit to IRA (from taxable)
    - Kept index funds, real estate syndications in taxable
    - Tax savings: $2,200/year
3. Systematic tax-loss harvesting
    - Harvested $25K+ losses annually (2022-2023 bear market)
    - Offset $25K gains elsewhere
    - Tax savings: $5,000/year
4. Donor-Advised Fund
    - Bunched $50K (5 years' giving) in high-income year
    - Saved $18,500 immediately vs. spreading
5. Real estate 1031 exchange
    - Sold rental property, $180K gain
    - Rolled into syndication via 1031
    - Deferred $36K+ tax
6. QOZ investment
    - Invested $100K capital gains in Qualified Opportunity Zone
    - Deferred gain + potential tax-free growth

Annual tax bill (2024): $14,000

Annual savings: $42,000

30-year projection:

- Without optimization: Pay $1.68M in taxes
- With optimization: Pay $420K in taxes
- Savings: $1.26M

That $1.26M compounds at 8% over 30 years → adds $3.8M to final wealth

Tax optimization alone nearly doubled James's eventual wealth.

Your Tax Optimization Action Plan

Phase 1: Foundation (Implement immediately)

- Max all tax advantaged accounts (401k, IRA, HSA)

- Set up automatic contributions
- Document for $_____ annual tax savings

Phase 2: Asset Location (Implement over 6-12 months)

- Audit current holdings and account types
- Identify misplaced assets (tax-inefficient in taxable accounts)
- Reposition systematically (avoid triggering large gains)
- Target for $_____ annual tax savings

Phase 3: Active Management (Implement ongoing)

- Set up tax-loss harvesting (manual or automated)
- Create capital gains realization strategy
- Plan charitable giving (DAF, QCD when eligible)
- Target for $_____ annual tax savings

Phase 4: Advanced Strategies (Implement as needed)

- Evaluate entity structures (LLC, trust) if net worth >$1M
- Real estate: Use 1031 exchanges, cost segregation
- Estate planning if net worth >$5M
- Work with CPA/attorney on QOZ, GRATs, SLATs
- Target for $_____ annual tax savings

Total annual tax savings goal: $_____

30-year compound value: $_____ (use 8% growth rate)

This is wealth you're leaving on the table if you ignore tax optimization.

The Ultimate Tax Principle

It's not what you earn. It's what you keep.

Two investors:

- Investor A: 12% gross returns, 35% tax burden = 7.8% net returns
- Investor B: 10% gross returns, 15% tax burden = 8.5% net returns

Investor B wins despite lower gross returns.

Tax optimization isn't about aggression or gaming the system. It's about using legal strategies Congress designed to incentivize behavior (retirement saving, real estate investment, charitable giving, entrepreneurship).

The tax code is a 4,000-page instruction manual for legally reducing taxes. Use it.

Key Takeaways:

- Taxes reduce returns by 2-3% annually; over 30 years, this compounds to millions lost
- Three optimization layers: Tax-advantaged accounts (foundation), asset location (intermediate), strategic management (advanced)
- Max all tax-advantaged space first: 401(k), IRA, HSA, Roth—saves $5-15K annually
- Asset location: Tax-inefficient assets (bonds, REITs, private credit) in IRAs; tax-efficient (index funds, real estate) in taxable accounts
- Tax-loss harvesting adds 0.5-1% annual return through systematic loss realization
- Real estate offers unique benefits: depreciation, cost segregation, 1031 exchanges, step-up basis
- Strategic withdrawal sequencing (Roth first, then gains, then IRA) can reduce retirement taxes to near-zero
- Entity structures (LLC, trusts) provide asset protection and tax planning for $1M+ portfolios
- Charitable giving optimization (DAF, QCD, donating appreciated stock) multiplies impact while reducing taxes
- Tax optimization can add $15-50K annually in savings, compounding to $1-3M+ over decades

CHAPTER 16:

BUILDING FOR VOLATILITY

March 2020. The world shut down. Markets collapsed 34% in 33 days—the fastest bear market in history.

Two investors watched their portfolios:

Investor A:

- 100% stocks
- Portfolio: $800K → $528K (-34%)
- Panic-sold at the bottom: "I can't watch this anymore"
- Missed the recovery
- Portfolio one year later: $580K (still down 27% from start)

Investor B:

- Diversified architect portfolio (30% core, 40% income, 20% growth, 10% asymmetric)
- Portfolio: $800K → $692K (-13.5%)
- Calm: Income streams continued ($48K distributions)
- Used cash reserves to buy stocks at -30%
- Portfolio one year later: $950K (up 19% from start)

Same market. Different systems. Opposite outcomes.

This chapter is about building portfolios that don't just survive volatility—they thrive because of it.

The Inevitability of Crashes

Historical market crashes (S&P 500):

- 1929: -86% (Great Depression)
- 1973-1974: -48%

- 1987: -34% (Black Monday)
- 2000-2002: -49% (Dot-com bust)
- 2008-2009: -57% (Financial Crisis)
- 2020: -34% (COVID)
- 2022: -25% (Inflation/Rate hikes)

Average frequency: Major correction (10%+) every 1-2 years. Bear market (20%+) every 3-5 years.

If you invest for 30 years, you will experience:

- 15-30 corrections (10-20% drops)
- 6-10 bear markets (20%+ drops)
- 2-4 crashes (30%+ drops)
- Possibly 1 catastrophe (50%+ drop)

Volatility isn't a possibility. It's a certainty.

The question isn't whether markets will crash. It's whether your portfolio can handle it without destroying your life or forcing you to sell at the worst moment.

The Three Types of Volatility

Type 1: Price Volatility (Temporary)

What it is: Day-to-day, month-to-month price fluctuations

Characteristics:

- Constant (stocks fluctuate 15-25% annually)
- Mean-reverting (markets generally recover)
- Emotionally challenging but financially harmless (if you don't panic)

How to handle:

- Ignore daily prices
- Focus on underlying fundamentals
- Maintain long time horizon
- Never check portfolio during market panics

The architect's advantage: Income-producing portfolios reduce psychological impact—you're still receiving distributions even when prices swing

Type 2: Drawdown Volatility (Scary)

What it is: Sustained portfolio declines of 20-50%+

Characteristics:

- Infrequent (every 5-10 years)
- Duration: 6-24 months typically
- Psychologically devastating (watching wealth evaporate)
- Recovery: 2-7 years historically

How to handle:

- Diversification reduces severity (balanced portfolios fell 13-20% in 2020 vs. 34% for pure stocks)
- Income streams provide comfort and buying power
- Rebalancing forces buying low
- Emotional resilience from knowing it's temporary

The architect's advantage: Proper portfolio construction reduces drawdowns by 30-50% vs. all-stock portfolios.

Type 3: Permanent Impairment (Devastating)

What it is: Losing capital permanently—company bankruptcy, fraud, total loss

Characteristics:

- Rare at portfolio level if diversified
- Common at individual position level
- Cannot be recovered (position goes to zero)
- Avoided through diversification and due diligence

How to handle:

- Never put >5% in single position
- Diversify across 20+ holdings minimum
- Vet operators/managers thoroughly
- Accept that some positions will fail (especially startups)

The architect's advantage: Position sizing limits damage—if one $10K investment goes to zero in a $500K portfolio, it's 2% loss, not portfolio destruction.

The Antifragile Portfolio Framework

Nassim Taleb's concept: Things that benefit from disorder.

Fragile: Breaks under stress (all-stock portfolio in 2008) Robust: Survives stress (balanced portfolio in 2008) Antifragile: Grows stronger from stress (architect portfolio in 2008)

The Four Pillars of Antifragility

Pillar 1: Income Independence

Why it matters: If a portfolio generates income regardless of market prices, crashes become buying opportunities, not emergencies.

Implementation:

- 30-40% of portfolio in income-producing assets
- Target: Covering 60-100% of expenses through distributions
- Multiple income sources (6-10 different streams)

Example:

- Portfolio: $1M
- Income assets: $400K generating $32K/year (8% yield)
- Expenses: $50K/year
- Coverage: 64%

During crash:

- Portfolio drops to $800K (-20%)
- Income continues: $32K/year (distributions don't stop)
- Can live on income + some savings without selling depreciated assets
- Meanwhile, use excess cash to buy at depressed prices

This is antifragile: Crash creates opportunity rather than crisis.

Pillar 2: Liquidity Layering

Why it matters: Having cash available during crashes allows you to buy at generational lows.

The ladder:

- Tier 1 (Immediate): 3-6 months expenses in savings account
- Tier 2 (Quick): 5-10% of portfolio in cash or money market (1-week access)
- Tier 3 (Medium): 10-15% in bonds or liquid alternatives (1-month access)
- Tier 4 (Slow): 30-40% in semi-liquid alternatives (1-year access)
- Tier 5 (Locked): 35-45% in illiquid investments (3-10 year holds)

Example $1M portfolio:

- $30K: Emergency fund (checking/savings)
- $75K: Money market (Tier 2)
- $125K: Bonds/liquid alts (Tier 3)
- $350K: Real estate, private credit (Tier 4)
- $420K: PE/VC, long-term positions (Tier 5)

During crash:

- Use Tier 2-3 ($200K) to buy stocks at -30%
- Don't touch Tier 4-5 (these are compounding)
- Replenish Tier 2-3 from income over next 12-24 months

Result: Deploy $200K at market lows, potentially generating $400K+ gain in recovery.

Pillar 3: Asymmetric Positioning

Why it matters: Small positions in assets that benefit from chaos provide portfolio insurance.

Chaos beneficiaries:

- Gold/precious metals (inverse to stocks during crashes)
- Volatility index (VIX) positions (profits from market fear)
- Tail-risk hedges (options strategies that pay off in crashes)
- Distressed debt (buy assets cheap during panics)
- Cash (gains purchasing power when assets are on sale)

Conservative approach (5% allocation):

- 3% Gold/commodities
- 2% Cash above normal reserves

Moderate approach (8% allocation):

- 4% Gold/commodities
- 2% Managed futures or trend-following strategies
- 2% Cash above normal reserves

Aggressive approach (12% allocation):

- 5% Gold/commodities
- 3% Tail-risk hedges
- 2% Volatility strategies
- 2% Distressed/opportunistic funds

During crash:

- Gold might rise 20% while stocks fall 30%
- Volatility positions might double or triple
- Sell these positions at highs, buy stocks at lows

Example:

- $50K in gold (5% of $1M portfolio)
- Market crashes -30%, gold rises 25%
- Gold now worth $62.5K
- Sell gold, buy $62.5K of stocks at -30% discount
- When stocks recover, that $62.5K becomes $89K+
- $39K gain from rebalancing during volatility

Pillar 4: Uncorrelated Diversification

Why it matters: When everything moves together, diversification fails. True diversification means assets that move independently.

Correlation spectrum:

- = Perfect correlation (move identically)
- 0.5 = Moderate correlation (often move together)
- = No correlation (move independently)
- -0.5 = Moderate negative correlation (often move oppositely)
- -1.0 = Perfect negative correlation (always move oppositely)

Asset correlations to S&P 500 (historical):

- International stocks: 0.85 (very high—not true diversification)
- Investment-grade bonds: 0.15 (low—good diversification)
- Real estate: 0.55 (moderate—some diversification)
- Commodities: 0.20 (low—good diversification)
- Private equity: 0.65 (moderate-high)
- Hedge funds: 0.30 (low-moderate—good diversification)

Building uncorrelated portfolio:

- Don't just own different stocks (all highly correlated)
- Own different asset classes with low/negative correlations
- Own private assets (real estate, PE) that don't mark-to-market daily
- Own alternatives (royalties, farmland) with unique return drivers

Example uncorrelated portfolio:

- 25% S&P 500 (baseline)
- 15% Bonds (correlation 0.15)
- 25% Real estate (correlation 0.55)
- 15% Commodities/gold (correlation 0.20)
- 10% Private credit (correlation 0.30)
- 10% Alternatives (royalties, farmland, correlation ~0.10)

Portfolio volatility: ~9% (vs. 18% for all-stocks)

During 2008 crash:

- All-stock portfolio: -57%
- This portfolio: -25% (bonds +5%, commodities +15%, real estate -30%, stocks -57%)
- Recovery time: 2.5 years vs. 6 years for all-stocks

The Barbell Strategy

The concept: Extreme safety + extreme aggression, nothing in the middle

How it works:

- 80-90% in ultra-safe, income-producing, low-volatility assets
- 10-20% in high-risk, asymmetric, potentially explosive assets
- Avoid the "moderately risky" middle (corporate bonds, value stocks, etc.)

The logic:

- Safe portion protects you from ruin
- Aggressive portion captures outliers
- Middle is "risky without reward" (can lose 20-30% but lacks 10x upside)

Example $1M barbell portfolio:

Safe (85% = $850K):

- $300K: Treasury bonds
- $200K: Private credit (senior debt)
- $250K: Core real estate (stable, cash-flowing)
- $100K: Cash

Aggressive (15% = $150K):

- $75K: Early-stage venture capital
- $50K: Cryptocurrency (Bitcoin/Ethereum)
- $25K: Emerging technology (AI, biotech)

Performance during crash:

- Safe portion: -5% ($850K → $807.5K)
- Aggressive portion: -40% ($150K → $90K)
- Total: -10.25% ($1M → $897.5K)

But aggressive portion positioned for 5-10x upside during recovery

vs. Traditional 60/40:

- Crash: -20% ($1M → $800K)
- Upside: Limited (2x maybe)

Barbell protects downside while maintaining asymmetric upside.

Volatility as Opportunity: The Deployment Strategy

The mindset shift: Most investors fear volatility. Architects welcome it.

Why? Because crashes create the best buying opportunities of a lifetime.

The deployment rules:

Rule 1: Never deploy all at once

Even at market "lows," prices can fall further. Deploy in tranches.

Example: $100K to deploy during crash:

- Market down 15%: Deploy $25K
- Market down 25%: Deploy $25K more
- Market down 35%: Deploy $30K more
- Market down 45%+: Deploy remaining $20K

This ensures you buy more at better prices without timing the exact bottom.

Rule 2: Buy quality at discount, not junk

Crashes make bad companies cheap and great companies cheaper. Don't be fooled.

Avoid:

- Highly leveraged companies (may go bankrupt)
- Speculative businesses with no profits
- Fads that were overvalued even before crash

Buy:

- Blue-chip companies with strong balance sheets
- Index funds (diversified quality)
- Real estate in solid markets with good sponsors
- Established businesses temporarily beaten down

Rule 3: Maintain reserves

Don't deploy 100% of dry powder. Keep 20-30% for "just in case it gets worse."

Rule 4: Income first, growth second

During crashes, prioritize income-producing assets:

- Dividend aristocrats (companies that raised dividends for 25+ years)
- Private credit opportunities (distressed lending at high rates)

- Real estate at discounts (cash-flowing properties)

These provide immediate income while you wait for recovery.

The Drawdown Budget

The concept: Know in advance how much loss you can tolerate before making changes.

Why it matters: Removes emotion from crisis decision-making.

How to calculate:

Step 1: Maximum tolerable drawdown

"At what portfolio decline would I panic-sell or not sleep at night?"

- Conservative: 15-20%
- Moderate: 20-30%
- Aggressive: 30-40%

Step 2: Design portfolio for that threshold

If your maximum tolerable drawdown is 25%, build a portfolio that won't drop more than 25% even in severe crashes.

Allocation to meet 25% max drawdown:

- 40% low-volatility (bonds, cash, gold): -5% in crash
- 35% moderate-volatility (real estate, private credit): -15% in crash
- 20% high-volatility (stocks): -35% in crash
- 5% very-high-volatility (venture, crypto): -60% in crash

Weighted drawdown: (0.40 × -5%) + (0.35 × -15%) + (0.20 × -35%) + (0.05 × -60%) = -15.25%

This portfolio won't drop more than ~15% even in severe crashes, well within your 25% tolerance.

Step 3: Commit to the plan

Write down: "If my portfolio drops more than __%, I will [specific action]."

Example actions:

- Do nothing (if within tolerance)
- Deploy opportunity fund (if have dry powder)
- Reduce spending temporarily (if needed)
- Increase allocation to safe assets (if psychological need)

Never: Panic-sell everything and go to cash

Stress-Testing: The Scenario Analysis

Run your portfolio through worst-case scenarios.

Scenario 1: The 2008 Repeat

Assumptions:

- Stocks: -50%
- Bonds: -10%
- Real estate: -35%
- Private equity: -30%
- Venture: -40%
- Commodities: +15%
- Cash: 0%

Your portfolio:

- 25% stocks: → $187.5K (from $250K)
- 10% bonds: → $90K (from $100K)
- 30% real estate: → $195K (from $300K)
- 15% PE: → $105K (from $150K)
- 10% venture: → $60K (from $100K)
- 5% commodities: → $57.5K (from $50K)
- 5% cash: → $50K (unchanged)

Total: $745K (from $1M) = -25.5% drawdown

Can you tolerate this? Can you live on income during this? Do you have cash to deploy?

Scenario 2: The 1970s Stagflation

Assumptions:

- Stocks: -25% (stagnant decade)
- Bonds: -20% (inflation kills fixed income)
- Real estate: +10% (inflation hedge)
- Commodities: +50% (inflation surge)
- Cash: -30% real value (inflation)

Your portfolio:

- 25% stocks: → $187.5K
- 10% bonds: → $80K
- 30% real estate: → $330K
- 5% commodities: → $75K
- 30% other alternatives: Assume flat → $300K
- 5% cash: → $50K (but worth $35K real value)

Total: $1.022M (up nominally, down ~15% real terms)

Can you handle slow erosion + high inflation?

Scenario 3: The Personal Crisis

Assumptions:

- You lose your job
- Portfolio drops 20%
- Need to live on portfolio for 18 months
- Cannot access illiquid investments

Your portfolio:

- Portfolio value: $800K (from $1M)
- Liquid assets: 40% = $320K
- Annual expenses: $70K
- 18 months expenses: $105K

Can you withdraw $105K from $320K liquid assets without destroying your portfolio?

If yes, you're resilient. If not, you need more liquidity.

Crisis Management: The Decision Tree

When markets crash and your portfolio drops 20%+:

Step 1: Check Your Freedom Index

Question: Is your passive income still covering 50%+ of expenses?

If YES:

- You're financially stable
- You don't need to sell anything
- This is temporary mark-to-market pain
- Action: Stay calm, rebalance, potentially deploy

If NO:

- You're dependent on portfolio value for living
- Temporary losses create real impact
- May need to reduce spending or access liquid reserves
- Action: Assess liquid reserves, consider spending reductions

Step 2: Assess Liquidity

Question: Do you have 12+ months expenses in liquid reserves?

If YES:

- You have runway without selling at losses
- Markets typically recover within 1-2 years
- Action: Live on reserves, let portfolio recover

If NO:

- You may need to sell at inopportune time
- Risk of permanent impairment
- Action: Immediately reduce spending, possibly sell non-core positions

Step 3: Emotional Check

Question: Are you making this decision from fear or strategy?

Fear-based decisions:

- "I can't take this anymore"
- "What if it goes lower?"
- "Everyone is selling, I should too"

Strategy-based decisions:

- "My plan says if portfolio drops >30%, I rebalance into stocks"
- "I'll deploy $X from opportunity fund at 25% decline"
- "I'll reduce spending 20% and wait for recovery"

If fear-based → Do nothing for 48 hours. Talk to advisor/trusted friend. Don't make permanent decisions in temporary circumstances.

If strategy-based → Execute the plan.

Step 4: The Rebalancing Opportunity

Question: Are any positions >15% above or below target?

If YES:

- Sell overweight positions (likely defensive assets that held up)
- Buy underweight positions (likely stocks/growth assets that crashed)
- This forces "buy low, sell high"

Example:

- Target: 30% stocks, 40% income, 20% growth, 10% cash
- Current: 20% stocks (down -35%), 45% income (down -10%), 18% growth (down -25%), 17% cash (repositioned for safety)
- Action: Sell 5% income + 7% cash, buy stocks back to 30% target

This is how you profit from volatility systematically.

Building Emotional Resilience

Volatility isn't just a financial challenge. It's a psychological one.

The strategies that preserve wealth during crashes:

Strategy 1: Stop checking prices

During crashes, checking your portfolio daily causes:

- Anxiety and poor sleep
- Emotional decision-making
- Increased likelihood of panic-selling

Instead:

- Check monthly or quarterly only
- Focus on income received (distributions continue)
- Read books/avoid financial news during panics

Strategy 2: Zoom out

Every crash in history has been recovered. Every. Single. One.

Historical recovery times:

- 1987 crash: 2 years
- 2000-2002 dot-com: 7 years
- 2008 financial crisis: 4 years
- 2020 COVID: 5 months
- 2022 inflation crash: 2 years

Average: 2-4 years. Your investment horizon is 20-40 years. This is noise.

Strategy 3: Reframe losses

Instead of: "I lost $200K" Think: "My net worth temporarily declined 20%, and I'm accumulating assets at a 20-30% discount"

The mark-to-market loss is only real if you sell. If you hold, it's temporary pain followed by gain.

Strategy 4: Process with trusted advisor

Don't: Call your broker in a panic demanding they sell everything Do: Talk to spouse/partner, fee-only advisor, trusted friend who's been through this

Often just verbalizing fears and hearing "this is normal, you're OK" is enough to prevent bad decisions.

Strategy 5: Remember your "why"

Why are you investing?

- Financial autonomy for your family?
- Early retirement to pursue passion?
- Legacy for your children?
- Funding philanthropic mission?

The temporary pain of a crash is worth the permanent gain of achieving your purpose.

Remind yourself: "Short-term volatility is the price of long-term freedom."

Case Study: Thriving Through 2008

Investor: Robert, age 38 in 2007, $450K portfolio

Portfolio allocation (2007):

- 30% Index funds
- 35% Real estate syndications
- 20% Private credit
- 10% Cash
- 5% Commodities

2008 crash impact:

- Index funds: -50% ($135K → $67.5K)
- Real estate: -25% ($157.5K → $118K, slower repricing)
- Private credit: -5% ($90K → $85.5K, continued paying)
- Cash: $45K (unchanged)
- Commodities: +20% ($22.5K → $27K)

Portfolio: $450K → $343K (-24% vs. -57% for S&P 500)

Robert's income streams:

- Real estate distributions: $12K/year (reduced but continuing)

- Private credit: $8.5K/year (continuing)
- Total: $20.5K/year (covered 32% of his $65K expenses)

His actions:

- Stayed calm: Income continued, he could cover expenses with salary + some income
- Deployed cash: Used $40K to buy index funds at -50% discount
- Continued contributions: $2,000/month from salary into stocks at depressed prices
- Sold commodities: Sold $25K in commodities (at +20%), bought more stocks

2009-2012 recovery:

- Index funds recovered: $67.5K original + $65K deployed = $132.5K → $300K+ by 2012
- Real cstate recovered: $118K → $180K
- Private credit: Continued paying, $85.5K → $95K
- Total portfolio 2012: $675K (+50% from pre-crash peak)

Key to success:

- Diversification reduced crash severity (-24% vs. -57%)
- Income continued, reducing need to sell
- Cash reserves allowed buying at lows
- Emotional resilience (he never panic-sold)
- Systematic deployment during panic

2007-2012 compounded annual return: 8.4% despite experiencing worst crash since 1929

vs. average investor who panic-sold in 2008 and bought back in 2010: -3.2% CAGR

Your Volatility Preparation Plan

Action Step 1: Calculate Your Drawdown Tolerance

"I can psychologically tolerate a portfolio decline of ___% before I would panic-sell."

Most people: 20-30%

Action Step 2: Stress-Test Current Portfolio

Using 2008-level crash assumptions:

- My portfolio would decline approximately ____%
- My income streams would decline approximately ____%
- I would need $_____from liquid reserves to cover 18 months expenses

If projected decline > tolerance: Reduce risk (more bonds, cash, stable income assets)

Action Step 3: Build Opportunity Fund

"I will maintain $_____ in cash (separate from emergency fund) specifically to deploy during market crashes."

Target: 5-10% of portfolio

Action Step 4: Set Deployment Triggers

"When S&P 500 drops **%, I will deploy $**___ into _____."

Example:

- -20%: Deploy $25K into index funds
- -30%: Deploy $25K more into index funds
- -40%: Deploy $30K into individual quality stocks

Action Step 5: Create "If-Then" Rules

"If portfolio drops >25%, I will [specific action]." "If passive income drops >20%, I will [specific action]." "If I feel panic, I will [call advisor/wait 48 hours/review this chapter]."

Action Step 6: Review Liquidity Ladder

- Immediate reserves: $_____
- Quick liquidity: $_____
- Medium liquidity: $_____
- Total liquid in crisis: $_____
- Months of expenses covered: _____

Target: 12+ months

Action Step 7: Annual Volatility Drill

Once per year, simulate a crash:

- "If my portfolio dropped 30% tomorrow, what would I do?"
- Walk through decision tree
- Confirm comfort with plan
- Update triggers/rules as needed

This prevents panic when a real crash happens—you've already mentally prepared.

The Ultimate Volatility Truth

Markets are volatile. That will never change.

But volatility is only destructive if:

- You're forced to sell during downturns
- You panic and sell voluntarily
- You're over-concentrated in one asset
- You have no income streams

Build a portfolio that eliminates all four risks:

- ✓ Income covers expenses (no forced selling)
- ✓ Emotional plan prevents panic (systematic rules)
- ✓ Diversification protects against concentration (20+ positions, uncorrelated assets)
- ✓ Multiple income streams provide stability (6-10 sources)

When you do this, volatility transforms from enemy to ally.

Every crash becomes a sale. Every panic becomes an opportunity. Every bottom becomes a generational buying moment.

The investors who build wealth aren't the ones who avoid volatility (impossible).

They're the ones who build systems that thrive *because of* it.

Key Takeaways:

- Volatility is certain: Expect 6-10 bear markets, 2-4 crashes over 30-year investing career
- Three volatility types: Price (temporary), Drawdown (scary), Permanent impairment (devastating)
- Antifragile portfolio four pillars: Income independence, liquidity layering, asymmetric positioning, uncorrelated diversification
- Barbell strategy: 80-90% ultra-safe + 10-20% ultra-aggressive, avoid risky middle
- Crashes are opportunities: Deploy cash in tranches (25% at -15%, 25% at -25%, 30% at -35%)
- Know your drawdown tolerance: Build portfolio that won't exceed your psychological breaking point
- Stress-test portfolio: Run through 2008, stagflation, and personal crisis scenarios
- Crisis decision tree: Check Freedom Index → Assess liquidity → Emotional check → Rebalance
- Emotional resilience: Stop checking prices, zoom out, reframe losses, process with advisors
- Income streams transform crashes from catastrophes to opportunities

SECTION V

THE LEGACY

Wealth Beyond Money

CHAPTER 17:

THE KUBERA FRAMEWORK

In Hindu mythology, Kubera is the god of wealth—not just money, but all forms of prosperity: material, intellectual, spiritual.

The Kubera Framework is a 10-step methodology to design your personalized wealth system, aligned with your purpose, values, and life stage.

This is the culmination of everything we've covered—turning principles into practice, theory into reality.

Step 1: Define Your Purpose

The foundational question: What is money enabling?

Not "How much do I want?" but "What do I want money to make possible?"

Common purposes:

- Autonomy: Freedom from work dependency
- Security: Peace of mind for family
- Impact: Funding causes I care about
- Experience: Travel, learning, adventure
- Creation: Building businesses, art, projects
- Legacy: Providing for future generations
- Time: Buying back hours/days/years

Exercise: The Eulogy Test

Imagine your funeral. What do you want people to say about how you used your wealth?

"He accumulated $10 million" or "He funded education for 1,000 kids"? "She retired at 45" or "She built a business that employed her community"? "They died rich" or "They lived free"?

Your purpose statement:

"I am building wealth to ____."

This becomes your North Star. Every investment decision is evaluated against this purpose.

Step 2: Calculate Your Numbers

Five critical numbers:

1. Your Freedom Number Annual passive income needed to cover lifestyle = $______

2. Your Capital Target Capital required to generate Freedom Number (Income ÷ Target Yield) = $______

3. Your Current Position Net worth today = $______ Passive income today = $______ /year

4. Your Freedom Index (Current Passive Income ÷ Annual Expenses) × 100 = ______%

5. Your Timeline Years until financial autonomy based on savings rate and returns = ______ years

Example:

1. Freedom Number: $75,000/year
2. Capital Target: $75,000 ÷ 0.07 = $1,071,000
3. Current Position: $280,000 net worth, $15,000 passive income
4. Freedom Index: $15,000 ÷ $75,000 = 20%
5. Timeline: 12 years (saving $50K/year, 10% returns, reaching $1.1M)

These aren't guesses. These are your mission parameters.

Step 3: Design Your Allocation

Based on your stage, timeline, and risk tolerance, design your target portfolio.

The Portfolio Architecture Pyramid™:

Foundation Layer (25-40%): Purpose: Stability, liquidity, ballast Assets: Index funds, bonds, cash, core REITs Target return: 4-7%

Income Layer (30-40%): Purpose: Cash flow generation, funding freedom Assets: Real estate syndications, private credit, dividend stocks, royalties Target return: 7-12% (yield + appreciation)

Growth Layer (15-25%): Purpose: Wealth accumulation, compounding Assets: Private equity, growth stocks, value-add real estate Target return: 12-20%

Asymmetric Layer (5-15%): Purpose: Moonshot potential, outlier returns Assets: Venture capital, startups, emerging tech, crypto Target return: 0-100x (binary outcomes)

Your allocation (fill in %):

- Foundation: ____%
- Income: ____%
- Growth: ____%
- Asymmetric: ____%
- Total: 100%

Allocation evolves with life stage:

- Age 25-35: 30% foundation, 25% income, 30% growth, 15% asymmetric
- Age 35-45: 30% foundation, 35% income, 25% growth, 10% asymmetric
- Age 45-55: 35% foundation, 40% income, 20% growth, 5% asymmetric
- Age 55+: 40% foundation, 40% income, 15% growth, 5% asymmetric

Step 4: Establish Your Income Strategy

Goal: Build multiple streams that collectively cover 100%+ of expenses

Income sources matrix:

Source	Current $	Target $	Timeline
Dividends	_____	_____	_____
RE distributions	_____	_____	_____
Private credit	_____	_____	_____
Royalties	_____	_____	_____
Preferred equity	_____	_____	_____

Business income	_____	_____	_____
Other	_____	_____	_____
TOTAL	_____	_____	_____

Target: 6-10 diverse sources, each representing <25% of total income

Step 5: Create Your Deployment Plan

Systematic capital deployment over next 12-36 months:

Available capital:

- Current savings: $_____
- Monthly savings: $_____
- Expected windfalls (bonus, inheritance, sale): $_____
- Total 12-month deployment capacity: $_____

Deployment priorities:

Quarter 1:

- Emergency fund gap (if <6 months): $_____
- Max tax-advantaged accounts: $_____
- Deploy into allocation: $_____

Quarter 2:

- Continue tax-advantaged: $_____
- Add income position (real estate/credit): $_____
- Deploy into allocation: $_____

Quarter 3:

- Continue tax-advantaged: $_____
- Add growth position (PE/VC fund): $_____
- Deploy into allocation: $_____

Quarter 4:

- Continue tax-advantaged: $_____

- Opportunistic deployment: $_____
- Rebalance if needed: $_____

This removes decision fatigue. You know what you're deploying and where, quarters in advance.

Step 6: Optimize for Tax Efficiency

Tax optimization checklist:

1. Maxing tax-advantaged space (401k, IRA, HSA)
    - Amount: $_____/year
    - Tax savings: $_____/year
2. Asset location optimized
    - Tax-inefficient assets (bonds, REITs, private credit) → IRAs
    - Tax-efficient assets (index funds, real estate) → Taxable
    - Highest growth potential → Roth IRA
3. Tax-loss harvesting system
    - Automated or manual quarterly review
    - Expected annual benefit: $_____
4. Entity structures (if net worth >$1M)
    - LLC for real estate holdings?
    - Trust for estate planning?
    - Cost: $_____ | Tax savings: $_____
5. Charitable strategy (if giving >$5K/year)
    - Donor-Advised Fund?
    - QCD (if age 70.5+)?
    - Donating appreciated stock?

Total annual tax optimization: $_____ saved

30-year compounded value: $_____ (use 8% growth rate)

Step 7: Build Resilience

Resilience = ability to withstand worst-case scenarios

Scenario testing:

Test 1: Job Loss

- Liquid reserves: $_____
- Monthly passive income: $_____
- Months of runway: _____
- Action if <12 months: Increase cash reserves

Test 2: Market Crash (-30%)

- Projected portfolio value: $_____
- Projected income reduction: _____%
- Can I avoid selling? Yes / No
- Action if no: Reduce risk allocation

Test 3: Health Crisis

- Insurance coverage: $_____
- Out-of-pocket max: $_____
- Emergency fund covers: Yes / No
- Action if no: Increase emergency fund or insurance

Test 4: Prolonged Bear Market (5 years flat)

- Can I maintain a lifestyle on income alone? Yes / No
- Would I need to reduce spending? _____%
- Acceptable? Yes / No
- Action if no: Increase income allocation

Resilience score:

- 4/4 tests passed: Antifragile
- 3/4 tests passed: Resilient
- 2/4 tests passed: Vulnerable
- 1/4 tests passed: Fragile

Goal: Be resilient minimum, antifragile ideal

Step 8: Automate Everything

The Wealth Operating System (Wealth OS™):

Automated contributions:

- Paycheck → 401(k): ____%
- Auto-transfer → Roth IRA: $_____/month
- Auto-transfer → Taxable investment: $_____/month
- Auto-transfer → Opportunity fund: $_____/month

Automated investing:

- Contributions automatically deploy to target allocation: Yes / No
- Dividend/distribution reinvestment: On / Off (On until Freedom Number achieved)

Automated rebalancing:

- Frequency: Quarterly
- Threshold: When allocation >10% off target
- Tax-smart: Rebalance with new contributions first, avoid selling winners in taxable

Automated tax optimization:

- Tax-loss harvesting: Automated (via robo-advisor) or Manual quarterly
- Year-end tax moves: Calendar reminder December 1

Automated reviews:

- Monthly check-in: 15 minutes
- Quarterly deep dive: 1 hour
- Annual strategy session: 4 hours

Total active management time: <20 hours/year

The system runs itself 99% of the time.

Step 9: Continuously Compound Knowledge

Wealth compounds. Knowledge compounds. Network compounds.

Knowledge plan:

Weekly (1-2 hours):

- Podcast: [Investment podcast during commute]
- Reading: 30 minutes on investing/business

Monthly (2-4 hours):

- Book: 1 investing/business/personal finance book
- Community: Participate in online investment forum

Quarterly (4-8 hours):

- Course/webinar: Deep dive on new asset class or strategy
- Conference: Attend investment conference (annually minimum)

Annually (8-16 hours):

- Review: Analyze all investments, document lessons learned
- Strategy: Update investment thesis and allocation

Network plan:

Join:

- Online community: [Real estate syndication forum, angel investor group, etc.]
- Local group: [Meetup, mastermind, investment club]

Engage:

- Provide value first (answer questions, share insights)
- Build relationships (coffee meetings, virtual calls)
- Collaborate (co-investing, deal sharing)

Outcome:

- Year 1-3: Learn from others, build foundation
- Year 4-7: Deal flow begins, access improves
- Year 8+: You become source of capital, first access to opportunities

Knowledge and network compound slower than money but often provide greater leverage.

Step 10: Align with Values

Purpose-driven wealth is sustainable. Misaligned wealth creates emptiness.

Values alignment checklist:

Investment values: Do my investments align with my beliefs?

- Impact: Am I supporting businesses/industries I believe in?
- Ethics: Am I avoiding businesses that conflict with my values?
- Sustainability: Am I considering environmental/social impact?

Lifestyle values: Is my spending aligned with what matters?

- Time: Am I buying time freedom or just stuff?
- Experience: Am I investing in memories or possessions?
- Relationships: Is wealth enhancing or straining connections?

Contribution values: Am I using wealth for good beyond myself?

- Family: Supporting those I love?
- Community: Improving local surroundings?
- Causes: Funding issues I care about?

Legacy values: What will I leave behind?

- Financial: Passing wealth to heirs?
- Educational: Teaching others what I learned?
- Impact: Creating lasting positive change?

If you answer "no" to any question, course-correct. Money without meaning is just numbers.

The Kubera Compass™: Investment Evaluation Tool

Before committing to any investment, score it across 6 dimensions (1-10 scale):

1. Financial Return (1-10)

Expected risk-adjusted return relative to alternatives

- <5%: 1-3 points
- 5-8%: 4-6 points
- 8-12%: 7-8 points
- 12%+: 9-10 points

Score: ___/10

2. Portfolio Fit (1-10)

How well does this diversify existing holdings?

- Highly correlated to existing: 1-3
- Somewhat correlated: 4-6
- Low correlation: 7-8
- Negative correlation: 9-10

Score: ___/10

3. Risk Profile (1-10)

Risk level appropriate for portfolio position?

- Excessive risk for allocation: 1-3
- Moderate risk: 4-7
- Appropriate risk-reward: 8-10

Score: ___/10

4. Liquidity Match (1-10)

Does liquidity match my needs?

- Too illiquid for situation: 1-3

- Adequate liquidity: 4-7
- Optimal liquidity: 8-10

Score: ___/10

5. Comprehension (1-10)

How well do I understand this?

- Don't understand fully: 1-3
- Understand basics: 4-6
- Deep understanding: 7-8
- Expert level: 9-10

Score: ___/10

6. Values Alignment (1-10)

Does this align with my purpose/values?

- Conflicts with values: 1-3
- Neutral: 4-6
- Partially aligned: 7-8
- Fully aligned: 9-10

Score: ___/10

TOTAL SCORE: ___/60

Decision matrix:

- 50-60 points: Strong yes, full allocation
- 40-49 points: Qualified yes, 50-75% allocation
- 30-39 points: Maybe, pilot with 25-50% allocation
- <30 points: Pass

This removes emotion. You have objective criteria for every investment.

The Complete Kubera Framework Summary

Your personalized wealth system:

1. Purpose: [Your one-sentence purpose statement]
2. Numbers: Freedom Number = $, *Capital Target = $*, Current Freedom Index = ____%
3. Allocation: Foundation ___%, Income ___%, Growth ___%, Asymmetric ___%
4. Income: Current $, *Target $*, # of streams = _____
5. Deployment: $/*month systematic, $*/year total
6. Tax: $_____ annual savings through optimization
7. Resilience: Score ___/4, vulnerabilities addressed: [list actions]
8. Automation: ___% of portfolio on autopilot
9. Knowledge: ___hours/month learning, communities joined: [list]
10. Values: Alignment score ___/10, areas to improve: [list]

This is your blueprint. This is your system. This is your path to freedom.

Case Study: The Kubera Framework in Action

Investor: Starting net worth $340K, Income $215K

The Kubera Framework (Built in 2020):

1. Purpose: "I am building wealth to achieve work-optional by age 50, travel 4 months/year, and fund education for underserved youth."

2. Numbers:

- Freedom Number: $85,000/year
- Capital Target: $1,214,000 (at 7% yield)
- Current: $340K, $14K/year passive income
- Freedom Index: 16%
- Timeline: 11 years to goal (age 50)

3. Allocation:

- Foundation: 30% ($102K)
- Income: 40% ($136K)
- Growth: 20% ($68K)
- Asymmetric: 10% ($34K)

4. Income Strategy: Target 7 streams by 2031:

- Real estate distributions (3 properties)
- Private credit fund
- Dividend growth stocks
- Preferred equity
- Music royalties
- Part-time consulting (optional)
- Charitable fund distributions

5. Deployment Plan:

- $5,000/month systematic ($60K/year)
- Max 401k: $20,500/year
- Max Roth IRA: $6,500/year
- Taxable: $33K/year into income/growth assets

6. Tax Optimization:

- Annual tax savings: $16,000
- 30-year value: $1.2M

7. Resilience:

- 18 months expenses in liquid reserves
- Income covers 25% of expenses (growing)
- Portfolio designed for <25% max drawdown
- Score: 3.5/4 (resilient)

8. Automation:

- 95% automated (contributions, investing, rebalancing)
- <2 hours/month active management

9. Knowledge:

- 6 hours/month: Books, podcasts, courses
- Communities: Real estate syndication forum, women investor group
- Annual conference attendance

10. Values:

- Impact investing: 15% of portfolio
- Supporting education charities: $5K/year
- Teaching financial literacy: Volunteers monthly
- Alignment score: 9/10

Results (2020-2025):

→ 2020: $340K portfolio, $14K income
→ 2021: $455K portfolio, $22K income (Freedom Index: 26%)
→ 2022: $510K portfolio, $28K income (despite market crash, continued deploying)
→ 2023: $640K portfolio, $38K income (Freedom Index: 45%)
→ 2024: $775K portfolio, $48K income (Freedom Index: 56%)
→ 2025: $920K portfolio, $58K income (Freedom Index: 68%)

On track: Will hit $1.2M+ and 100% Freedom Index by age 49 (ahead of schedule)

Why it worked:

- Clear purpose drove discipline
- Systematic deployment removed emotion
- Tax optimization added $80K+ over 5 years
- Automation prevented mistakes
- Knowledge compounding improved returns
- Values alignment sustained motivation

Reflection: "The framework gave me a complete system. I'm not guessing or hoping—I have a blueprint and I'm executing it. For the first time, financial freedom feels inevitable, not aspirational."

Your Kubera Implementation Timeline

Week 1: Foundation

- Define purpose statement
- Calculate all five numbers
- Share with spouse/partner (if applicable)

Week 2: Design

- Design target allocation
- Map income strategy

- Create Kubera Compass for evaluating investments

Week 3: Execution

- Set up automation (contributions, auto-invest)
- Open/fund accounts as needed
- Make first systematic deployment

Week 4: Optimization

- Implement tax strategies
- Stress-test portfolio
- Document decision rules

Month 2: Knowledge

- Join investment communities
- Start learning plan
- Read 1-2 key books

Month 3: Review

- First quarterly review
- Adjust based on learnings
- Celebrate progress

Year 1: Refinement

- Four quarterly reviews
- Annual strategy session
- Measure Freedom Index growth

Years 2-5: Momentum

- System running smoothly
- Knowledge compounding
- Network providing deal flow
- Freedom Index climbing steadily

Years 5-10: Achievement

- Approaching 100% Freedom Index
- Decision: Continue working by choice vs. necessity
- Shift from accumulation to legacy

The Kubera Framework isn't a one-time exercise. It's a living system that evolves with you.

The Framework Review Cadence

Quarterly (1 hour):

- Check progress against numbers
- Review allocation drift
- Deploy new capital
- Update Freedom Index

Annually (4 hours):

- Deep performance review
- Strategy adjustment
- Goal recalibration
- Values alignment check

Every 3-5 years (8+ hours):

- Complete framework overhaul
- Life stage transition
- Major allocation shift
- Legacy planning begins

The framework provides structure. You provide the discipline.

Key Takeaways:

- The Kubera Framework: 10-step methodology to design personalized wealth system
- Step 1: Define purpose (what money enables, not just accumulation goal)
- Step 2: Calculate five numbers (Freedom Number, Capital Target, Net Worth, Freedom Index, Timeline)
- Step 3: Design allocation across four layers (Foundation, Income, Growth, Asymmetric)

- Step 4: Establish income strategy (6-10 diverse streams targeting 100%+ expense coverage)
- Step 5: Create deployment plan (systematic quarterly/annual capital allocation)
- Step 6: Optimize taxes (maximize tax-advantaged accounts, asset location, loss harvesting)
- Step 7: Build resilience (stress-test against job loss, crashes, health crisis, bear markets)
- Step 8: Automate everything (contributions, investing, rebalancing—system runs itself)
- Step 9: Compound knowledge (weekly learning, monthly community, quarterly courses)
- Step 10: Align with values (ensure investments, lifestyle, giving reflect purpose)
- Kubera Compass: Six-dimension scoring system for evaluating any investment opportunity
- Framework is living system: Quarterly reviews, annual strategy sessions, 3-5 year overhauls

CHAPTER 18:

THE FREEDOM INDEX

Net worth is a terrible measure of financial progress.

Person A: $2.5M net worth, $0 passive income, works 60 hours/week, terrified of losing job

Person B: $800K net worth, $65K passive income, works 15 hours/week, completely autonomous

Who's wealthier? Who's freer? Who designed a better life?

Traditional finance celebrates Person A. Architects know Person B is winning.

This chapter redefines success—from accumulation metrics to freedom metrics.

The Flaws of Net Worth

Net worth = Assets - Liabilities

Simple. Clear. Wrong metric.

Why net worth fails:

Problem 1: Includes non-productive assets

- $500K primary residence (you live there, generates $0)
- $100K cars (depreciating, generate $0)
- $50K jewelry (sitting in safe, generates $0)
- $650K of net worth generating zero freedom

Problem 2: Ignores income generation

- $1M in growth stocks generating $20K/year
- $1M in income-producing assets generating $80K/year

- Same net worth, 4x different freedom

Problem 3: Backward-looking

- Net worth tells you where you've been
- Doesn't tell you if you're on track to goals
- Doesn't measure progress toward autonomy

Problem 4: Highly volatile

- Fluctuates 20-30% with markets
- Creates unnecessary anxiety
- False sense of progress/failure based on temporary valuations

Problem 5: Encourages wrong behavior

- Optimizing for net worth = accumulation for accumulation's sake
- Doesn't consider: Time freedom, stress levels, lifestyle quality, purpose alignment

We need better metrics.

The Freedom Index: Your True Wealth Score

Freedom Index = (Annual Passive Income ÷ Annual Expenses) × 100

This single number tells you:

- How financially autonomous you are
- How much longer you must work (if at all)
- Whether you're making actual progress
- If your investments are working

Example:

- Annual passive income: $45,000
- Annual expenses: $72,000
- Freedom Index: ($45,000 ÷ $72,000) × 100 = **62.5%**

Interpretation: You're 62.5% financially free. Work is funding 37.5% of your life. Passive income funds the rest.

The Freedom Stages

Stage 1: Dependent (0-25%)

Status: Entirely reliant on active income

Characteristics:

- Passive income covers <25% of expenses
- Job loss = immediate crisis
- No optionality
- Full-time work is mandatory

Psychology: Scarcity mindset, financial stress, trapped

Example:

- Income: $65K salary, $8K passive
- Expenses: $55K
- Freedom Index: 14.5%

Goal: Build emergency fund + increase income-producing assets

Stage 2: Cushioned (25-50%)

Status: Meaningful passive income, but not sufficient alone

Characteristics:

- Passive income covers 25-50% of expenses
- Job loss is stressful but survivable 6-12 months
- Some optionality (could take lower-paying work you enjoy)
- Full-time work still necessary

Psychology: Reduced anxiety, growing confidence, seeing progress

Example:

- Income: $72K salary, $28K passive
- Expenses: $70K

- Freedom Index: 40%

Goal: Continue building income streams systematically

Stage 3: Flexible (50-75%)

Status: Substantial passive income, approaching autonomy

Characteristics:

- Passive income covers 50-75% of expenses
- Job loss is manageable (1-2 years runway)
- Significant optionality (part-time work, sabbaticals, career changes)
- Work is becoming optional

Psychology: Abundance mindset, reduced stress, career flexibility

Example:

- Income: $80K salary, $52K passive
- Expenses: $75K
- Freedom Index: 69%

Goal: Push through to 100%—you're close

Stage 4: Autonomous (75-100%)

Status: Nearly or fully financially independent

Characteristics:

- Passive income covers 75-100% of expenses
- Job loss is irrelevant (indefinite runway)
- Complete optionality (work by choice, not necessity)
- Work is entirely optional

Psychology: Freedom, peace, gratitude

Example:

- Income: $0 salary (retired/optional work), $68K passive
- Expenses: $70K

- Freedom Index: 97%

Goal: Maintain or exceed 100%, optimize lifestyle

Stage 5: Abundant (100-150%+)

Status: Financial independence with margin

Characteristics:

- Passive income exceeds expenses by 25-50%+
- Surplus for lifestyle expansion, giving, reinvestment
- Generational wealth building
- Legacy considerations

Psychology: Contribution-focused, mentorship, impact

Example:

- Income: $0 salary, $95K passive
- Expenses: $70K
- Freedom Index: 136%

Goal: Define legacy, teach others, maximize impact

The Three Secondary Metrics

Freedom Index is primary, but three supporting metrics complete the picture:

Metric 1: Liquidity Ratio

Liquidity Ratio = Liquid Assets ÷ Annual Expenses

Measures: How many years you can survive without income

Formula: (Cash + Bonds + Stocks + Liquid Alternatives) ÷ Annual Expenses

Example:

- Liquid assets: $180K
- Annual expenses: $65K
- Liquidity Ratio: 2.77 years

Interpretation:

- <0.5 years: Dangerous (one emergency from crisis)
- 0.5-1 year: Fragile
- 1-2 years: Adequate
- 2-3 years: Comfortable
- 3+ years: Abundant

Goal: Maintain 1.5-3 years minimum, even when building long-term wealth

Metric 2: Income Diversity Score

Income Diversity Score = Number of Meaningful Income Sources

Meaningful = generates >5% of total passive income

Example income sources:

1. Dividends from index funds: $8,000 (12%)
2. Real estate syndication A: $12,000 (18%)
3. Real estate syndication B: $9,000 (13%)
4. Real estate syndication C: $7,500 (11%)
5. Private credit fund: $15,000 (22%)
6. Music royalties: $4,000 (6%)
7. Preferred equity: $10,000 (15%)
8. Part-time consulting: $2,000 (3% - doesn't count as <5%)

Income Diversity Score: 7

Interpretation:

- 1-2 sources: Dangerous (concentration risk)
- 3-4 sources: Adequate
- 5-7 sources: Good
- 8-10 sources: Excellent
- 10+ sources: Exceptional

Goal: 5+ sources, none representing >25% of total

Metric 3: Optionality Score

Optionality Score = Calculated across 5 dimensions (0-20 scale)

Dimension 1: Career Freedom (0-4 points)

- 0: Must keep current job
- 1: Could change jobs in same field
- 2: Could change careers entirely
- 3: Could work part-time
- 4: Work is entirely optional

Dimension 2: Location Freedom (0-4 points)

- 0: Tied to current location
- 1: Could relocate within region
- 2: Could relocate anywhere in country
- 3: Could live abroad temporarily
- 4: Complete location independence

Dimension 3: Time Freedom (0-4 points)

- 0: Work 50+ hours/week mandatory
- 1: Work 40-50 hours/week
- 2: Work 30-40 hours/week
- 3: Work 15-30 hours/week
- 4: Complete time sovereignty

Dimension 4: Relationship Freedom (0-4 points)

- 0: Financial stress strains relationships
- 1: Financial stability, minor stress
- 2: Financial comfort, no stress
- 3: Financial surplus enables generosity
- 4: Complete financial alignment in relationships

Dimension 5: Impact Freedom (0-4 points)

- 0: No capacity for giving/impact
- 1: Occasional small donations
- 2: Regular meaningful giving
- 3: Significant giving/volunteering
- 4: Major philanthropic impact

Total Optionality Score: ___/20

Interpretation:

- 0-5: Constrained life
- 6-10: Limited freedom
- 11-15: Meaningful freedom
- 16-18: Substantial freedom
- 19-20: Complete sovereignty

Example:

- Career: 4 (work is optional)
- Location: 3 (could live abroad)
- Time: 4 (complete sovereignty)
- Relationship: 4 (financial alignment)
- Impact: 3 (significant giving)
- Total: 18/20

The Complete Freedom Dashboard

Your quarterly scorecard:

FREEDOM DASHBOARD - Q__ 20__

PRIMARY METRIC:
Freedom Index: ___% (Target: 100%)
Change from last quarter: +/- ___%

SECONDARY METRICS:
Liquidity Ratio: ___ years (Target: 2+ years)
Income Diversity: ___ sources (Target: 5+ sources)
Optionality Score: ___/20 (Target: 15+ points)

FINANCIAL METRICS (Context):
Net Worth: $_____
Passive Income (annual): $_____
Annual Expenses: $_____
Savings Rate: ___%

PROGRESS INDICATORS:
✓ On track to 100% by: [date]
✓ Quarterly income growth: +___%
✓ New income stream added: [Yes/No]
✓ Major milestones hit: [list]

NEXT QUARTER GOALS:
1. [Specific action]
2. [Specific action]
3. [Specific action]

This dashboard tells you everything net worth doesn't:

- Are you actually progressing toward freedom?
- Is your portfolio working (generating income)?
- Are you diversified (income sources)?
- Are you resilient (liquidity)?
- Are you free (optionality)?

Track this quarterly. Celebrate every percentage point gain in the Freedom Index.

The Freedom Index Growth Strategies

How to increase your Freedom Index:

Strategy 1: Increase Passive Income (Numerator)

Tactics:

- Deploy new capital into income-producing assets
- Reinvest all distributions for compounding
- Add new income streams (real estate, private credit, royalties)
- Optimize existing positions (refinance, improve operations)
- Increase allocation to income layer (from 30% to 40%)

Impact: Direct increase in Freedom Index

Example:

- Current: $40K income ÷ $70K expenses = 57%
- Add $150K to income assets yielding 8% = +$12K income
- New: $52K income ÷ $70K expenses = 74% (+17 points)

Strategy 2: Decrease Expenses (Denominator)

Tactics:

- Eliminate wasteful spending (subscriptions, impulse purchases)
- Optimize major expenses (housing, transportation, food)
- Geographic arbitrage (move to lower cost area)
- Lifestyle design (intentional spending on what matters)

Impact: Increases Freedom Index + reduces capital needed

Example:

- Current: $48K income ÷ $72K expenses = 67%
- Reduce expenses to $60K (eliminate $12K waste)
- New: $48K income ÷ $60K expenses = 80% (+13 points)

Bonus: Lower Freedom Number ($60K vs. $72K) means reaching 100% faster

Strategy 3: Simultaneous Attack

Most powerful: Increase income AND decrease expenses

Example:

- Current: $40K income ÷ $72K expenses = 56%
- Add $15K income + reduce expenses to $60K
- New: $55K income ÷ $60K expenses = 92% (+36 points!)

This is how people jump from 50% to 100% in 3-5 years instead of 10.

Strategy 4: Income Acceleration

Increase earned income temporarily to accelerate passive income growth

Tactics:

- Side hustle/freelancing (deploy 100% into investments)
- Negotiate raise/promotion
- Job change to higher comp
- One-time projects (speaking, consulting)

Example:

- Increase salary from $85K to $110K (+$25K)
- Maintain $60K lifestyle (don't lifestyle-inflate)
- Deploy extra $25K annually into income assets
- At 8% yield, generates +$2K passive income year 1
- Compounds over time

Use earned income to buy passive income, then passive income buys freedom.

Case Study: 12% to 108% in 7 Years

Investor: Marcus, started age 37, pharmacist

Starting point (Year 0):

- Net worth: $125K (mostly 401k)
- Passive income: $3,800/year (dividends)
- Expenses: $52,000/year
- Freedom Index: 7.3%
- Liquidity: 0.8 years
- Income sources: 1
- Optionality: 4/20

Year 1-2: Foundation

- Automated savings: $30K/year
- Built emergency fund to 1.5 years
- First real estate syndication: $25K
- Added private credit position: $15K
- Passive income: $6,200
- Freedom Index: 12%

Year 3-4: Acceleration

- Increased savings to $40K/year (lifestyle stayed flat despite raises)
- Added 2 more real estate positions
- Started angel investing ($10K total)
- Optimized taxes (saved $8K/year)
- Passive income: $14,800
- Freedom Index: 28%

Year 5: Inflection

- First syndication exited (2.1x return)
- Redeployed proceeds into 2 new income investments
- Side consulting (extra $15K, all deployed)
- Reduced expenses to $48K (moved to lower cost area)
- Passive income: $24,500
- Freedom Index: 51%

Year 6: Momentum

- Portfolio: $485K
- Income sources: 7 (real estate x4, private credit x2, dividends)
- Passive income: $38,000
- Freedom Index: 79%

Year 7 (Current):

- Portfolio: $590K
- Income sources: 8
- Passive income: $52,000
- Expenses: $48,000 (geographic arbitrage + intentional spending)
- Freedom Index: 108%
- Liquidity: 2.4 years
- Optionality: 17/20

Marcus at age 44:

- Reduced pharmacy work to 25 hours/week
- Spends 15 hours/week on passion project (teaching financial literacy)
- Travels 3 months/year
- Stress levels: Minimal
- Life satisfaction: 9/10

Keys to 7-year transformation:

- Aggressive savings rate (40-50%)
- Every raise/bonus deployed (no lifestyle inflation)
- Systematic income-building (prioritized cash flow)
- Geographic arbitrage reduced expenses 20%
- Tax optimization added $56K over 7 years
- Compounding kicked in around year 5

Reflection: "The first 3 years felt slow. Years 4-5 felt like momentum. Years 6-7 felt inevitable. Now I'm free and it's surreal."

The Freedom Milestones

Celebrate progress at these critical thresholds:

25% Freedom: "The Foundation"

- You have meaningful passive income
- Job loss isn't immediate catastrophe
- You've proven the system works
- Celebration: Take a weekend trip funded by passive income

50% Freedom: "The Inflection"

- You're halfway there
- Work is becoming more optional
- Could take significant pay cut for passion work
- Celebration: Take a month exploring what you'd do if work were optional

75% Freedom: "The Horizon"

- The finish line is visible
- Major life changes become possible
- Career flexibility is real
- Celebration: Make one major life decision based on freedom (move, career change, sabbatical)

100% Freedom: "The Threshold"

- Financial autonomy achieved
- Work is entirely optional
- Your system supports you indefinitely
- Celebration: Define your "second act"—what you'll do with freedom

150% Freedom: "The Abundance"

- Surplus for lifestyle, giving, legacy
- Wealth serves greater purpose
- Teaching others becomes focus
- Celebration: Major philanthropic commitment or mentorship program

Tracking Freedom Index: The Spreadsheet

Create a simple tracker:

Quarter	Passive Income	Expenses	Freedom Index	Change	Notes
Q1 2024	$18,500	$65,000	28.5%	+3.2%	Added RE position
Q2 2024	$21,200	$64,000	33.1%	+4.6%	First full quarter of new income
Q3 2024	$23,800	$63,500	37.5%	+4.4%	Reduced housing costs
Q4 2024	$26,500	$64,200	41.3%	+3.8%	Year-end distributions
Q1 2025	$28,900	$65,800	43.9%	+2.6%	Added credit fund

Key insights from tracking:

- Average quarterly growth: 3.7 percentage points
- At this rate: 100% in ~4 years
- Income growing faster than expenses (critical)
- System is working

This visibility creates motivation. You see progress. You stay disciplined.

When Freedom Index Declines

Sometimes your Freedom Index will drop. Don't panic.

Common reasons:

Temporary income decline:

- Real estate property sold (income pauses until redeployed)
- Dividend cut during recession
- Investment underperforming temporarily

Solution: Focus on long-term trajectory. Temporary dips are normal.

Lifestyle inflation:

- Expenses increased faster than income
- Moved to higher cost area
- Major life change (kids, health issue)

Solution: Conscious choice. If lifestyle increase is intentional and funded, fine. If unconscious creep, correct it.

Major expense year:

- Home renovation
- Medical bills
- Family support

Solution: Temporary. Return to baseline next year.

Market crash:

- Portfolio values down, distributions cut

Solution: Continue deploying. Crashes are temporary. Your income sources should be diversified enough that not all cut simultaneously.

The rule: Don't obsess over quarter-to-quarter fluctuations. Track year-over-year trend.

If Freedom Index is higher this year than last year, you're winning.

Freedom Index vs. Net Worth: The Comparison

Real example: Two investors, both age 45

Investor A (Net Worth Focused):

- Net worth: $2.1M
- Passive income: $18K/year (0.9% yield)
- Expenses: $95K/year
- Freedom Index: 19%
- Works 55 hours/week, stressed
- "I need to keep working to protect my wealth"

Investor B (Freedom Focused):

- Net worth: $950K
- Passive income: $68K/year (7.2% yield)
- Expenses: $58K/year
- Freedom Index: 117%
- Works 0-20 hours/week, by choice
- "I do work I find meaningful because I want to, not because I have to"

Who's wealthier?

By net worth: A is "richer" By any meaningful measure: B has achieved what A is working toward

The lesson: Optimize for freedom, not net worth.

The Freedom Index in Retirement

Traditional retirement: Live on 4% withdrawals

- $1M portfolio → $40K/year
- Pray portfolio lasts 30 years
- Reduce spending if markets crash
- Anxiety throughout retirement

Freedom Index retirement: Live on income

- $1M income-producing portfolio → $70K/year
- Income continues regardless of market valuations
- Never sell principal
- Peace throughout retirement

Example:

- Portfolio: $1.2M
- Allocation: 30% core, 45% income, 20% growth, 5% asymmetric
- Income generated: $78K/year
- Expenses: $72K/year
- Freedom Index: 108%

Retirement strategy:

- Live on $72K income
- Reinvest $6K surplus
- Principal continues growing
- Pass larger estate to heirs

vs. 4% rule:

- Withdraw $48K/year from $1.2M
- Hope it lasts 30 years
- Reduce spending in down years
- Principal depletes over time

Freedom Index approach is superior in every dimension: stability, sustainability, legacy.

Your Freedom Index Action Plan

Step 1: Calculate baseline

- Current passive income: $_____
- Current annual expenses: $_____
- Current Freedom Index: _____%

Step 2: Set milestone targets

- 25% Freedom by: [date]
- 50% Freedom by: [date]
- 75% Freedom by: [date]
- 100% Freedom by: [date]

Step 3: Identify growth levers

- Increase income by: $_____ annually
- Decrease expenses by: $_____ annually
- Deploy capital of: $_____ annually

Step 4: Track quarterly

- Create spreadsheet
- Calculate Freedom Index every quarter
- Document progress and learnings

Step 5: Celebrate milestones

- Define celebration for each 25% threshold
- Share progress with accountability partner
- Reflect on what freedom enables

Step 6: Adjust as needed

- Life changes? Recalculate expenses
- Major windfall? Accelerate plan
- Setback? Extend timeline but maintain direction

The Freedom Index is your North Star. Track it. Grow it. Achieve it.

Key Takeaways:

- Net worth is flawed metric: Includes non-productive assets, ignores income, backward-looking
- Freedom Index = (Passive Income ÷ Annual Expenses) × 100—measures true financial autonomy
- Five freedom stages: Dependent (0-25%), Cushioned (25-50%), Flexible (50-75%), Autonomous (75-100%), Abundant (100%+)
- Three secondary metrics: Liquidity Ratio (years of expenses in liquid assets), Income Diversity (number of sources), Optionality Score (freedom across 5 dimensions)
- Track Freedom Dashboard quarterly: Monitor progress, adjust strategy, celebrate milestones
- Increase Freedom Index through three strategies: Increase income (numerator), decrease expenses (denominator), or both simultaneously
- Freedom Index growth accelerates: Years 1-3 slow, years 4-5 momentum builds, years 6+ feels inevitable
- Celebrate milestones: 25% (Foundation), 50% (Inflection), 75% (Horizon), 100% (Threshold), 150% (Abundance)
- Optimize for Freedom Index, not net worth—freedom is the goal, accumulation is just the means
- Track year-over-year trend, not quarter-to-quarter fluctuations

CHAPTER 19:

FAMILY, VALUES AND CONTINUITY

Cornelius Vanderbilt died in 1877 as the richest American, worth $100 million (roughly $200 billion in today's dollars).

By 1973, at the first Vanderbilt family reunion, not a single millionaire remained among 120 descendants.

One of history's greatest fortunes dissipated in three generations.

Why? No system. No education. No values. No purpose beyond accumulation.

This chapter is about building wealth that lasts—not just financially, but meaningfully—across generations.

The 90% Failure Rate

Research (Williams Group): 90% of wealthy families lose their wealth by the third generation.

The pattern:

- **Generation 1 (Builder):** Creates wealth through sacrifice, hard work, skill, or luck
- **Generation 2 (Sustainer):** Maintains wealth, benefits from it but didn't build it
- **Generation 3 (Destroyer):** Loses wealth through entitlement, poor decisions, family conflict

Why it fails:

Reason 1: No financial education

- Generation 2 never learned how wealth was built
- Generation 3 has no concept of wealth creation
- Money is "just there" until it isn't

Reason 2: Entitlement mindset

- Children raised with wealth but not responsibility
- Expect lifestyle without understanding its cost
- No appreciation for work/discipline/sacrifice

Reason 3: Family conflict

- Inheritance battles
- Unequal treatment creating resentment
- No clear governance or decision framework

Reason 4: Lack of purpose

- Wealth exists for its own sake
- No mission beyond "having money"
- Next generation asks "Why bother?" and squanders it

Reason 5: Poor structure

- No trusts, governance, or protection
- Vulnerable to lawsuits, divorces, bad decisions
- One generation's mistake destroys everything

The antidote: Intentional wealth transfer with education, values, structure, and purpose.

Teaching Financial Literacy to Your Children

The goal: Raise financially capable adults, not entitled dependents

Age 3-7: Foundation Concepts

Lessons:

- Money is earned through work
- Saving vs. spending
- Delayed gratification
- Needs vs. wants

Activities:

- Allowance for age-appropriate chores (not for existing, for contributing)
- Three jars: Save, Spend, Give
- Let them make small purchase decisions
- Teach: If you want the toy, save your allowance

Avoid:

- Buying everything they ask for
- Using money as punishment/reward for behavior
- Hiding financial reality ("we can't afford that" when you can)

The message: Work → money → choices

Age 8-12: Money Management

Lessons:

- Budgeting basics
- Compound interest
- Investing concepts
- Entrepreneurship

Activities:

- Larger allowance with more responsibility (budgeting for clothes, activities)
- Open savings account in their name, show interest accumulating
- Explain your investments simply: "We own part of this building that pays us monthly"
- Encourage small businesses (lemonade stand, lawn mowing, crafts)

Avoid:

- Rescuing them from poor spending decisions
- Paying for everything (let them experience trade-offs)
- Lecturing without letting them experience consequences

The message: Your money decisions have consequences. Learn through small stakes now.

Age 13-17: Real-World Practice

Lessons:

- Investing (stocks, funds)
- Taxes and deductions
- Credit and debt
- Income vs. wealth

Activities:

- Open custodial brokerage account, teach them to invest
- First job: Show them paycheck deductions (taxes, FICA)
- Credit card with low limit (teach responsible use)
- Explain family finances age-appropriately: "Here's what things cost, here's how we invest"

Avoid:

- Preventing them from making financial mistakes
- Paying for everything in college
- Giving them credit cards without teaching budgeting

The message: Money is a tool. Master it now while mistakes are small.

Age 18-25: Independence

Lessons:

- Retirement accounts (401k, IRA)
- Student loans and debt management
- Rent, utilities, real costs of living
- Building credit score

Activities:

- Match their retirement contributions (incentivize saving)
- If you pay for college, require them to work part-time (skin in the game)
- Gradually reduce financial support (transition to independence)
- Share your investment strategy: "Here's our portfolio, here's why"

Avoid:

- Continuing to fund their entire lifestyle
- Bailing them out of every mistake
- Keeping wealth "secret" (breeds resentment or entitlement later)

The message: You're an adult. These are adult responsibilities.

Age 25+: Collaboration

Lessons:

- Advanced investing strategies
- Tax optimization
- Estate planning
- Philanthropy

Activities:

- Involve them in family investment discussions
- Create family governance structure
- Discuss inheritance plans openly
- Collaborate on charitable giving

The message: You're now a steward of family wealth, not just a beneficiary.

The Family Wealth Mission Statement

Purpose: Define why your family's wealth exists beyond accumulation

Components:

1. Origin Story: "This wealth was created by [how], through [values], for [purpose]."

Example: "This wealth was created through 40 years of disciplined saving and investing, through the values of hard work, education, and delayed gratification, for the purpose of providing our family with choices and the ability to contribute meaningfully to the world."

2. Core Values: What principles guide your family's relationship with money?

Examples:

- Hard work and self-reliance

- Education as foundation
- Generosity and contribution
- Stewardship (we're caretakers, not owners)
- Responsibility and accountability

3. Purpose: What should this wealth enable?

Examples:

- Financial autonomy for all family members
- Education funding for all generations
- Support for entrepreneurial pursuits
- Philanthropic impact in [specific area]
- Security without entitlement

4. Expectations: What's expected of family members?

Examples:

- Financial literacy education by age 25
- Self-sufficiency (earning income, not living off inheritance)
- Participation in family governance
- Contribution to family mission/philanthropy
- Teaching next generation

5. Governance: How are decisions made?

Examples:

- Annual family meetings
- Investment committee structure
- Voting rights and thresholds
- Dispute resolution process
- Trustee/successor designation

Sample Family Wealth Mission Statement:

"The [Family Name] wealth was built through decades of hard work, disciplined investing, and sacrifice. It exists to provide our family with choices, education, and the ability to pursue meaningful work without financial pressure. We value self-reliance, education, generosity, and stewardship.

This wealth is meant to amplify our family's positive impact on the world, not to fund idle luxury. Each generation is expected to contribute productively to society, educate themselves financially, and pass these values to the next generation.

We govern this wealth collectively, with transparency, mutual respect, and the understanding that we are stewards for future generations we'll never meet."

Create this document. Share it. Live it. Update it as the family evolves.

The Trust Structures for Wealth Transfer

Purpose: Protect wealth from taxes, lawsuits, and bad decisions

Revocable Living Trust (Basic)

What it is: Trust that holds assets during your life, avoids probate at death

Benefits:

- Avoids probate (saves time, money, privacy)
- Maintains control during life (you're the trustee)
- Easy to modify (revocable)
- Smooth transition to beneficiaries

Downsides:

- No tax benefits (treated as your assets)
- No asset protection (creditors can still access)
- Not dynasty wealth tool

Best for: Everyone with assets >$100K. Basic estate planning.

Cost: $1,500-$3,000

Irrevocable Life Insurance Trust (ILIT)

What it is: Trust that owns life insurance policy, removing death benefit from taxable estate

Benefits:

- Life insurance proceeds pass tax-free to heirs

- Protected from estate taxes (if structured correctly)
- Protected from creditors

Downsides:

- Cannot modify (irrevocable)
- You give up control
- Must gift premiums to trust annually

Best for: High net worth ($3M+) with large life insurance policies

Cost: $2,500-$5,000 setup

Dynasty Trust (Multigenerational)

What it is: Irrevocable trust designed to last multiple generations

Benefits:

- Assets pass estate-tax-free across generations
- Protected from creditors, divorces, lawsuits
- Can last 100+ years (depending on state)
- Beneficiaries receive distributions but don't own assets (creditor protection)

Downsides:

- Complex and expensive
- You give up control permanently
- Requires careful planning and ongoing management

Best for: Ultra-high net worth ($10M+) focused on multigenerational legacy

Cost: $10,000-$25,000 setup + annual trustee fees

Qualified Personal Residence Trust (QPRT)

What it is: Transfer home to trust, continue living in it, removes from estate after term

Benefits:

- Reduces estate taxes (gifting home at discounted value)

- Continue living in home during trust term
- Home appreciation passes tax-free to heirs

Downsides:

- Must outlive trust term (or it fails)
- After term, must pay rent or move out
- Complex IRS rules

Best for: High net worth with valuable primary residence

Charitable Remainder Trust (CRT)

What it is: Donate assets to trust, receive income for life, remainder to charity at death

Benefits:

- Immediate tax deduction
- Income for life
- Removes assets from estate
- Supports charitable cause

Downsides:

- Assets ultimately go to charity (not heirs)
- Irrevocable
- Complex administration

Best for: Wealthy, charitably-inclined, wanting income + tax benefits

Work with an estate attorney to determine appropriate structures for your situation and state.

The Family Governance Model

For families with $2M+ net worth, formal governance prevents disaster.

The Family Council

Purpose: Forum for communication, education, decision-making

Structure:

- Quarterly or annual meetings
- All adult family members participate
- Facilitator keeps discussions productive
- Document decisions and action items

Agenda:

- Financial education session (teach next generation)
- Portfolio review (performance, strategy updates)
- Major decisions (significant investments, estate planning changes)
- Philanthropic activities (charitable giving decisions)
- Family matters (supporting members, resolving conflicts)

This creates:

- Transparency (everyone understands the wealth)
- Education (learning happens formally)
- Unity (shared mission and values)
- Accountability (decisions documented)

The Investment Committee

Purpose: Oversee family wealth management**

Structure:

- 3-5 family members with financial competency
- Meets quarterly minimum
- Reviews portfolio performance
- Approves major investment decisions
- Hires/fires advisors as needed

Responsibilities:

- Maintain target allocation
- Evaluate new opportunities
- Rebalance portfolio
- Monitor advisor performance
- Report to Family Council

This creates:

- Professional oversight (not emotional decisions)
- Continuity (process outlasts individuals)
- Accountability (committee structure, not dictatorship)

Succession Planning

Question: What happens when the wealth builder dies or becomes incapacitated?

Critical documents:

- Will (basic asset distribution)
- Trust documents (detailed trust management)
- Power of Attorney (financial decision-making if incapacitated)
- Healthcare Directive (medical decisions)
- Letter of Intent (non-binding guidance on wishes)

Trustee succession:

- Who becomes trustee after you?
- Who's back up if they can't serve?
- What powers do they have?
- How are disputes resolved?

Financial information binder:

- List of all accounts (with account numbers)
- Passwords and access instructions
- Advisor contact information (attorney, CPA, financial advisor)
- Insurance policies
- Real estate holdings
- Business interests
- Digital assets (crypto wallets, domain names, etc.)

Update annually. Store securely. Share location with trusted family member.

Many fortunes are lost not through bad investing but through lack of succession planning.

Teaching Adult Children About Wealth

The conversation most families avoid:

"We need to talk about money."

When to have it: Before inheritance, not after.

What to cover:

1. The Numbers: "Here's what exists. Here's how it's structured. Here's what you'll inherit."

- Be specific (not vague "we're comfortable")
- Explain current structure (trusts, accounts, allocations)
- Discuss timeline (now vs. after death)
- Answer questions honestly

Why: Surprises after death cause conflict. Transparency creates trust.

2. The Values: "Here's why this wealth exists and what it's meant to enable."

- Share family wealth mission
- Discuss your values around money
- Explain your expectations (education, self-sufficiency, contribution)
- Discuss philanthropy and giving

Why: Without context, money becomes just money. Values give it meaning.

3. The Responsibilities: "Here's what we expect from you as a beneficiary."

- Financial literacy requirements
- Employment/self-sufficiency expectations
- Participation in family governance
- Contribution to family mission
- Education of your own children

Why: Rights without responsibilities create entitlement.

4. The Structure: "Here's how it works legally and practically."

- Explain trusts (what they can/can't do)

- Discuss distributions (when, how much, under what conditions)
- Review governance (who makes decisions, how)
- Clarify roles (trustees, executors, beneficiaries)

Why: Understanding structure prevents confusion and legal battles.

5. The Question: "What do you need to know? What concerns do you have?"

- Listen more than talk
- Address fears (about dependence, about pressure, about fairness)
- Discuss individual situations (some children may need more/less)
- Revisit conversation annually

Why: Dialogue builds trust. Monologue builds resentment.

The Incentive Trust Structure

Problem: Unconditional inheritance can destroy motivation

Solution: Structure distributions around positive behaviors

Common Incentive Provisions:

Education incentives:

- Match earnings $ for $ while in school
- Bonus distribution upon degree completion
- Graduate degree funding

Employment incentives:

- Match earned income (if you earn $50K, trust distributes $50K)
- Business startup funding (up to $X for entrepreneurial ventures)
- Sabbatical funding (if you've worked X years)

Lifestyle milestones:

- First home down payment (up to $X)
- Wedding funding (reasonable amount)
- Childcare support (per grandchild)

Contribution incentives:

- Match charitable giving 2:1
- Fund volunteer sabbaticals
- Support mission-aligned work (even if lower-paying)

Example Incentive Trust Language:

"Beneficiary shall receive annual distributions equal to 100% of earned income, up to $100,000 annually, provided the beneficiary is employed full-time or actively pursuing education.

Beneficiary may receive business startup capital up to $250,000 for entrepreneurial ventures, subject to business plan approval by the Investment Committee.

Trust shall match beneficiary's charitable contributions at 2:1 ratio, up to $50,000 annually.

Upon completion of a graduate degree, the beneficiary receives a one-time distribution of $100,000.

Trust shall provide first home down payment assistance up to $150,000, for primary residence only."

The balance:

- Incentivize productive behavior
- Don't create hoops that feel controlling
- Allow flexibility for individual paths
- Review and adjust as values/situations evolve

Caution: Consult attorney. Poorly drafted incentive provisions can create conflict or fail legally.

The Philanthropy Plan

Purpose: Teach giving, create impact, unify family

The Family Foundation (For $5M+ Families)

Structure:

- Private foundation or Donor-Advised Fund
- Family members serve on board
- Annual grant-making to chosen charities
- Educational component (learning about causes)

Benefits:

- Tax deduction at funding
- Family governance practice
- Teaches values to next generation
- Creates lasting impact beyond family

Example process:

- Each family member nominates causes
- Research and present to family
- Vote on annual grants ($X budget)
- Visit organizations receiving grants
- Track impact over time

This teaches:

- Research and decision-making skills
- Empathy and social awareness
- Financial stewardship
- Collaborative governance

Even modest giving ($5K-$10K annually) creates family unity and teaches values.

The Giving Pledge (For $10M+ Families)

Concept: Commit to giving away majority of wealth to charity

Purpose: Signal values, prevent entitlement, create meaning

Warren Buffett and Bill Gates initiative—over 200 billionaires have pledged

You don't need billions to apply the concept:

- Commit to giving X% of wealth during life or at death
- Involve family in how it's distributed
- Document reasoning for future generations

Message to children: "We're leaving you enough to do anything, but not enough to do nothing."

Case Study: The Five-Generation Plan

Family: The Chen Family, net worth $8.5M

Generation 1 (Grandparents, ages 75 and 73):

- Built wealth through business ownership + disciplined investing
- Created family wealth mission statement
- Established dynasty trust holding $5M
- Continued control during life

Generation 2 (Children, ages 45-52):

- Three children, all employed and self-sufficient
- Participated in creating family governance structure
- Serve on Investment Committee
- Received financial education from parents
- Annual family council meetings
- Each child has $1M allocated in sub-trusts

Generation 3 (Grandchildren, ages 15-28):

- Financial education program starting at age 12
- Custodial investment accounts ($25K each)
- Employment incentives (trust matches earned income)
- College fully funded
- Graduate degree funding for those pursuing
- Invited to family council at age 25
- Six grandchildren, total $1.5M allocated

Generation 4 (Great-grandchildren, ages 0-5):

- Education trusts established
- Each receives $10K at birth, compounds until age 18
- Will participate in family governance when adults
- Four great-grandchildren so far

The Structure:

Dynasty Trust ($5M core):

- Invested per family allocation (Foundation 35%, Income 40%, Growth 20%, Asymmetric 5%)
- Generates $325K annually
- Distributions:
    - 40% to family foundation (philanthropy)

  - 30% to beneficiaries (based on incentive provisions)
  - 30% retained/reinvested (grows perpetually)

Family Foundation ($2M, growing):

- Annual grants: $80-100K
- Focus areas: Education, community development
- All family members vote on grants
- Educational site visits annually

Incentive Trust Provisions:

- Education match: $1 for $1 while in school
- Income match: $1 for $1 up to $100K earned income
- Business funding: Up to $250K for ventures
- Home purchase: Up to $200K assistance
- Charitable match: 2:1 up to $50K

Family Governance:

- Quarterly Investment Committee (reviews portfolio)
- Annual Family Council (all adults, education + decisions)
- Biannual family retreat (strengthens relationships)
- Monthly philanthropy committee (grant decisions)

Results after 10 years:

- Trust value grew from $5M to $7.8M (despite distributions)
- 15 family members educated in financial literacy
- $850K donated to charities
- Zero family conflict (clear governance prevented disputes)
- All Generation 3 grandchildren employed and self-sufficient
- Wealth mission embraced by all generations

Grandparents' reflection: "We didn't just want to pass money down. We wanted to pass values, skills, and purpose. The structure ensures our grandchildren and great-grandchildren we'll never meet will benefit from what we built—but only if they contribute productively to the world."

This is multigenerational wealth done right.

Your Family Wealth Continuity Plan

Action steps:

Step 1: Create Family Wealth Mission

- Draft with spouse/partner
- Involve adult children in refinement
- Document and share
- Review annually

Step 2: Educate Current Generation

- Age-appropriate financial literacy for children
- Open conversations about wealth with adult children
- Involve them in investment decisions gradually

Step 3: Structure Legally

- Consult estate attorney
- Create appropriate trusts
- Draft incentive provisions if applicable
- Establish succession plan

Step 4: Implement Governance

- Schedule first Family Council meeting
- Create Investment Committee if wealth >$2M
- Document decision-making processes
- Hold annual reviews

Step 5: Plan Philanthropy

- Determine giving strategy
- Involve family in decisions
- Create foundation or DAF if appropriate
- Make giving collaborative and educational

Step 6: Document Everything

- Financial information binder

- Passwords and access
- Trust documents organized
- Letter of intent with values/wishes

Step 7: Communicate Regularly

- Annual wealth conversations
- Quarterly updates if Investment Committee exists
- Transparent about numbers, structure, expectations
- Listen to concerns and adjust

This isn't a one-time task. It's an ongoing commitment to ensuring wealth serves your family for generations.

Key Takeaways:

- 90% of family wealth lost by third generation due to lack of education, entitlement, conflict, no purpose, poor structure
- Teach financial literacy age-appropriately: Ages 3-7 (basics), 8-12 (management), 13-17 (investing), 18-25 (independence), 25+ (collaboration)
- Create Family Wealth Mission: Define origin, values, purpose, expectations, governance
- Use appropriate trust structures: Revocable Living (basic), Dynasty (multigenerational), ILIT (life insurance), CRT (charitable)
- Implement family governance: Family Council (quarterly/annual), Investment Committee (oversight), succession planning
- Have "the conversation" with adult children before inheritance: Discuss numbers, values, responsibilities, structure, answer questions
- Consider incentive trusts: Match earned income, fund education/business, reward contribution, avoid entitlement
- Plan family philanthropy: Teach giving, create impact, unify family around shared mission
- Document everything: Financial binder, trust documents, succession plan, passwords, advisor contacts
- Review and update annually: Family situations change, structures need adjustment, communication is ongoing

CHAPTER 20:

THE ARCHITECT'S MINDSET

We've covered frameworks, strategies, allocation models, tax optimization, and wealth transfer.

But none of it matters without the right mindset.

This final chapter is about the mental models, principles, and perspectives that separate successful architects from everyone else.

The Fundamental Shift

From Consumer → to Investor

Most people are trained as consumers:

- Earn money
- Spend money
- Repeat

Investors think differently:

- Earn money
- Convert into assets
- Assets generate more money
- Reinvest
- Compound indefinitely

The shift: Money isn't for spending. It's for deploying.

Every dollar is a soldier. Do you send it to die (spending) or to recruit more soldiers (investing)?

This doesn't mean deprivation. It means intention.

Buy the experience that creates memories. Skip the status symbol that impresses nobody. Invest the difference.

The 10 Principles of the Architect's Mindset

Principle 1: Systems Over Goals

Goals are outcomes. Systems are processes.

Goal-focused: "I want to be a millionaire"

- Vague
- Binary (achieved or not)
- Doesn't tell you what to do today

System-focused: "I invest $X monthly into Y allocation, rebalance quarterly, and increase contributions annually"

- Specific
- Daily/weekly/monthly actions
- Guarantees progress

The truth: You don't achieve goals. You follow systems that produce inevitable outcomes.

If your system is:

- Save $60K/year
- Invest in 7-10% returning assets
- Reinvest all distributions
- Continue for 15 years

The outcome is inevitable: You will accumulate $1.5-2M+.

Focus on system excellence. Outcomes take care of themselves.

Principle 2: Compounding Over Cleverness

- Most investors try to be clever:
- Time the market
- Pick winning stocks
- Find the next Bitcoin

- Beat professional investors

Architects choose compounding:

- Consistent contributions
- Long time horizons
- Reinvesting distributions
- Letting systems run

Warren Buffett's genius isn't stock-picking—it's letting compounding work for 70+ years.

His net worth at age 50: $376M His net worth at age 90: $118B

99.7% of his wealth came after age 50. From compounding, not brilliance.

The lesson: Time in the market beats timing the market. Discipline beats intelligence.

Principle 3: Asymmetry Over Symmetry

Symmetrical bet: Risk $100 to make $100 (1:1) Asymmetric bet: Risk $100 to make $1,000+ (10:1 or better)

Architects seek asymmetry:

- Limited downside (you can only lose 100%)
- Unlimited upside (you can gain 10x, 50x, 100x)

How to find asymmetry:

- Early-stage startups ($5K investment, potential 50x return)
- Contrarian value plays (buying quality assets during panic)
- Skill-based investing (private markets where research creates edge)
- Options strategies (when used carefully)

The 80/20 approach:

- 80% safe, compounding assets (protect downside)
- 20% asymmetric bets (capture upside)

One 50x winner in your asymmetric allocation pays for 49 losses and transforms your portfolio.

Position sizing enables asymmetry: If you bet $1,000, losing everything is tolerable. If you bet $100,000, you can't afford asymmetric risk.

Principle 4: Income Over Appreciation

Traditional wisdom: Buy assets that appreciate, sell when needed

Architect wisdom: Buy assets that pay you forever, never sell

The math:

Appreciation-only:

- $500K portfolio growing at 8% annually
- Must sell 4% per year ($20K) to fund life
- Portfolio slowly depletes
- Vulnerable to sequence-of-returns risk

Income-focused:

- $500K portfolio generating 7% income ($35K annually)
- Never sell principal
- Portfolio continues growing
- Income likely grows with inflation

Same capital. Different strategy. Opposite outcomes.

The goal: Build a portfolio that feeds you indefinitely while growing independently.

Principle 5: Time Over Money

The ultimate wealth question: Can you buy back your time?

Most people trade time for money their entire lives:

- Work 40+ years
- Accumulate wealth
- Retire with money but without health/energy

Architects trade money for time as early as possible:

- Build passive income

- Achieve autonomy in 40s or 50s
- Use prime years for meaning, not money

The calculation:

Traditional path:

- Age 25-65: Work (80,000 hours)
- Age 65-85: Retire (40,000 hours leisure, declining health)

Architect path:

- Age 25-45: Work + build systems (40,000 hours)
- Age 45-85: Financial autonomy (80,000 hours freedom, peak health)

Same effort. Double the freedom. Better health during freedom years.

Ask constantly: "Am I trading time for money, or money for time?"

Principle 6: Process Over Results

Results are noisy. Process is controllable.

You cannot control:

- Market returns this year
- Whether your startup investment succeeds
- Timing of real estate sales
- Economic cycles

You can control:

- Your savings rate
- Your allocation decisions
- Your due diligence quality
- Your emotional discipline
- Your tax optimization
- Your reinvestment strategy

Focus on process excellence:

- Did I stick to my allocation?

- Did I rebalance as planned?
- Did I deploy capital systematically?
- Did I avoid emotional decisions?
- Did I learn from this investment?

If you execute excellent process consistently, excellent results become inevitable over time.

Judge yourself on what you control, not what you don't.

Principle 7: Optionality Over Optimization

Optimization: Finding the single best solution Optionality: Creating multiple good solutions

Example:

Optimized portfolio: 100% in the highest-returning asset class

- Problem: If that asset class crashes, you're ruined
- Problem: Requires perfect prediction (impossible)

Optionality portfolio: Diversified across uncorrelated assets

- If one fails, others continue
- Multiple paths to success
- Resilient to unknown futures

Optionality in life:

- Passive income = option to quit job
- Liquidity = option to capitalize on opportunities
- Skills = option to earn in multiple ways
- Network = option to access deals

Architects build optionality, not optimization.

The world is uncertain. Multiple options are more valuable than one "optimal" choice.

Principle 8: Antifragility Over Stability

Three responses to stress:

Fragile: Breaks under stress (all-stock portfolio in 2008) Robust: Survives stress (balanced portfolio in 2008) Antifragile: Grows stronger from stress (architect portfolio with cash deployed during 2008)

How to build antifragility:

- Income streams that continue during crashes
- Cash reserves to deploy during panics
- Asymmetric positions that benefit from chaos
- Emotional systems that prevent panic

The mindset shift:

Fragile investor: "I hope markets don't crash" Robust investor: "I can survive a crash" Antifragile investor: "I hope markets crash so I can buy cheap"

Volatility isn't your enemy. It's your opportunity—if you're positioned correctly.

Principle 9: Learning Over Certainty

Certainty is an illusion. Learning is real.

The investor who thinks they know everything:

- Stops learning
- Becomes overconfident
- Makes larger bets with less diligence
- Eventually gets crushed by the market

The investor who embraces uncertainty:

- Learns continuously
- Stays humble
- Properly sizes risk
- Adapts to new information
- Survives and thrives

The best investors are students forever:

- Reading constantly
- Studying failures (especially their own)
- Updating beliefs with new evidence

- Admitting mistakes quickly

Your knowledge compounds like your capital—but only if you keep depositing into it.

Wisdom isn't knowing everything. It's knowing how much you don't know.

Principle 10: Purpose Over Profit

Money without meaning is empty.

Two investors, both wealthy:

Investor A: Accumulated $5M through discipline

- But has no purpose beyond accumulation
- Feels empty despite success
- Fears losing it (because that's all there is)
- Dies wealthy but unfulfilled

Investor B: Built $2M aligned with purpose

- Wealth enables meaningful work
- Supports causes she cares about
- Feels abundant despite less wealth
- Lives and dies fulfilled

Who's richer?

Purpose gives wealth meaning:

- Financial autonomy to pursue passion work
- Capacity to support family
- Ability to fund causes that matter
- Teaching others what you learned
- Creating lasting impact

Without purpose, wealth is just a score. With purpose, wealth is a tool for contribution.

Start with "why" and the "how much" becomes clear.

The Architect's Daily Practices

Your mindset isn't built in a day. It's built in daily repetitions.

Morning Practice (15 minutes)

Gratitude:

- What am I grateful for financially? (income, investments, opportunities)
- What progress have I made? (even small wins)

Intention:

- What financial decision faces me today?
- Am I operating from fear or strategy?
- What would my future self want me to do?

Learning:

- Read 10 pages of investing/business book
- Listen to 20-minute podcast on commute

This primes your mind for disciplined decisions throughout the day.

Weekly Practice (1 hour)

Review:

- Check account balances (awareness, not obsession)
- Note any investment distributions received
- Confirm automated contributions executed

Planning:

- Any capital to deploy this week?
- Any investment opportunities to research?
- Any financial decisions to make?

Learning:

- Finish 50+ pages of current book

- Participate in online investment community

This maintains momentum without consuming your life.

Monthly Practice (2-3 hours)

Portfolio Check:

- Calculate current Freedom Index
- Review allocation vs. targets
- Note any significant changes

Deployment:

- Deploy available capital per system
- Research new opportunities
- Update investment pipeline

Learning:

- Finish 1 book
- Attend webinar or course
- Connect with 2-3 investors in your network

This ensures system is on track and knowledge is growing.

Quarterly Practice (4-6 hours)

Deep Review:

- Full portfolio performance analysis
- Rebalancing if thresholds exceeded
- Tax-loss harvesting opportunities
- Freedom Index tracking and celebration

Strategy:

- Any allocation adjustments needed?
- Any new asset classes to explore?
- Any investments to exit?

Learning:

- Document lessons from last quarter
- Update investment thesis
- Set next quarter goals

This creates accountability and continuous improvement.

Annual Practice (8+ hours)

Comprehensive Review:

- Year-over-year progress
- Performance vs. benchmarks
- Freedom Index growth
- All lessons learned

Strategy Session:

- Update Kubera Framework
- Adjust allocations for life stage
- Tax planning for upcoming year
- Estate plan review

Goal Setting:

- Next year's targets
- New learning goals
- Network expansion plans

This ensures you're still on track toward your long-term vision.

The Common Mental Traps (And How to Avoid Them)

Trap 1: Comparison Anxiety

The trap: Comparing your portfolio to others', feeling behind

Why it happens: Social media, friends, financial media create false benchmarks

The antidote:

- Your only competition is your past self
- Everyone's situation, timeline, and goals differ

- Focus on your Freedom Index, not their net worth

The mantra: "Am I freer than I was last year? Then I'm winning."

Trap 2: Paralysis by Analysis

The trap: Researching endlessly, never deploying capital

Why it happens: Fear of making wrong choice, seeking perfection

The antidote:

- Perfect information doesn't exist
- Waiting has a cost (missed compounding)
- Start small, learn, adjust
- Done beats perfect

The mantra: "I will make small bets, learn fast, and improve continuously."

Trap 3: Recency Bias

The trap: Believing recent trends continue forever

Why it happens: Human brains overweight recent experience

Examples:

- 2021: "Stocks only go up" → crash in 2022
- 2022: "Inflation is permanent" → inflation fell in 2023
- Post-crash: "Markets will never recover" → they always have

The antidote:

- Study full market cycles (80+ years of history)
- Remember: Trees don't grow to the sky
- Mean reversion is real

The mantra: "This too shall pass—booms and busts alike."

Trap 4: Loss Aversion

The trap: Fearing losses more than valuing gains (psychologically, losses hurt 2x more)

Why it happens: Evolutionary wiring (avoiding danger)

The result:

- Holding losers too long (hoping to break even)
- Selling winners too early (locking in gains)
- Avoiding good risks (might lose!)

The antidote:

- Losses are feedback, not failure
- Position sizing makes losses tolerable
- Focus on process, not individual outcomes

The mantra: "I size positions so losses are learning, not ruin."

Trap 5: Overconfidence After Wins

The trap: A few wins convince you you're a genius, take bigger risks, get crushed

Why it happens: Success feels like skill even when it's luck

The result:

- Larger position sizes
- Less due diligence
- Riskier bets
- Eventual blowup

The antidote:

- Attribute wins honestly (skill vs. luck)
- Maintain discipline regardless of recent results
- Position sizing rules always apply

The mantra: "Good results don't make me smart. Good process over time makes me successful."

The Architect's Creed

I am building wealth for freedom, not status.

I measure progress by autonomy gained, not dollars accumulated.

I design systems that compound without my constant intervention.

I take asymmetric risks with capital I can afford to lose entirely.

I build income streams that fund my life indefinitely.

I optimize for time sovereignty, not maximum returns.

I learn continuously, admit mistakes quickly, and adapt constantly.

I protect my wealth through diversification, structure, and discipline.

I share my knowledge, mentor others, and contribute to purposes larger than myself.

I am not clever. I am systematic.

I am not lucky. I am patient.

I am not a speculator. I am an architect.

I am building financial freedom—for myself, my family, and future generations I'll never meet.

The Final Word: From Here to Freedom

You've reached the end of this book. But you're at the beginning of your journey.

You now know:

- Why traditional portfolios no longer work
- How to design your wealth blueprint
- How to allocate across asset classes
- How to generate passive income
- How to optimize for taxes
- How to build for volatility
- How to measure true progress

- How to create multigenerational wealth

But knowledge isn't wealth. Action is.

Your next steps:

This week:

- Calculate your Freedom Number and Freedom Index
- Define your purpose statement
- Set up automatic contributions

This month:

- Design your target allocation
- Make your first alternative investment (or research opportunities)
- Join an investment community

This quarter:

- Deploy capital systematically
- Implement tax optimization strategies
- Schedule quarterly review

This year:

- Build 3+ income streams
- Increase Freedom Index by 10+ percentage points
- Document your system

Next 5 years:

- Achieve 50-75% Freedom Index
- Master 2-3 alternative asset classes
- Build network that provides deal flow

Next 10 years:

- Cross 100% Freedom Index threshold
- Achieve financial autonomy
- Begin teaching others

The path to freedom isn't complicated. It's:

- Save aggressively
- Invest systematically
- Compound patiently
- Build income streams
- Stay disciplined

Do this for 10-20 years and financial autonomy is inevitable.

Not because you got lucky. Not because you timed the market. Not because you found a secret.

Because you built a system. And systems work.

The Beginning

The investors who achieve financial freedom aren't the smartest, luckiest, or wealthiest.

They're the most systematic.

They design portfolios that serve their purpose. They build income that funds their lives. They compound patiently. They avoid fatal mistakes. They learn continuously. They adapt to changing markets.

They are architects—of wealth, of freedom, of lives well-lived.

You can't predict markets, but you can design freedom.

You've read the blueprint. Now build your masterpiece.

Welcome to the rest of your life.

You are the architect.

EPILOGUE: A Letter to Your Future Self

Ten years from now, you'll open this book again.

You'll remember where you were when you first read it. The uncertainty. The hope. The determination.

You'll calculate your Freedom Index and smile.

Maybe you're at 75% and can see the finish line clearly. Maybe you've crossed 100% and work has become truly optional. Maybe you're at 150% and teaching your children what you've learned.

Wherever you are, you'll be grateful you started.

Because the hardest part of any journey is the first step. And you took it.

You chose to be intentional about your wealth rather than leaving it to chance. You chose to design a system rather than hoping for luck. You chose freedom over accumulation. You chose to be an architect.

And that choice—that single decision to start—changed everything.

Your future self is thanking you right now.

Don't disappoint them.

Start building.

Key Takeaways:

- The architect's mindset: 10 core principles that separate successful investors from everyone else
- Principle 1: Systems over goals (process creates inevitable outcomes)
- Principle 2: Compounding over cleverness (discipline beats intelligence)
- Principle 3: Asymmetry over symmetry (limited downside, unlimited upside)
- Principle 4: Income over appreciation (assets that pay forever vs. selling principal)
- Principle 5: Time over money (buying back years, not just accumulating wealth)
- Principle 6: Process over results (control what you can control)
- Principle 7: Optionality over optimization (multiple good solutions vs. one perfect solution)
- Principle 8: Antifragility over stability (benefit from chaos, not just survive it)
- Principle 9: Learning over certainty (continuous adaptation vs. false confidence)
- Principle 10: Purpose over profit (wealth as tool for meaning, not just accumulation)
- Daily practices build the mindset: morning intention, weekly reviews, monthly deployment, quarterly deep dives, annual strategy

- Common mental traps: comparison anxiety, paralysis by analysis, recency bias, loss aversion, overconfidence
- The Architect's Creed: systematic over clever, patient over lucky, builder over speculator
- Action plan: This week (calculate numbers), this month (design allocation), this quarter (deploy capital), this year (build income streams), 10 years (achieve autonomy)

Made in the USA
Monee, IL
12 November 2026

a1d3230b-ae19-43d4-975d-35f0c9f8e8b8R01